2020 North Carolina Real Estate Exam Prep. Questions and Answers

Study Guide to Passing the Salesperson Real Estate License Exam Effortlessly

D1568564

Written by

Real Estate Exam Professionals, Ltd.

Table of Contents

INTRODUCTION

Thank you for purchasing this Real Estate Exam Prep. book. We hope you will learn a great deal from our study guide and that you will study well and pass your exam. It is our purpose to provide you with the most up to date information for your state real estate exam. We have made every effort to present this material as the closest possible example to what you will see on your actual state exam. At times, it will appear to be exactly what you will see on the exam. We have tried very hard to make this book as error and typo free as possible. However, we are not without our faults. Real estate exam material and the real estate exams change rapidly and we are continuously updating this book as these changes occur. You may find a typo here and there, but do not be alarmed. We assure you that if you find one, it will be obvious and it will not prevent you from being able to tell what the correct answer is.

You will find that after you have studied this material as instructed in the *How to Use this Guide Effectively*, you will discover that this is all you need to pass the real estate exam. There are many real estate schools out there such as Allied Real Estate School, Anthony Real Estate School and Kaplan that, although they are good schools, also offer exam cram or exam preparation materials, but are extremely overpriced. Their materials can cost into the $100 and $300 ranges and provide a lot of extra "fluff" material that will not help you pass the exam and will waste your time. This book offers all the same materials in a condensed and precise manner with no fluff. Once you have taken the department of real estate certified classes and passed them, qualified to for a state exam date then you do not need those classroom materials anymore. All you will need are the answers to the state and national real estate exam questions. Study those, nothing else, memorize them, and you will pass your exam on the 1st try. There is no need to buy expensive materials from other schools, no need to sit in live exam cram courses, and there is no need for the Real Estate Exam for Dummies books. We have been offering this material to thousands of licensees for over 10 years with a tremendous amount of positive reviews and feedback.

Please be aware that the materials in this book including any bonus item you have received with this book are copyrighted. No part of this book in part or in whole may be duplicated, distributed or resold without consent of the publishers. Our staff actively searches the internet everyday for sales of real estate media on thousands of websites and online auctions. If our program is found being copied, distributed or resold we will prosecute to the fullest extent of the law.

How To Use This Guide Effectively

Here you will find tried and true steps to help you use this guide effectively and to get the best results while minimizing your study time. Please understand that as you go through the real estate questions we have prepared for you, you may come across a few that you have never seen before. Do not be alarmed. These are questions that are on the state exam, but were never given to you in the real estate class you took or in your class textbooks. This is why there is such a high failure rate for the real estate exam. The actual questions on the state or national real estate exams are NOT created by the same agency that created the college courses or text books. These college courses are designed by regional college accreditation agencies and the state real estate exams are created by the individual state's department of real estate or real estate commissions. It is very frustrating, we know. That is why there publishers like us who create exam cram courses and applications to "bridge the gap" of knowledge for the real estate exams.

STEP 1: Read and understand the VOCABULARY section first. These are very important terms. The key to successful knowledge of real estate is understanding and knowing the vocabulary used. Review them until you are confident to go onto the questions. Do not continue to the questions until you know these terms well.

STEP 2: Now go to the STUDY SECTION and read all the real estate questions with their correct answers and explanations in each exam. There are a lot of questions. Pace yourself and allow time to understand and memorize the correct answers.

STEP 3: Go back to the VOCABULARY section and review. Again, they are VERY important. You must know these forwards and backwards.

STEP 4: Repeat step 2 until you feel you are scoring 90% or better. Then review the VOCABULARY section again.

STEP 5: Now begin the MATH only portion of the STUDY SECTION. Read the questions with the answers and explanations until you have mastered them just as you did with the regular real estate questions. Make sure you set aside a separate time of the day to ONLY study the math. The reason for this is that the analytical/math function of the human brain works on math problems from different areas of the brain than word problems. When studying it takes approx. 10 min. for the brain to fully switch to a pure analytical/math function. If you are studying word problems and math problems in the same study session, you will be wasting a lot of time and overworking your brain. Time is key here, especially when it comes to the day of the exam, more about that later.

STEP 6: Repeat the MATH ONLY portion in the STUDY SECTION until you feel you are scoring at least 90% or better.

STEP 7: Now you are ready to go on to the TEST SECTION of this book. These questions will simulate what you will find on the actual state exam. You will have a limited time to complete the exam. Set a timer to the amount of time that your state allows for you to complete the state exam. Begin taking one of the exams and write your answers on a blank sheet of paper. When you are finished, check your answers with the correct answers shown in the same exams from the STUDY SECTION and score yourself. Now continue to Step 8.

STEP 8: Did you score 90% or better? If so, congratulations! You are ready to take the actual state exam and pass on your first try. If you did not score 90% or better, review the questions you missed using the STUDY SECTION. Study them, and retake the corresponding exam in the TESTING SECTION.

Continue doing this and review the Vocabulary, if needed, until you are scoring 90% or better.

IMPORTANT!!!

REMEMBER THIS ON THE DAY YOU TAKE YOUR STATE EXAM…

DO NOT ANSWER, OR EVEN READ, THE FIRST 5 QUESTIONS OF THE EXAM. DO THOSE SECOND TO LAST AND ANY MATH RELATED QUESTIONS, VERY LAST!!!

Write the numbers to these questions on a piece of paper to remember to do them later. The reason is that they have placed the hardest questions in the first 5 spots to distract you, make you nervous and frustrated while taking the test. So, do those just before doing the math questions. Do the math questions very last because as we explained earlier, psychologically it takes the brain about 5-10 minutes to go from comprehensive thinking to analytical mathematical thinking. You only have a limited amount of time to complete the real estate exam. Therefore, your time will be very valuable. Do not leave any question unanswered. An unanswered question will be scored as a wrong answer.

Be sure to read the section *"Secrets to Passing the Real Estate Exam"* this section was developed by ex-real estate exam proctors. It will give you more detailed steps and inside information on how to use the above method on the day of your exam. It will also show you how to answer a question correctly even if you have completely forgotten the answer.

Good luck and study well!

REAL ESTATE VOCABULARY

Due to the length of this Real Estate Glossary, we have included it as a link below. Please understand these are general real estate terms used in almost every state. This is here for review purposes and reference only.

http://www.realestateabc.com/glossary/

You may also download a PDF version here:

http://tinyurl.com/realestatevocab

STUDY SECTION

In this section you will have the Real Estate Vocabulary Exam, 2020 Real Estate Exam and Real Estate Math Exam. Read through all the questions in each exam according to the *How to Use this Guide Effectively* chapter and ONLY look at the correct answers in each exam. Start with the Vocabulary Exam and read question number one and then read ONLY the correct answer immediately. Continue to do this for each question until you have read all the questions in the first exam. If you go through each exam 3-4 times in this manner, you will then be able to recognize the correct answer right away when it comes to taking the actual exam. If your reading device has the ability to highlight the correct answer in each question, please utilize this feature. It will make it a little easier each time when reading through the exams in this section.

REAL ESTATE VOCABULARY EXAM

Please understand these are general real estate terms used in almost every state. This is here for practice and review purposes only. Some terms may not be on your exam.

1. Which of the following describes the term "appreciation"?

A.   Kind words expressed to someone about something they did
B.   An increase in the value of property
C.   An item of value owned by an individual
D.   None of the above

Answer: B. Appreciation is the increase in the value of a property due to changes in market conditions, inflation, or other causes.

2. When ownership of a mortgage is transferred from one company or individual to another, it is called

A.   an assumption
B.   an assignment
C.   an assessment

D.   all of the above

Answer: B. When ownership of a mortgage is transferred (assigned) from one company or individual to another, it is called an assignment.

3. A mortgage loan which requires the remaining balance be paid at a specific point in time is called a/an

A.   balloon mortgage
B.   early due mortgage
C.   mortgage of convenience
D.   promissory note

Answer: A. A mortgage loan that requires the remaining principal balance be paid at a specific point in time is a balloon mortgage.

4. The following reason accounts for why bridge loans are not used much anymore:

A.   More second mortgage lenders now will lend at a high loan to value
B.   Sellers would rather accept offers from Buyers who have already sold their property
C.   Neither A or B

D.   Both A and B

Answer: D. Bridge loans are not used much anymore because more second mortgage lenders now will lend at a high loan to value and sellers often prefer to accept offers from buyers who have already sold their property.

5. A title which is free of liens or legal questions as to ownership of the property is called a _____ title.

A.   good
B.   cloudy
C.   clear
D.   free

Answer: C. A title free of liens or legal questions as to ownership of the property is called a clear title. It is clear because there can be no challenges made to its legality.

6. What is the collateral in a home loan?

A.   The property itself
B.   A person's good name
C.   The amount of savings a person has
D.   The current automobile the person owns

Answer: A. The property itself is the collateral, and the borrower risks losing it if he does not repay according to the terms of the mortgage or deed of trust.

7. The adjustment date on an adjustable-rate mortgage is

A. the date the interest rate changes
B. the date the stock market goes up
C. 30 days from the date the mortgage was taken out
D. all of the above

Answer: A. The adjustment date is the date the interest rate changes (adjusts).

8. What is the deposit made by a potential buyer to show he is serious about buying a house called?

A. Serious money deposit
B. Earnest money deposit
C. "Nothing ventured, nothing gained" deposit
D. Down payment

Answer: B. The deposit made by a potential buyer to show they are in earnest about purchasing a house is called an earnest money deposit.

9. A right-of-way which gives persons other than the owner access to or over a property is known as an

A.   easement
B.   ingress
C.   egress
D.   none of the above

Answer: A. An easement is a right-of-way to persons other than the owner and gives them legal access.

10. Which best describes a "subdivision"?

A.   Houses in the same neighborhood similar in style and size
B.   A housing development created by dividing a tract of land into individual lots
C.   A development which is "substandard"
D.   None of the above

Answer: B. A subdivision consists of individual lots created from a larger tract (subdivided) and are offered for sale or lease.

11. When someone contributes to the construction or rehabilitation of a property with labor or services rather than cash, that contribution is called

A.   a personal contribution
B.   sweat equity

C. a big help to the contractors
D. toil and labor

Answer: B. Sweat equity is the contribution to the construction of or rehabilitation of a property in the form of labor or services rather than cash.

12. A two-step mortgage is defined as

A. an adjustable rate mortgage with one interest rate for the first five or seven years and a different rate for the remainder of the term.
B. a mortgage which is both adjustable and fixed
C. a mortgage which is named after a dance step
D. all of the above

Answer: A. A two-step mortgage starts out with one rate for the first five or seven years and then changes to a different rate for the remainder of the term of the mortgage amortization.

13. A legal document evidencing a person's right to or ownership of a property is called a:

A. quitclaim deed
B. title
C. yearly lease
D. accurate appraisal

Answer: B. A title is a legal document evidencing a person's right to or ownership of a property.

14. If you were buying a house that included furnishings, you would receive a written document transferring title to the personal property. This document is called a/an

A.   title
B.   deed
C.   bill of sale
D.   evidence of payment

Answer: C. A bill of sale is a written document that transfers personal property from one owner to another.

15. An oral or written agreement that is binding in a court of law is called a:

A.   gentlemen's agreement
B.   contract
C.   business deal
D.   promissory note

Answer: B. A contract can be oral or written and is binding in a court of law.

16. The part of the purchase price of a property that the buyer pays in cash and does not finance with the mortgage is

called the

A.   deposit
B.   second mortgage
C.   down payment
D.   deed of trust

Answer: C. The down payment is the amount paid down in cash as the initial upfront portion of the total amount due. It is usually given in cash at the time of finalizing the transaction.

17. A female named in a will to administer an estate is called an

A.   executor
B.   executrix
C.   individual representative
D.   able inheritor

Answer: B. The female executor named in a will to administer an estate is called an executrix.

18. The greatest possible interest a person can have in real estate is called

A.   fee complex
B.   fee simple
C.   no additional fees

D.   ownership

Answer: B. The greatest possible interest a person can have in real estate is called fee simple.

19. Required for properties located in federally designated flood areas, this type of insurance compensates for physical property damage resulting from flooding. It is called

A.   water damage insurance
B.   hurricane insurance
C.   there's no such thing
D.   flood insurance

Answer: D. Flood insurance is required in federally designated flood areas and does compensate for physical property damage resulting from flooding.

20. The following is true of a government loan:

A.   It is guaranteed by the Department of Veterans Affairs (VA)
B.   It is guaranteed by the Rural Housing Service (RHS)
C.   It is insured by the Federal Housing Administration (FHA)
D.   All of the above

Answer: D. Government loans are either insured by FHA,

guaranteed by VA or RHS. Mortgages that are not government loans are called conventional loans.

21. The person conveying an interest in real property is called

A.   the buyer
B.   the grantee
C.   the grantor
D.   the mortgagor

Answer: C. The grantor is the person conveying an interest in real property to another party.

22. Insurance that covers in the event of physical damage to a property from fire, wind, vandalism, or other hazards is called

A.   act of God insurance
B.   hazardous insurance
C.   hazard insurance
D.   there is no such insurance

Answer: C. Insurance covering physical damage to a property from fire, wind, vandalism, or other hazards is called hazard insurance.

23. A liquid asset is

A. an asset which is not in solid form
B. an asset which cannot be frozen
C. a cash asset or an asset easily turned into cash
D. an asset that is hard to get to

Answer: C. A liquid asset is either cash or something easily turned into cash.

24. Another term for the lender in a mortgage agreement is the

A. banker
B. mortgagee
C. mortgagor
D. private mortgage company

Answer: B. The mortgagee is the lender.

25. If you are buying a house and asking the Seller to provide all or part of the financing, you are asking for _____ financing.

A. special
B. owner
C. personal
D. non-bank

Answer: B. When the Seller provides all or part of the financing it is called owner financing.

26. A point is

A.   the part of the pen you sign a contract with
B.   a score in a basketball game
C.   the reason for telling the story
D.   1% of the amount of the mortgage

Answer: D. A point is 1% of the amount of the mortgage.

27. What does a power of attorney grant someone?

A.   The ability to attend law school
B.   Complete or limited authority on behalf of someone else
C.   Complete control over which medical facility someone uses
D.   The right to inherit an estate

Answer: B. A power of attorney derives power from a legal document and grants someone complete or limited authority on behalf of someone.

28. The principal is

A.   the amount borrowed or remaining unpaid

B.	part of the monthly payment that reduces the remaining balance of a mortgage

C.	an ethic or value

D.	both A and B

Answer: D. The principal is the amount borrowed or remaining unpaid, as well as the part of the monthly payment that reduces the remaining balance of a mortgage.

29. A promissory note is

A.	a written promise to repay a specified amount over a specified period of time

B.	an oral promise to repay a specified amount over a specified period of time

C.	a note passed back and forth in class

D.	a note you deliver to another telling them of your intentions

Answer: A. A promissory note is a written promise to repay a specific amount over a specified period of time.

30. Which of the following best describes a real estate agent?

A.	A licensed person who negotiates and transacts the sale of real estate

B.	The owner of a real estate firm

C.	A person who negotiates and transacts the sale of real

estate but is not licensed

D.   A person who sells both property and insurance

Answer: A. A real estate agent is a licensed person who negotiates and transacts the sale of real estate.

31. When does an assumption take place?

A.   When someone believes something and it turns out to be true
B.   When the buyer assumes the seller's mortgage
C.   When the seller assumes the buyer's mortgage
D.   All of the above

Answer: B. When the buyer assumes the seller's mortgage is a transaction called an assumption.

32. A legal document conveying title to a property is called a/an

A.   sales contract
B.   option to purchase
C.   deed
D.   contract for deed

Answer: C. A deed is a legal document conveying title to property.

33. If you have a loan and transfer the title to another individual without informing the lender, it is likely that the lender will demand payment of the outstanding loan balance. He is able to do this because of a clause in your mortgage called the

A.   due on demand clause
B.   acceleration clause
C.   amortization schedule
D.   both A and B

Answer: B. An acceleration clause allows the lender to demand payment, most commonly if the borrower defaults on the loan or transfers title to someone without informing the lender.

34. The most common type of bankruptcy is called

A.   Chapter 11 bankruptcy
B.   Chapter 11 no asset bankruptcy
C.   Chapter 7 no asset bankruptcy
D.   Chapter 7 bankruptcy

Answer: C. The most common type for an individual is a "Chapter 7 No Asset" bankruptcy, which relieves the borrower of most types of debts.

35. Which of the following best describes a "broker"?

A.   Someone who owns a real estate firm
B.   Some real estate agents working for brokers
C.   Someone who acts as an agent and brings two parties together for a transaction and earns a fee for this
D.   All of the above

Answer: D. A broker can own a real estate firm, work for another broker who owns the firm, broker loans in the mortgage industry, but basically is defined as anyone who acts as an agent, bringing two parties together for any type of transaction and earns a fee.

36. A normal contingency in a real estate contract would be that the

A.   purchaser is able to obtain a satisfactory home inspection from a qualified inspector.
B.   seller is allowed to come back and spend 2 weeks in the house each year
C.   purchaser is able to have occupancy as soon as the sales contract is signed
D.   seller is allowed to dig up some of the landscaping and take it with him

Answer: A. A normal contingency in a sales contract would be that the purchaser is able to obtain a satisfactory home inspection from a qualified inspector. This condition has to be met before the contract is legally binding.

37. If you go to a bank or mortgage company to apply for a home, what type of mortgage would you be applying for?

A.   Government
B.   Conventional
C.   American
D.   Adjustable rate

Answer: B. Home loans which are not VA or FHA are called conventional loans.

38. A report of someone's credit history which is prepared by a credit bureau and used by a lender in the loan qualification process is called a

A.   personal affidavit
B.   credit card history
C.   savings account history
D.   credit report

Answer: D. A report of an individual's credit prepared by a credit bureau and used by a lender in determining a loan applicant's creditworthiness is called a credit report.

39. If you have not made your mortgage payment within 30

days of the due date, the mortgage is considered to be in

A.   arrears
B.   default
C.   trouble
D.   bankruptcy

Answer: B. Failure to make the mortgage payment within a specified period of time, usually 30 days for first mortgages or first trust deeds, causes the loan to be in default.

40. A term used by appraisers to estimate the physical condition of a building. It may be different from the building's actual age.

A.   Estimated age
B.   Longevity
C.   Preferred age
D.   Effective age

Answer: D. An appraiser's estimate of the physical condition of a building is called effective age. Its actual age may be shorter or longer than the effective age.

41. The difference between the fair market value of a property and the amount still owed on the mortgage and other liens is the owner's financial interest in the property and is called his

A.   equity
B.   balance due
C.   indebtedness
D.   none of the above

Answer: A. A homeowner's financial interest in a property is called his equity. It is the difference between fair market value and what is still owed on the mortgage and any other liens.

42. You put in a new driveway to your property, but in the process the paving goes across your property line onto your neighbor's property a few inches. This is called an

A.   illegal driveway
B.   extra benefit for your neighbor
C.   encroachment
D.   easement

Answer: C. An improvement that intrudes illegally on another's property is called an encroachment. An easement would be a LEGAL intrusion.

43. A government loan that is not a VA loan would be a/an

A.   FHA mortgage
B.   FDA mortgage
C.   This type loan does not exist

D.   ARM mortgage

Answer: A. A mortgage which is insured by the Federal Housing Administration (FHA) and is the other type of government loan besides a VA loan is an FHA mortgage.

44. If you convey an interest in real property to a relative, that person is known as the

A.   receiver
B.   mortgagor
C.   grantee
D.   lucky relative

Answer: C. The person to whom an interest in real property is conveyed is the grantee.

45. You decide you want to buy a boat and you want to borrow against the equity in your home. You would get a mortgage loan up to a specified amount which is in second position to your first mortgage. This arrangement is called a

A.   perfectly acceptable way to buy a boat
B.   leverage against your house
C.   home equity line of credit
D.   line of credit for personal purposes

Answer: C. A mortgage loan, usually in second position, which allows the borrower to obtain cash drawn against the equity of his home, up to a predetermined amount, is known as a home equity line of credit.

46. You are your sister are joint tenants in a home your mother left you. Your sister has three children in her will and you have one. If she dies first, who does the property go to?

A.   It is divided equally between her three children
B.   It goes entirely to you
C.   It is divided equally between her three children and your one
D.   It goes into her estate

Answer: B. In the event of death in joint tenancy, the survivor owns the property in its entirety.

47. What is the best description of a lien?

A.   Something that doesn't stand up straight in a house
B.   Something that's illegal
C.   A legal claim against property that must be paid off when it's sold
D.   None of the above

Answer: C. A lien, such as a mortgage or first trust deed, is a legal claim against a property that must be paid off when it is sold.

48. What is a lock-in?

A.   A gated community which locks the gate at midnight
B.   An agreement from a lender guaranteeing a specific interest rate for a specific time at a certain cost
C.   What parents do with wayward children
D.   A type of key available at most hardware stores

Answer: B. A lock-in is a rate guaranteed by the lender for a certain period of time at a certain cost to the buyer.

49. The right of a government to take private property for public use upon payment of its fair market value. It is the basis for condemnation proceedings.

A.   Eminent domain
B.   Governmental domain
C.   Encroachment
D.   Both A and B

Answer: A. Eminent domain is the right of the government to take private property for public use upon payment of its fair market value.

50. A mortgage with a lien position subordinate to the first

mortgage on a piece of property is called a

A.   second mortgage
B.   first subordinate mortgage
C.   mortgage which isn't legal
D.   lien position mortgage

Answer: A. A second mortgage is a mortgage with a lien position subordinate to the first mortgage.

51. An adjustable-rate mortgage, also known as an ARM is

A.   one in which the interest rate is fixed over time
B.   one in which the interest rate changes periodically, depending on index changes
C.   one in which the interest rate changes periodically, depending on the stock market
D.   a type of mortgage that the mortgagor can adjust himself

Answer: B. An adjustable rate mortgage in one in which the interest rate adjusts periodically, according to corresponding fluctuations in an index.

52. A schedule that shows how much of each payment will be applied to principal and how much toward interest over the life of the loan is called a/n

A.   amortization schedule
B.   annual percentage rate
C.   assumption
D.   both A and C

Answer: A. An amortization schedule is a table showing how much of each payment is applied to interest and how much to principal. It also shows the gradual decrease of the loan balance until it reaches zero.

53. The term applied to a mortgage in which you make the payments every two weeks, thereby making thirteen payments a year rather than twelve. This mortgage is paid off faster than a normal mortgage.

A.   Twice-monthly mortgage
B.   Accelerated mortgage
C.   Bi-weekly mortgage
D.   None of the above

Answer: C. A mortgage in which you make payments every two weeks instead of once a month is called a bi-weekly mortgage.

54. The limitation of how much an adjustable rate mortgage may adjust over a six-month period, annual period, and over the life of the loan is called a

A. buy-down
B. high point
C. top stop
D. cap

Answer: D. The limitation on how much the loan may adjust over a period of time and for the life of the loan is a cap.

55. When is a real estate transaction considered to be "closed"?

A. When the buyer has signed all the sales contracts
B. When the closing documents have been recorded at the local recorder's office
C. When all the documents are signed and money changes hands
D. Both B and C.

Answer: D. In some states "closed" means when the documents are recorded at the courthouse, and in others it is a meeting where the documents are signed and money changes hands.

56. A record of an individual's repayment of debt, reviewed by mortgage lenders in determining credit risk is called a

A. credit affidavit
B. credit history

C.   there is no such record
D.   credit worthiness

Answer: B. A record of an individual's repayment of debt is called a credit history.

57. If you sell your property to a neighbor and the lender demands repayment in full, this means you have a _____ in your mortgage.

A.   seller pays all provision
B.   buyer pays all provision
C.   due-on-sale provision
D.   none of the above

Answer: C. A provision in a mortgage which allows the lender to demand repayment in full if the borrower sells the property that serves as security for the mortgage is called a due-on-sale provision.

58. The sum total of all the real and personal property owned by an individual at time of death is called their

A.   estate
B.   probate
C.   will
D.   all of the above.

Answer: A. The sum total of all the real and personal property owned by an individual at time of death is called an estate.

59. If you list your property with a real estate agent and sign a written agreement that they are the only ones entitled to a listing for a specific time you have given them an

A.   exclusive listing
B.   exclusive right to advertise
C.   exclusive right to show
D.   inclusive listing

Answer: A. A written contract giving a licensed real estate agent the exclusive right to sell a property for a specified time is called an exclusive listing.

60. Fair market value could be defined as

A.   how much a property is worth, determined by a realtor's market analysis
B.   the most a buyer, willing, but not compelled to buy, would pay
C.   the least a seller, willing, but not compelled to sell, would take
D.   both B and C

Answer: D. Fair market value is the highest price that a buyer, willing but not compelled to buy, would pay, and the lowest a seller, willing but not compelled to sell, would accept.

61. If a lender agrees to make a loan to a specific borrower on a specific property, he has made a

A.   decision to make the loan
B.   statement that both the buyer and the property pass inspection
C.   firm commitment
D.   both B and C

Answer: C. A lender's agreement to make a loan to a specific borrower on a specific property is called a firm commitment.

62. If you buy a house and build cabinets into the wall, then sell that house, the cabinets stay because they have become a

A.   type of attachment
B.   fixture
C.   part of the house
D.   none of the above

Answer: B. Personal property becomes real property when attached in a permanent manner to real estate and is called a fixture.

63. A home inspection is

A.   a thorough inspection by a professional which evaluates the structural and mechanical condition of a property
B.   not required by law
C.   often a contingency in a contract that it turns out satisfactorily
D.   both A and C

Answer: D. A home inspection is a thorough inspection by a professional that evaluates the structural and mechanical condition of the property. A satisfactory home inspection is often a contingency.

64. An insurance policy which combines personal liability insurance and hazard insurance coverage for a dwelling and its contents is called

A.   homeowner's insurance
B.   buyer's insurance
C.   errors and omissions insurance
D.   all of the above

Answer: A. Homeowner's insurance combines personal liability insurance and hazard insurance coverage for a dwelling and its contents.

65. Which of the following is true of a lease-option?

A.   It is an alternative financing option
B.   Each month's rent may also consist of an additional amount applied toward the purchase
C.   The price is already set in the beginning
D.   All of the above

Answer: D. A lease-option is an alternative financing option that allows home buyers to lease a home with an option to buy. Each month's rent payment may consist of not only the rent, but an additional amount which can be applied toward the down payment on an already specified price.

66. In simple terms, a sum of borrowed money (principal) usually repaid with interest is called a

A.   mortgage
B.   loan
C.   conventional loan
D.   alternative mortgage

Answer: B. A sum of borrowed money generally repaid with interest is simply a loan.

67. A property description which is recognized by law and is sufficient to locate and identify the property without oral testimony is known as the property's

A.   address
B.   911 address
C.   legal description
D.   identifying information

Answer: C. A legal description describes the property and is recognized by law. It is sufficient to locate and identify the property without oral testimony.

68. The date on which the principal balance of a loan, bond, or other financial instrument becomes due and payable is called

A.   its due date
B.   maturity
C.   end of the paper trail
D.   delivery

Answer: B. The date on which the principal balance of a loan, bond, or other financial instrument becomes due and payable is called maturity.

69. The person borrowing money in a mortgage agreement is called the

A.   mortgagor
B.   mortgagee

C. borrower

D. lessee

Answer: A. The borrower in a mortgage agreement is called the mortgagor.

70. Which of the following is true about an origination fee?

A. It applies to both government and conventional loans

B. It is usually 1% on a government loan

C. It is usually 2% on a conventional loan

D. Both A and B

Answer: D. Origination fees apply to government and conventional loans. A government loan origination fee is one percent of the loan amount, but additional points may be charged which are called "discount points". In a conventional loan, the origination fee refers to the total number of points a borrower has to pay.

71. Which of the following falls under the term "personal property"?

A. A garage attached to a house

B. A sofa

C. The front porch of a home

D.   The windows in a home

Answer: B. Personal property is any property that is not part of the real property. A, C, an D are all parts of the house.

72. In some cases if a borrower pays off a loan before it is due he may encounter a penalty called a

A.   penalty for early withdrawal
B.   loan to value penalty
C.   prepayment penalty
D.   there is never a penalty for paying a loan off early

Answer: C. A fee that may be charged to a borrower who pays off a loan before it is due is known as a prepayment penalty.

73. Which of the following statements is true regarding the term "pre-approval"?

A.   It applies only to the property
B.   It is done before the loan application is complete
C.   It s a loosely used term
D.   None of the above

Answer: C. Pre-approval is a loosely used term generally taken to mean a borrower has completed a loan application and provided debt, income, and savings documentation which an underwriter has reviewed and approved.

74. PITI reserves applies to

A.   a cash amount the borrower must have on hand after down payment and closing Costs.
B.   an amount which is financed with the mortgage
C.   both A and B
D.   none of the above

Answer: A. PITI reserves must equal the cash amount that the borrower would have to pay for principal, interest, taxes, and insurance for a predefined number of months.

75. Why would a public auction take place?

A.   It's a good way to buy property
B.   To inform the public about property for sale
C.   To help auctioneers get employment
D.   To sell property to repay a mortgage in defaults

Answer: D. A public auction is a meeting in an announced public location to sell property to repay a mortgage that is in default.

76. The term "realtor" applies to

A. any real estate agent who has passed the state exam
B. any real estate agent whose license is active
C. any real estate agent who is a member of a local real estate board affiliated with the National Association of Realtors.
D. any real estate agent who belongs to his local board

Answer: C. A realtor is defined as an agent, broker, or associate who holds active membership in a local real estate board which is affiliated with the National Association of Realtors.

77. "Remaining term" refers to

A. the remaining school term for a real estate class
B. the original amortization term minus the number of payments that have been applied
C. the months left in a pregnancy
D. all of the above

Answer: B. The remaining term applies to the original amortization term minus the number of payments that have been applied.

78. Which of the following is not true of a "revolving debt"?

A. It is a type of credit arrangement, like a credit card
B. It revolves around no interest for the first six months
C. A customer borrows against a pre-approved line of credit

D.   The customer is billed for the amount borrowed plus any interest due

Answer: B. Revolving debt is a credit arrangement, such as a credit card, which allows a customer to borrow against a pre-approved line of credit when purchasing goods and services. The borrower is billed for the amount that is actually borrowed plus any interest due.

79. Which of the following does a survey not show?

A.   Precise legal boundaries of a property
B.   Location of improvements, easements, rights of way
C.   Encroachments
D.   Location of furnishings within the dwelling

Answer: D. A survey is a drawing or map showing the precise legal boundaries of a property, the location of improvements, easements, rights of way, encroachments, and other physical features.

80. What is meant by "seller carry-back"?

A.   The seller physically carries his furnishings out of the house on the day of closing
B.   The seller agrees to be on the mortgage with the buyer
C.   the seller provides financing, often in combination with

an assumable mortgage

D.   The seller carries the principal, but not the interest on a loan

Answer: C. A seller carry-back is an agreement in which the owner of a property provides financing, often in combination with an assumable mortgage.

81. A title company is one which

A.   is usually not needed in a real estate transaction
B.   is not called upon until one year after the sale is closed
C.   specializes in examining and insuring titles to real estate
D.   specializes in preparing deeds and deeds of trust

Answer: C. A title company specializes in examining and insuring titles to real estate.

82. A state or local tax which is payable when title passes from one owner to another is called a

A.   title tax
B.   transfer tax
C.   revenue stamps
D.   real estate tariff

Answer: B. State or local tax payable when title passes from one owner to another is called a transfer tax.

83. What is Truth-in-Lending?

A.   A state law requiring lenders to fully disclose in writing all terms and conditions of a mortgage
B.   A federal law requiring lenders to fully disclose in writing all terms and conditions of a mortgage
C.   A local law requiring lenders to fully disclose in writing all terms and conditions of a mortgage
D.   None of the above

Answer: B. Truth-in-Lending is a federal law requiring lenders to fully disclose in writing the terms and conditions of a mortgage, including the annual percentage rate and other charges.

84. A VA mortgage

A.   is a conventional mortgage for the state of Virginia
B.   is guaranteed by the Department of Veterans Affairs
C.   originates in Texas but ends up in Virginia
D.   in available to anyone applying for a mortgage

Answer: B. A VA mortgage is guaranteed by the Department of Veterans Affairs.

85. Which of the following is not true of "amortization"?

A. Over time the interest portion increases as the loan balance decreases
B. Over time the interest portion decreases as the loan balance decreases
C. Over time the amount applied to principal increases so the loan is paid off in the specified time
D. None of the above

Answer: A. The loan payment consists of a portion which will be applied to pay the accruing interest on a loan, with the remainder being applied to the principal. Over time the interest portion decreases as the loan balance decreases and the amount applied to principal increases so that the loan is paid off (amortized) in the specified time.

86. The valuation placed on property by a public tax assessor for taxation purposes is called

A. real value
B. fair market value
C. assessed value
D. predicted value

Answer: C. The valuation placed on property by a public tax assessor for purposes of taxation is called assessed value.

87. If a veteran is eligible for a VA loan, he or she would receive a document from the VA called

A. Certificate of Authenticity
B. Certificate of Approval
C. Certificate of Met Requirements
D. Certificate of Eligibility

Answer: D. A certificate of eligibility is a document issued by the Veteran's Administration that certifies a veteran's eligibility for a VA loan.

88. Which of the following usually earns the largest commissions in a real estate transaction?

A. Attorneys
B. Realtors
C. Loan officers
D. Home warranty companies

Answer: B. Realtors generally earn the largest commissions, followed by lenders.

89. An unwritten body of law based on general custom in England and used to an extent in some states is called

A. common law
B. uncommon law

C.   casual law

D.   it isn't law if it's not written down

Answer: A. An unwritten body of law based on general custom in England and used to an extent in some states is called common law.

90. If a real estate agent is trying to determine the market value of a property, one thing they would use is recent sales of similar properties or

A.   neighbors' estimates of the value of the property

B.   records from several years back in the same neighborhood

C.   comparable sales

D.   sales they estimate to happen in the future

Answer: C. Recent sales of similar properties in nearby areas and used to help determine the market value of a property are called comparable sales, or "comps."

91. A person to whom money is owed is known as a

A.   debtor

B.   creditor

C.   mortgagee

D.   lender

Answer: B. A creditor is a person to whom money is owed.

92. Discount points refer to

A.   a system of figuring out how much the property will be discounted

B.   points paid in addition to the one percent loan origination fee

C.   usually only FHA and VA loans

D.   both B and C

Answer: D. This term is usually used in reference to only government loans (FHA and VA). Discount points are any points paid in addition to the one percent loan origination fee.

93. Which of the following can the Equal Credit Opportunity Act (ECOA) not discriminate against?

A.   Race, color or religion

B.   National origin

C.   Age, sex, or marital status

D.   All of the above

Answer: D. ECOA is a federal law requiring lenders and other creditors to make credit equally available without discrimination based on race, color, religion, national origin, age, sex, marital status, or receipt of income from public assistance programs.

94. An exclusive listing is one which gives a licensed real estate agent the exclusive right to sell a property

A.   until it sells
B.   until the owner takes it off the market
C.   for a specified period of time
D.   none of the above

Answer: C. An exclusive listing gives a licensed real estate agent the exclusive right to sell a property for a specified period of time.

95. Which of the following is true about Fannie Mae's Community Home Buyer's Program?

A.   It is an income-based community lending model
B.   It has flexible underwriting guidelines to increase low to moderate income family's buying power
C.   Borrows who participate must attend pre-purchase home-buyer education sessions
D.   All of the above

Answer: D. Fannie Mae's Community Home Buyer's Program is an income-based community lending model, under which mortgage insurers and Fannie Mae offer flexible underwriting guidelines to increase a low or moderate income family's buying power and to decrease the total amount of cash needed to purchase a home. Participating borrows are required to attend pre-purchase home-buyer education sessions.

96. The mortgage that is in first place among any loans recorded against a property and usually refers to the date in which loans are recorded, but not always, is called a

A.   primary mortgage
B.   first in line mortgage
C.   first mortgage
D.   both A and B

Answer: C. The mortgage that is in first place is a first mortgage.

97. The legal process by which a borrower in default under a mortgage is deprived of his or her interest in the mortgaged property is called a

A.   takeover by the mortgage company
B.   public auction
C.   foreclosure
D.   proceeds sale

Answer: C. The legal process by which a borrower in default under a mortgage is deprived of his or her interest in the mortgaged property is called a foreclosure.

98. Loans against 401K plans are

A.   not allowed for down payments on property
B.   an acceptable source of down payment for most types of loans
C.   too great a risk for most people to take
D.   only allowed if you're accumulated $50,000 in the plan

Answer: B. Some administrators of 401(k)/403B plans allow for loans against the monies you have accumulated in these plans. Loans against 401k plans are an acceptable source of down payment for most types of loans.

99. A late charge is

A.   the penalty a borrower pays when a payment is late a stated number of days
B.   usually put into play when the payment is fifteen days late on a first mortgage
C.   usually not applicable to most people
D.   both A and B

Answer: D. A late charge usually kicks in after fifteen days on a first mortgage and is a penalty a borrower must pay.

100. A person's financial obligations are known as his

A.   payments
B.   assets
C.   liabilities
D.   credit risks

Answer: C. A person's financial obligations are called liabilities and include long-term and short-term debt and any other amounts owed to others.

101. Which of the following is not true of annual percentage rate (APR)?

A.   It is the note rate on your loan
B.   It is not the note rate on your loan
C.   It is a value created according to a government formula intended to reflect the true cost of borrowing and expressed as a percentage
D.   It is always higher than the actual note rate on your loan

Answer: A. Annual percentage rate is not the note rate on your loan. It is a value created according to a government formula intended to reflect the true annual cost of borrowing, expressed as a percentage. The APR is always higher than the actual note rate on your loan.

102. An individual qualified by education, training, and experience to estimate the value of real property and personal property and who usually works independently is called an

A.   estimator of value
B.   appraiser
C.   on-site inspector
D.   underwriter

Answer: B. An appraiser is an individual qualified by education, training, and experience to estimate the value of real and personal property. Some work for lenders, but most are independent.

103. Which of the following best describes a "balloon payment"?

A.   Payment delivered with a "bang"
B.   First of many payments on a mortgage
C.   The final lump sum payment due at the termination of a balloon mortgage
D.   Payments which go higher and higher each year

Answer: C. A balloon payment is the final lump sum payment due at the termination of a balloon mortgage.

104. When a borrower refinances his mortgage at a higher amount than the current loan balance with the intention of pulling out money for personal use, it is referred to as a

A.   refinance extra
B.   cash-out refinance
C.   home equity refinance
D.   adjustable lump sum refinance

Answer: B. A cash-out refinance is when a borrow refinances his mortgage at a higher amount than the current loan balance because he wants to pull our money for personal use.

105. A certificate of deposit is

A.   the same as a down payment
B.   a liquid asset
C.   a deposit held in a bank paying a certain amount of interest to the depositor over a certain time
D.   a deposit held in a bank which pays double the amount of normal interest over time

Answer: C. A certificate of deposit is a time deposit held in a bank which pays a certain amount of interest to the depositor.

106. Common area assessments are

A.   sometimes called Homeowners Association Fees
B.   paid by individual owners of condominiums or planned
unit developments
C.   used to maintain the property and common areas
D.   all of the above

Answer: D. Common area assessments are also sometimes
called Homeowners Association Fees and are paid by the
individual owners of condos or planned unit developments and
are used to maintain the property and common areas.

**107. A short-term interim loan for financing the cost of
construction is called a**

A.   flexible loan
B.   convertible loan
C.   construction loan
D.   not a loan, but a promissory note

Answer: C. A short-term interim loan for financing the cost of
construction is called a construction loan. The lender makes
payments to the builder at periodic intervals as the work

progresses.

108. In simple terms, debt is

A.   credit extended to someone
B.   an amount owed to another
C.   an amount owed to another with interest
D.   repayable

Answer: B. Debt is an amount owed to another

109. Which of the following is not true of the term "depreciation"?

A.   It is a decline in the value of property
B.   It is an accounting term showing the declining monetary value of an asset
C.   It is a true expense where money is actually paid
D.   Lenders add back depreciation expense for self-employed borrowers and count it as income

Answer: C. Depreciation is not a true expense where money is actually paid. It is a decline in the value of property and an accounting term showing the declining monetary value of an asset. Lenders add back depreciation expense for self-employed borrowers and count it as income.

110. Which of the following would not be paid by escrow disbursements?

A.   Real estate taxes
B.   Hazard insurance
C.   Mortgage insurance
D.   Personal property taxes

Answer: D. Personal property taxes are not a typical escrow disbursement, but real estate taxes, hazard insurance and mortgage insurance are.

111. The lawful expulsion of an occupant from real property is called

A.   conviction
B.   divorce from bed and board
C.   eviction
D.   there is no way to lawfully remove an occupant from real property

Answer: C. The lawful expulsion of an occupant from real property is called eviction.

112. If you have a loan in which the interest rate does not change during the term of the loan you have a _____ mortgage.

A. fixed-rate
B. conventional fixed-rate
C. owner financing
D. all of the above

Answer: A. A loan in which the interest rate does not change during the term is called a fixed-rate mortgage.

113. The following is true of a Home Equity Conversion Mortgage (HECM).

A. It is also known as reverse annuity mortgage
B. You don't make payments to the lender, the lender makes payments to you
C. It enables older homeowners to convert their equity into cash
D. All of the above

Answer: D. Usually called a reverse annuity mortgage, this mortgage is unique in that instead of making payments to a lender, the lender makes payments to you, allowing older homeowners to convert their equity to cash. The loan does not have to be repaid until the borrower no longer occupies the property.

114. A written agreement between property owner and

tenant stipulating the conditions under which the tenant may possess the property for a specified period of time and the payment due is called a/an

A.   contract
B.   option
C.   lease
D.   lease-option

Answer: C. A written agreement between property owner and tenant laying out the terms of the agreement including payment and period of time is called a lease.

115.   A lender is

A.   the firm making the loan
B.   the individual representing the firm making the loan
C.   the individual offering owner financing
D.   both A and B

Answer: D. A lender is the firm making the loan or an individual representing the firm making the loan.

116. A margin is

A.   a measurement of error
B.   an artificial line not to write in on a loan document
C.   both A and B

D.   the difference between the interest rate and the index on an adjustable rate mortgage

Answer: D. A margin is the difference between the interest rate and the index on an adjustable rate mortgage which remains stable over the life of the loan.

117. Which of the following is the best definition of a mortgage broker?

A.   A mortgage company which originates loans, then places with other lending institutions
B.   A mortgage company which originates loans, then keeps them in house
C.   An individual which originates loans, then sells on the secondary market
D.   Much like a real estate broker, receives a commission on loans

Answer: A. A mortgage broker is a mortgage company which originates loans, then places with a variety of other lending institutions with whom they usually have pre-established relationships.

118. The term "note rate" refers to:

A.   the speed at which a musician plays scales

B.   the interest rate stated on a mortgage note
C.   the interest rate stated on a personal loan
D.   the rate at which a note is amortized

Answer: B. Note rate means the interest rate stated on a mortgage note.

119. If you have not made your mortgage payment, you are likely to receive which of the following?

A.   Notice of non-payment
B.   A written eviction notice
C.   Notice of default
D.   A letter from an attorney

Answer: C. You are likely to receive a formal written notice, called a notice of default, that a default has occurred and legal action may be taken.

120. A payment that is not sufficient to cover the scheduled monthly payment on a mortgage loan is called a

A.   late payment
B.   partial payment
C.   "too little, too late" payment
D.   a drop in the bucket

Answer: B. A payment insufficient to cover the scheduled monthly payment on a mortgage loan is a partial payment, normally not accepted by the lender, but in times of hardship a borrower can make a request of the loan servicing collection department.

121. PITI stands for

A.   principal, interest, taxes and insurance

B.   principle, interest, taxes and insurance
C.   prepayment, interest, tariff and insurance
D.   none of the above

Answer: A. PITI is principal, interest, taxes and insurance.

122. Which of the following describes "prepayment"?

A.   An amount paid to reduce the interest on a loan before the due date
B.   An amount paid to reduce the principal on a loan before the due date
C.   Can result from a sale, owner's decision to pay off the loan, or foreclosure
D.   Both B and C

Answer: D. A prepayment reduces the principal on a loan before the due date and can result from a sale, the owner's decision to pay off the loan early, or foreclosure.

123. What is private mortgage insurance?

A.   Mortgage insurance that is arranged for by the buyer privately

B.   Mortgage insurance provided by a private mortgage insurance company
C.   Insurance required for loans with a loan-to-value percentage in excess of 80%
D.   Both B and C

Answer: D. A prepayment reduces the principal on a loan before the due date and can result from a sale, the owner's decision to pay off the loan early, or foreclosure.

124. If you were trying to buy a home you and the seller would need to sign a written contract called a/an

A.   purchase agreement
B.   down payment agreement
C.   option to purchase
D.   all of the above

Answer: A. A written contract signed by buyer and seller stating the terms and conditions under which a property will be sold is called a purchase agreement.

125. What is a recorder?

A.   A public official who keeps records of real property transactions
B.   The county clerk
C.   The registrar of deeds
D.   All of the above.

Answer: D. A recorder is a public official who keeps records of real property transactions in their area and is also known by the names "county clerk" and "registrar of deeds".

126. The principal balance on a mortgage is

A.   the outstanding balance of principal and interest
B.   the outstanding balance of principal only
C.   the amount the mortgage has been paid down
D.   none of the above

Answer: B. The principal balance is the outstanding balance of principal only on a mortgage and does not include interest or any other charges.

127. Which of the following is not true about qualifying ratios?

A.   There are two types of ratios—"top" or "front" and "back" or "bottom"

B.   The "top" ratio is a calculation of the borrower's monthly housing costs (principal, taxes, insurance, mortgage insurance, homeowners' association fees) as a percentage of monthly income

C.   the "back" ratio includes all monthly costs as well as "back" taxes

D.   Both calculations are used in determining whether a borrower can qualify for a mortgage

Answer: C. The "back" or "bottom" ratio includes housing costs as well as all other monthly debt.

128. The definition of "real" property is

A.   property that has nothing artificial on it, only natural materials

B.   land and appurtenances, including anything of a permanent nature such as structures, trees and minerals

C.   things located within houses such as furniture, accessories, appliances, and clothing

D.   all of the above

Answer: B. Real property is defined as land and appurtenances, including anything of a permanent nature such as structures, trees, minerals, and the interest, benefits, and inherent rights thereof.

129. In joint tenancy, if one person dies and the other inherits the property, this is called

A.   tenants in common
B.   whatever is stated in the will
C.   following the wishes of the deceased
D.   right of survivorship

Answer: D. In joint tenancy the right of survivors to acquire the interest of a deceased joint tenant is called right of survivorship.

130. A secured loan is

A.   backed by collateral
B.   when the borrower promises something of value to the lender
C.   when the bank is not in danger of failing
D.   when the bank has been bailed out

Answer: A. A secured loan is backed by security, also called collateral.

131. A mortgage or other type of lien that has a priority lower than that of the first mortgage is called

A.   a second mortgage
B.   subordinate financing
C.   first subordinate financing
D.   all of the above

Answer: B. Subordinate financing is any mortgage or other lien that has a priority lower than the first mortgage.

132. If you were buying a house and wanted to protect yourself against any loss arising from disputes over ownership of your property, you would purchase

A.   hazard insurance
B.   errors and omissions insurance
C.   title insurance
D.   deed insurance

Answer: C. Insurance that protects the lender (lender's policy) or the buyer (owner's policy) against loss arising from disputes over ownership of a property is title insurance.

133   Which of the following is true of the Veteran's

Administration (VA)?

A.   It encourages lenders to make mortgages to veterans
B.   It is an agency of the federal government which guarantees residential mortgages made to eligible veterans
C.   The guarantee protects the lender against loss
D.   All of the above

Answer: D. An agency of the federal government, the VA guarantees residential mortgages made to eligible veterans of the military services. This guarantee protects the lender against loss and thus encourages lenders to make mortgages to veterans.

134. The form used to apply for a mortgage loan, which contains information about a borrower's income, savings, assets, debts, and more is called a/an

A.   application for funds
B.   income documentary
C.   both A and B
D.   application

Answer: A. The form used to apply for a mortgage loan containing information about a borrower's income, savings, assets, debts, and more is called an application.

135. An assessment does which of the following?

A.　　Places a value on property for the purpose of real estate sales

B.　　Is the same as a competitive market analysis

C.　　Places a value on property for the purpose of taxation

D.　　Is usually carried out by the mayor of a town

Answer: C. An assessment places a value on property for the purpose of taxation.

136. Which of the following is not true about the "bond market"?

A.　　It refers to the daily buy and selling of thirty-year treasury bonds

B.　　Lenders do not usually follow this market closely

C.　　The same factors that affect the bond market affect mortgage rates at the same time

D.　　Fluctuations in this market cause mortgage rates to change daily

Answer: B. Lenders actually do follow this market closely because the same factors that affect the Treasury Bond market also affect mortgage rates at the same time.

137. What does the term "buydown" mean?

A.   Usually refers to a fixed rate mortgage where the interest rate is "bought down" for a temporary period, usually one to three years.

B.   A lump sum is paid and held in an account used to supplement the borrower's monthly payment

C.   These funds can sometimes come from the seller to induce someone to buy their property

D.   All of the above

Answer: D. A buy-down refers to a fixed rate mortgage where the interest rate is "bought down" for a temporary period. The funds for this can come from the seller, the lender, or some other source. The lump sum is paid and held in an account used to supplement the borrower's monthly payment for a time and after that time the borrower's payment is calculated at the note rate.

138. Certificate of Reasonable Value (CRV) applies to

A.   an FHA loan
B.   a conventional loan
C.   a VA loan
D.   a car loan

Answer: C. Once the appraisal has been done on a property being bought with a VA loan, the VA issues a CRV.

139. If you are buying a piece of property and have someone else who is obligated on the loan and is on the title to the property, that person is called a

A.   spouse
B.   family member or friend who shares the property and payments with you
C.   co-borrower
D.   none of the above

Answer: C. An additional individual who is both obligated on the loan and is on the title to the property is called a co-borrower.

140. How would you define "collection"?

A.   A plate, usually at church, where money is donated
B.   It goes into effect when a borrower falls behind
C.   It applies to several or many things in the same category on a loan application
D.   It only applies to trash

Answer: B. When a borrower falls behind, the lender contacts them in an effort to bring the loan current. The loan then goes to "collection" and the lender must mail and record certain documents in case they have to foreclose on the property.

141. Which of the following is true of "condominium"?

A.   It applies to ownership, not to construction or development
B.   It is a type of ownership where all of the owners own each other's interior units
C.   It is an ownership where owners own the property, common areas, and buildings together
D.   both A and C

Answer: D. A condominium is real property where all the owners own the property, common areas and building together, with the exception of the interior of the unit to which they have title. Mistakenly referred to as a type of construction or development, it actually refers to type of ownership.

142. An organization which gathers, records, updates, and stores financial and public records information about the payment records of individuals being considered for credit is called a

A.   credit repository
B.   credit reporting agency
C.   mortgage company
D.   bank

Answer: A. A credit repository is an organization which gathers, records, updates, and stores financial and public records information about the payment records of individuals being considered for credit.

143. In some states a recorded mortgage is replaced by a

A.   contract for deed
B.   promissory note
C.   deed of trust
D.   deed

Answer: C. Some states do not record mortgages but do record a deed of trust which is essentially the same thing.

144. If you have failed to pay mortgage payments when they are due, it is called

A.   delinquency
B.   foreclosure
C.   collections
D.   no big deal

Answer: A. Failure to make mortgage payments when they are due is called delinquency. Most are due on the first day of the month, and even though they may not charge a "late fee" for a number of days, the payment is considered to be late and the loan delinquent.

145. Which of the following would not be considered an "encumbrance", limiting the fee simple title, on a piece of property?

A.   Leases
B.   Mortgages
C.   Easements or restrictions
D.   Furniture not paid for

Answer: D. Encumbrances include mortgages, easements, leases, or restrictions.

146. An earnest money deposit is put into this until delivered to the seller when the transaction is closed.

A.   the realtor's bank account
B.   the attorney's bank account
C.   the buyer's bank account
D.   an escrow account

Answer: D. An earnest money deposit is put into escrow until delivered to the seller when the transaction is closed.

147. Which of the following is true of the Federal National

Mortgage Association (Fannie Mae)?

A.   It is the nation's largest supplier of mortgages
B.   It is congressionally chartered, shareholder owned
C.   It is the same as Freddie Mac
D.   both A and B

Answer: D. Fannie Mae is a congressionally chartered, shareholder-owned company that is the nation's largest supplier of home mortgage funds.

148. An employer-sponsored investment plan allowing individuals to set aside tax-deferred income for retirement or emergency purposes is called a _____ plan.

A.   436(k)/401B
B.   339(k)/372B
C.   401(k)/403B
D.   both A and B

Answer: C. 401(k)/403B plans are employer-sponsored investment plans allowing individuals to set aside tax-deferred income for retirement or emergency purposes. Private corporations provide 401(k) plans; 403B plans are provided by not for profit organizations.

149. Which of the following is true of the Government National Mortgage Association, also known as Ginnie Mae?

A. It is government owned
B. It was created by Congress on September 1, 2002
C. Provides funds to lenders for making home loans
D. Both A and C

Answer: D. Ginnie Mae is government owned, created by Congress on September 1, 1968. Ginnie Mae performs the same roles as Fannie Mae and Freddie Mac in providing funds to lenders for home loans, but it provides funds for government loans (FHA and VA).

150. At what amount is a loan considered to be a "jumbo" loan, which exceeds Fannie Mae's and Freddie Mac's loan limits? It is also known as a non-conforming loan.

A. $417,000
B. $227,150
C. $300,000
D. Jumbo refers to the percentage borrowed, not the amount

Answer: A. A jumbo loan is anything over $417,000.

151. Usually part of a homeowner's insurance policy, this type insurance offers protection against claims alleging that

a property owner's negligence or inappropriate action resulted in bodily injury or property damage to another party.

A.   Malpractice insurance
B.   Liability insurance
C.   Hazard insurance
D.   Collision insurance

Answer: B. Liability insurance protects against claims against a property owner for negligence or bodily injury or property damage to another party.

152. A lender refers to the process of getting new loans as

A.   selling his product
B.   loan origination
C.   his bread and butter
D.   more than just a job

Answer: B. A lender refers to the process of getting new loans as loan origination.

153. The percentage relationship between the amount of the loan and the appraised value or sales price (whichever is lower) is called

A. value to loan
B. first-time homebuyer's loan
C. loan to value
D. both B and C

Answer: C. The percentage relationship between the amount of the loan and the appraised value or sales price is called loan to value.

154. If you are applying for a loan, the lender gives and guarantees you a specific interest rate for a specific time. This period of time is called the

A. period of no return
B. rate-freeze period
C. lock-in period
D. period at which you cannot seek other financing

Answer: C. The time during which the lender has guaranteed a certain rate is called the lock-in period.

155. A credit report which reports the raw data pulled from two or more of the major credit repositories is called a

A. multi-credit report
B. merged credit report
C. this is not legal

D.   none of the above

Answer: B. A merged credit report reports the raw data pulled from two or more of the major credit repositories.

156. Sometimes, called a first trust deed, this is a legal document pledging a property to the lender as security for payment of a debt.

A.   promissory note
B.   deed of trust
C.   owner financing document
D.   mortgage

Answer: D. A mortgage is a legal document pledging a property to the lender as security for payment of a debt.

157. Which of the following is not true of mortgage insurance?

A.   It covers the lender against some of the losses incurred resulting from default on a home loan
B.   It is sometimes is mistakenly referred to a PMI (private mortgage insurance)
C.   It is required on all loans having a loan to value of more than 90%
D.   No "MI" loans are usually made at higher rates

Answer: C. Mortgage insurance is required on all loans having a loan to value of more than 80%.

158   A no-point loan has an interest rate

A.   lower than if you pay one point
B.   the same as if you pay one point
C.   higher than if you pay one point
D.   a no-point loan does not exist

Answer: C. The interest rate on a "no points" loan is approximately a quarter percent higher than on a loan where you pay one point.

159. The total amount of principal owed on a mortgage before any payments are made is called the

A.   total amount due
B.   original principal balance
C.   a lot less than you'll actually pay
D.   your down payment times ten

Answer: B. The total amount of principal owed on a mortgage before any payments are made is called the original principal balance.

160. A planned unit development (PUD) is different from a condominium because

A.   a condominium usually has more amenities
B.   there are fewer units in a condominium development
C.   in a condominium the individual owns the airspace of the unit
D.   all of the above

Answer: C. A planned unit development is a type of ownership where individuals actually own the building or unit they live, but common areas are owned jointly with the other members of the development or association. In a condominium, an individual owns the airspace of his unit, but the buildings and common areas are owned jointly with the others in the development.

161. The term that means a limit on the amount that the interest rate can increase or decrease over the life of an adjustable rate mortgage is

A.   term cap
B.   life cap
C.   ARM cap
D.   none of the above

Answer: B. A life cap limits the amount the interest rate can increase or decrease over the life of the mortgage.

162. If a commercial bank or other financial institution extends you credit up to a certain amount for a certain time, you are receiving a

A.   line of credit
B.   personal loan
C.   unsecured loan
D.   both B and C

Answer: A. A line of credit is given by a commercial bank or other financial institution for a certain time and certain amount.

163. The term "modification" means

A.   a change in your mortgage without having to refinance
B.   a change in house plans before building begins
C.   the right of the bank to modify the interest rate without telling you
D.   both B and C

Answer: A. Occasionally a lender will agree to modify the terms of your mortgage without requiring you to refinance.

164. Which of the following is true of the term "mortgage banker"?

A.   They are generally assumed to originate and fund their own loans
B.   It is a loosely applied term to those who are mortgage brokers or correspondents
C.   They usually sell loans on the secondary market to Fannie Mae, Freddie Mac, or Ginnie Mae.
D.   All of the above.

Answer: D. A mortgage banker is generally assumed to originate and fund their own loans, which are then sold on the secondary market. Firms loosely apply this term to themselves, whether they are true mortgage bankers or simply mortgage brokers or correspondents.

165. Which of the following describes "prime rate"?

A.   It is the interest rate banks charge to their preferred customers
B.   The same factors that influence the prime rate also affect interest rates of mortgage loans
C.   Changes in the prime rate are usually not widely publicized in the news media
D.   Both A and B

Answer: D. Prime rate is the interest rate banks charge to their preferred customers. Changes in the prime rate are widely publicized in the news media and the same factors that influence prime rate also affect interest rates of mortgage loans.

166. A no cash-out refinance is

A.   intended to put cash in the hands of the borrower
B.   calculated to cover the balance due on the current loan and any costs associated with obtaining the new mortgage
C.   often referred to as a "rate and term refinance"
D.   both B and C

Answer: D. A no cash-out refinance is not intended to put cash in the hands of the buyer, but the new balance is calculated to cover the balance due on the current loan and any costs associated with obtaining the new mortgage. It is often referred to as a "rate and term refinance".

167. A legal document requiring a borrower to repay a mortgage loan at a stated interest rate during a specified period of time is called a

A.   note
B.   deed of trust
C.   mortgage
D.   both B and C

Answer: A. A note is a legal document requiring a borrower to repay a mortgage loan at a stated interest rate during a specified period of time.

168. The date when a new monthly payment amount takes effect on an adjustable-rate mortgage or graduated-payment mortgage is called the

A.   new payment date
B.   payment change date
C.   new payment due date
D.   change payment date

Answer: B. The date when a new monthly payment amount takes effect on an adjustable-rate mortgage or graduated-payment mortgage is called the payment change date.

169. A quitclaim deed does which of the following?

A.   Transfers with warranty whatever interest or title a grantor may have at the time the conveyance is made
B.   Transfers without warranty whatever interest or title a grantor may have at the time the conveyance is made
C.   Does not transfer interest at all
D.   Quitclaim deeds are no longer used

Answer: B. A quitclaim deed transfers without warranty whatever interest or title a grantor may have at the time the conveyance is made

170. In a refinance transaction, what happens?

A.   One loan is paid off with the proceeds from a new loan using the same property as security
B.   An additional loan is added to the present loan
C.   The loan's interest rate changes
D.   The term of the loan is increased

Answer: A. A refinance transaction is the process of paying off one loan with the proceeds from a new loan using the same property as security.

171. The amount of principal that has not yet been repaid is called the

A.   amount owed
B.   balance of the loan
C.   remaining balance
D.   all of the above

Answer: C. The amount of principal that has not yet been repaid is called the remaining balance.

172. If you made an arrangement to repay delinquent installments or advances, you would be setting up a

A.   good faith payment plan
B.   repayment plan
C.   another loan to pay off
D.   oral contract

Answer: B. A repayment plan is an arrangement made to repay delinquent installments or advances.

173. Your neighbor has given you a right of first refusal on a piece of land he plans to sell. What does this mean?

A.   He has given you the first opportunity to purchase it before he offers it for sale to others
B.   He expects you to refuse to buy it
C.   He expects you to pay more for it than anyone else
D.   None of the above

Answer: A. A right of first refusal is a provision in an agreement that requires the owner of a property to give another party the first opportunity to purchase or lease the property before he offers it for sale or lease to others.

174. You are selling the house you live in, but the house you're moving to is not completed. You need to stay on in

the house a while after closing. You work out a deal with the new purchaser called a

A.   no-rent lease agreement
B.   delayed possession for the new purchaser
C.   sale-leaseback
D.   lease for one year past closing

Answer: C. A sale-leaseback is a technique in which a seller deeds property to a buyer for a consideration, and the buyer simultaneously leases the property back to the seller.

175. In a tenancy in common

A.   ownership passes to the survivors in the event of death
B.   ownership does not pass to the survivors in the event of death
C.   there are no provisions made for the death of the owners
D.   when one person dies, the others have to move

Answer: B. In a tenancy in common ownership does not pass to the survivors in the event of death.

176. The duties of a "servicer" include

A.   collecting principal and interest payments from borrowers
B.   managing borrowers' escrow accounts

C.	usually a servicer services mortgages purchased by an investor in the secondary mortgage market
D.	all of the above

Answer: D. A servicer is an organization that collects principal and interest payments from borrowers and manages borrowers' escrow accounts. The servicer often services mortgages that have been purchased by an investor in the secondary mortgage market.

177. In "third-party origination"

A.	an independent political party originates a loan
B.	a lender uses another party to completely or partially originate, process, underwrite, close, fund, or package the mortgages it plans to deliver to the secondary mortgage market.
C.	three parties are involved in the loan process
D.	all of the above

Answer: B. A lender uses another party to completely or partially originate, process, underwrite, close, fund, or package the mortgages it plans to deliver to the secondary mortgage market.

178. A title search of a property would show the following to be true:

A.   the seller is the legal owner of the property
B.   there are no liens or other claims against the property
C.   the previous owners came over on the Mayflower
D.   both A and B

Answer: D. A title search would show that the seller is the legal owner and there are no outstanding liens or other claims against the property.

179. A trustee

A.   is known to be trustworthy
B.   is someone who has a great deal of trust in others
C.   is a fiduciary who holds or controls property for the benefit of another
D.   is usually a job for relatives

Answer: C. A trustee is a fiduciary who holds or controls property for the benefit of another.

180. When a person is "vested" he can

A.   use a portion of a fund such as an individual retirement fund
B.   use a portion of a fund without paying taxes on it
C.   have access to a bulletproof vest when in dangerous situations

D.   both A and C

Answer: A. A person who is "vested" can use a portion of a fund such as an individual retirement fund, but must pay taxes on funds that are withdrawn. If someone is 100% vested, they can withdraw all the funds set aside for them in a retirement fund.

181. Which of the following is not true of the term "appraised value"?

A.   It usually comes out lower than the purchase price when using comparable sales
B.   It is an opinion of a property's fair market value
C.   It is based on comparable sales
D.   None of the above

Answer: A. The appraised value usually comes out at the purchase price because the most recent sale is the one on the property in question.

182. If a buyer qualifies and is able to take over the seller's mortgage when buying his home, this type of mortgage is called

A.   "pass on down" mortgage
B.   assumable mortgage

C.   owner financing
D.   both B and C

Answer: B. A mortgage that can be assumed by the buyer when a home is sold is called an assumable mortgage. Usually the borrower must qualify in order to assume.

183. A call option is most similar to

A.   a lifetime cap
B.   a buy-down
C.   an acceleration clause
D.   all of the above

Answer: C. A call option is most similar to an acceleration clause.

184. A "chain of title" would show

A.   the transfers of title to a piece of property over the years
B.   members of the "chain gang" who had previously owned the property
C.   neither A nor B
D.   both A and B

Answer: A. A chain of title is an analysis of the transfers of title to a piece of property over the years.

185. Which of the following is true of a cloud on title?

A.   It usually cannot be removed except by deed, release, or court action

B.   It is the result of conditions revealed by a title search that adversely affect the title to real estate

C.   both A and B

D.   neither A nor B

Answer: C. A cloud on title is any condition revealed by a title search that adversely affects the title to real estate. Usually clouds cannot be removed except by deed, release, or court action.

186. Which of the following applies to "closing costs"?

A.   They are divided into two categories—"non-recurring closing costs" and "pre-paid items"

B.   Lenders try to estimate the amounts of non-recurring and pre-paids on a Good Faith Estimate shortly after receiving the loan application

C.   Pre-paids are items which recur over time, such as property taxes and homeowners insurance

D.   All of the above

Answer: D. Closing costs are either "non-recurring" or "pre-paids." "Pre-paids" occur over time, like property taxes and homeowners insurance. Lenders try to estimate both categories and give a Good Faith Estimate within three days of receiving a home loan application.

187. What is "community property"?

A.   Property that is owned by an entire condominium development
B.   Property that is owned by an entire subdivision of single-family homes
C.   Property acquired by a married couple during the marriage and considered to be jointly owned
D.   Both A and B

Answer: C. Community property, an outgrowth of the Spanish and Mexican heritage of the area, determines that property acquired by a married couple during their marriage is considered to be jointly owned.

188. If an apartment complex is converted to a condominium, this is called

A.   a condominium conversion
B.   an apartment conversion
C.   either an apartment or condominium conversion
D.   fewer options for people to rent

Answer: A. Changing the ownership of an existing building (usually a rental project) to the condominium form of ownership is called a condominium conversion.

189. This is an adjustable rate mortgage that allows the borrower to change the ARM to a fixed rate mortgage within a specific time.

A.   due-to-change ARM
B.   convertible ARM
C.   fixed rate ARM
D.   two-fold mortgage

Answer: B. A convertible ARM is an adjustable rate mortgage that allows the borrower to change the ARM to a fixed rate mortgage within a specific time.

190. If someone gives you "credit," you are

A.   agreeing to receive something of value in exchange for a promise to repay the lender at a later date
B.   getting something you deserve for something you did
C.   very lucky, because this doesn't happen often
D.   both B and C

Answer: A. Credit is an agreement in which a borrower receives something of value in exchange for a promise to repay the lender at a later date.

191. In an effort to avoid foreclosure (which may or may not happen), you might give the lender

A.   the payments he is due, all at one time
B.   your car and any other valuable personal property you have
C.   a "deed in lieu" (of foreclosure)
D.   a "deed in lieu" (of foreclosure), which then will not affect your credit badly

Answer: C. A "deed in lieu of foreclosure" conveys title to the lender when the borrower is in default and wants to avoid foreclosure. The lender may or may no stop foreclosure proceedings. Regardless, the avoidance and non-repayment of debt will most likely show on a credit history. The "deed in lieu" may prevent having the documents preparatory to a foreclosure becoming a matter of public record by being recorded.

192. When a lender performs this calculation annually to make sure the correct amount of money for anticipated expenditures is being collected, the lender is performing

A.   checks and balances
B.   an escrow analysis

C. a detailed loan analysis
D. lenders don't do this

Answer: B. Once a year your lender will perform an "escrow analysis" to make sure they are collecting the correct amount of money for the anticipated expenditures.

193. The report on the title of a property from the public records or an abstract of the title is called

A. a title report
B. an examination of title
C. an examination of deed, survey and title
D. title insurance

Answer: B. The report on the title of a property from the public records or an abstract of the title is called an examination of title.

194. A consumer protection law that regulates the disclosure of consumer credit reports by consumer/credit reporting agencies and establishes procedures for correcting mistakes on one's credit record is called the

A. Credit Reporting Act
B. Fair Credit Reporting Act
C. Consumer Protection Act

D.   Truth-in-Lending Act

Answer: B. The Fair Credit Reporting Act is a consumer protection law that regulates the disclosure of consumer credit reports by consumer/credit reporting agencies and establishes procedures for correcting mistakes on one's credit record.

195. If you inherit from someone, the best type of estate to inherit is called

A.   a fee simple estate
B.   general, all-encompassing estate
C.   life estate
D.   none of the above

Answer: A. A fee simple estate is an unconditional unlimited estate of inheritance that represents the greatest estate and most extensive interest in land that can be enjoyed and is of perpetual duration.

196. A homeowner's association does which the following?

A.   It manages the common areas of a condominium project or planned unit development
B.   It owns title to the common elements in a condominium development
C.   It doesn't own title to the common elements in a planned

unit development

D.   All of the above

Answer: A. A homeowner's association manages the common areas of a condominium project or planned unit development, owns title to the common elements in a planned unit development but doesn't in a condo development.

197. In simple terms a judgment is

A.   a personal opinion about real estate
B.   an individual's way of making decisions about legal matters
C.   a decision made by a court of law
D.   an opinion of an attorney

Answer: C. A judgment is a decision made by a court of law. In repayment of a debt, the court may place a lien against the debtor's real property as collateral for the judgment's creditor.

198. This is a way of holding title to a property wherein the mortgagor does not actually own the property but rather has a recorded long-term lease on it.

A.   contract for deed
B.   rent-to-own contract
C.   long-term lease

D.   leasehold estate

Answer: D. A leasehold estate is a way of holding title to a property when the mortgagor does not actually own the property but rather has a recorded long-term lease on it.

199. Which of the following are duties of a loan officer?

A.   The solicitation of loans
B.   Representation of the lending institution
C.   Representation of the borrower to the lending institution
D.   All of the above

Answer: D. A loan officer, sometimes called a lender, loan representative, loan "rep," or account executive solicits loans, represents the lending institution, and represents the borrower to the lending institution.

200. The amount paid by a mortgagor for mortgage insurance, either government or private is called

A.   mortgage insurance premium
B.   private mortgage insurance premium
C.   FHA insurance premium
D.   VA insurance premium

Answer: A. The mortgage insurance premium is paid by a

mortgagor for mortgage insurance, either to a government agency such as the Federal Housing Administration (FHA) or to a private mortgage insurance (MI) company.

201. Which of the following statements is not true of mortgage life and disability insurance?

A.   It begins immediately after someone becomes disabled

B.   It pays off the entire debt if someone dies during the life of the mortgage

C.   It is a type of term life insurance often bought by borrowers

D.   In this type insurance, the amount of coverage decreases as the principal declines

Answer: A. Be careful to read the terms of coverage because often it does not start immediately upon the disability, but after a specified period, sometimes forty-five days.

202. Which is the best definition of "multi-dwelling units"?

A.   They are properties that provide separate housing units for more than one family with several different mortgages

B.   They are properties that provide separate housing units for more than one family, but with a single mortgage

C.   They are properties that provide separate housing units for more than one family, but are leased rather than owned

D.   They are properties that provide separate housing units for more than one family on a lease-option basis

Answer: B. Multi-dwelling units provide separate housing units for more than one family, although they secure only a single mortgage.

203. Which of the following is true of "negative amortization"?

A.   It is also called "deferred interest"
B.   Because some ARM's allow the interest rate to fluctuate, the borrower's minimum payment may not cover all the interest
C.   The unpaid interest is added to the balance of the loan and the loan balance grows larger instead of smaller
D.   All of the above

Answer: D. Because some adjustable rate mortgages allow the interest rate to fluctuate independently of a required minimum payment, if a borrower makes the minimum payment it may not cover all the interest. The borrower is deferring the interest payment, called "deferred interest." It is then added to the balance, making it grow larger, and thus the term "negative amortization.

204. For someone to be determined to be "pre-qualified" for a loan, what has taken place?

A.   The person has given a written statement saying he can afford the loan

B.   A loan officer has given a written opinion of the borrower's ability to qualify based on debt, income, or savings

C.   The loan officer has reviewed a credit report on the borrower

D.   The information given to the loan officer is in the form of written documentation

Answer: B. Pre-qualification usually refers to the loan officer's written opinion of the ability of a borrower to qualify for a home loan, after the loan officer has made inquiries about debt, income, and savings. This information provided to the loan officer may have been presented verbally or in the form of documentation, and the loan officer may or may not have reviewed a credit report on the borrower.

205. The four components of a monthly mortgage payment on impounded loans are

A.   principal, interest, taxes, maintenance
B.   principal, interest, insurance, bank fees
C.   principal, interest, taxes, miscellaneous charge
D.   principal, interest, taxes, insurance

Answer: D. The four components of a monthly mortgage payment on impounded loans are principal, interest, taxes and insurance (PITI). While taxes and insurance are usually paid into an escrow account until they're due, principal refers to the part of the monthly payment that reduces the remaining balance and interest is the fee charged for borrowing money.

206. The term "periodic rate cap" refers to

A.   an adjustable rate mortgage
B.   a limit on the amount the interest rate can increase or decrease during any one adjustment period
C.   conventional fixed-rate loans
D.   both A and B

Answer: D. For an adjustable rate mortgage, a limit on the amount that the interest rate can increase or decrease during any one adjustment period, regardless of how high or low the index might be is called a periodic rate cap.

207. The acquisition of property through the payment of money or its equivalent is called

A.   a purchase money transaction
B.   having a down payment and mortgage
C.   simply, buying property
D.   a sales transaction

Answer: A. The acquisition of property through the payment of money or its equivalent is called a purchase money transaction.

208. What is a recording?

A. A sound file of music to study real estate by
B. Details of a properly executed legal document noted in the registrar's office
C. A document, such as a deed or mortgage note which becomes public record
D. Both B and C

Answer: D. The noting in the registrar's office of the details of a properly executed legal document, such as deed, mortgage note, satisfaction of mortgage, or extension of mortgage, thereby making it a part of the public record is called a recording.

209. If a landlord wants to protect himself against loss or rent or rental value due to fire or other casualty that would render the premises unusable for a time he would purchase

A. hazard insurance
B. fire insurance
C. rent-loss insurance
D. there is no such insurance

Answer: C. Rent loss insurance protects a landlord against loss or rent or rental value due to fire or other casualty that renders the leased premises unavailable for use and as a result of which the tenant is excused from paying rent.

210. The right to enter or leave designated premises is called

A.   the right of ingress or egress
B.   the right to enter or leave
C.   the right of non-trespass
D.   an easement

Answer: A. The right to enter or leave designated premises is called the right of ingress or egress.

211. "Secondary market" means

A.   a market which is not as important as the primary market
B.   the buying and selling of existing mortgages, usually as part of a "pool" of mortgages
C.   a market of lower real estate values
D.   none of the above

Answer: B. The buying and selling of existing mortgages, usually as a "pool," is called the secondary market.

212. The property that will be pledged as collateral for a loan is called

A. the back-up plan
B. the credit
C. security
D. the borrower's former home

Answer: C. Security is the property that will be pledged as collateral for a loan.

213. If you were purchasing a piece of property, either you or your bank would want to know if you were paying a fair price and would order

A. a market analysis by a realtor
B. an appraisal
C. survey
D. termite inspection

Answer: B. An appraisal is a written justification of the price paid for a property, primarily based on an analysis of comparable sales of similar homes nearby.

214. Which of the following is an example of "transfer of ownership"?

A. The purchase of property "subject to" the mortgage
B. Joint tenancy

C.   The assumption of the mortgage debt by the property purchaser

D.   Both A and C

Answer: D. Lenders consider the following to be a transfer of ownership: the purchase of a property "subject to" the mortgage, the assumption of the mortgage debt by the property purchaser, and any exchange of possession of the property under a land sales contract or any other land trust device.

215. Which of the following does not apply the Treasury index?

A.   An index used to determine interest rate changes for certain fixed-rate loans

B.   It is based on the results of auctions that the U. S. Treasury holds for its Treasury bills and securities

C.   derived from the U. S. Treasury's daily yield curve

D.   None of the above

Answer: A. The Treasury index is an index used to determine interest rate changes for certain adjustable rate loans.

216. What are assets?

A.   Items of value owned by an individual

B.   Items that can be quickly converted into cash are called "liquid assets"

C.   Real estate, personal property, and debts owed to someone by others

D.   All of the above.

Answer: D. Assets are items of value owned by an individual. Assets quickly converted to cash are considered "liquid assets" and include bank accounts, stocks, bonds, mutual funds, etc. Other assets include real estate, personal property, and debts owed to an individual by others.

217. One who establishes the value of a property for taxation purposes is called

A.   a government tax appraiser
B.   an assessor
C.   an appraiser
D.   all of the above

Answer: B. A public official who establishes the value of a property for taxation purposes is called an assessor.

218. A certificate of deposit index is

A.   one of the indexes used for determining interest rate changes on some adjustable rate mortgages

B.   is an average of what banks are paying on certificates of deposit

C.   both A and B

D.   neither A nor B

Answer: C. A certificate of deposit index is used for determining interest rate changes on some adjustable rate mortgages. It is an average of what banks are paying on certificates of deposit.

219. Which of the following is true of "common areas"?

A.   They include swimming pools, tennis courts, and other recreational facilities

B.   They are portions of a building, land, and amenities owned or managed by a planned unit development or condominium project's homeowners' association

C.   They have shared expenses by the project owners for the operation and maintenance

D.   all of the above

Answer: D. Common areas include portions of a building, land, and amenities owned by or managed by a planned unit development or condo project's homeowners' association (or a cooperative project's cooperative corporation) that are used by all of the unit owners, who share in the common expenses of their operation and maintenance. They include swimming pools,, tennis courts, and other recreational facilities, as well as common corridors of buildings, parking areas, means of ingress and egress, etc.

220. In a condominium hotel you would find the following:

A.   Rental or registrations desks
B.   Daily cleaning services
C.   No individual ownership
D.   Both A and B

Answer: D. Often found in resort areas, this is a condominium project with rental or registration desks, short-term occupancy, food and telephone services, and daily cleaning services. It is operated like a commercial hotel even though the units are individually owned.

221. A type of multiple ownership where the residents of a multi-unit housing complex own shares in the cooperative corporation that owns the property and gives each resident the right to occupy a specific apartment or unit is called

Λ.   an investment condominium
B.   an investment planned unit development
C.   a cooperative
D.   a government-run housing project

Answer: C. A cooperative (co-op) is a type of multiple ownership where the residents of a multi-unit housing complex own shares in the cooperative corporation that owns the property and gives each resident the right to occupy a specific unit.

222. Which is true of the cost of funds index (COFI)?

A.   It represents the weighted-average cost of savings, borrowings, and advances of the financial institutions such as banks and savings & loans in the 11th District of the Federal Home Loan Bank
B.   It is one of the indexes used to determine interest rate changes for certain government fixed rate mortgages
C.   It is an index used to determine interest rate changes for certain adjustable-rate mortgages
D.   Both A and C

Answer: D. The cost of funds index is one of the indexes used to determine interest rate changes for certain adjustable-rate mortgages. It represents the weight-average cost of savings, borrowings, and advances of the financial institutions such as banks and savings and loans, in the 11th District of the Federal Home Loan Bank.

223. Once you buy a house, the amount you pay each month includes an extra amount above principal and interest. This extra money is held in a special account to pay your taxes and homeowners insurance when it comes due. This account

is called

A. an escrow account
B. a savings account
C. a regular checking account
D. both B and C

Answer: A. Once you close your transaction, you probably have an escrow account with your lender which is composed of extra money taken from your monthly payments to be put in escrow and pay your taxes and insurance when they come due. The lender pays them with your money instead of you paying them yourself.

224. Which of the following does the Federal Housing Administration do?

A. Lends money and plans and constructs housing
B. Insures residential mortgage loans made by government lenders
C. Sets standards for construction and underwriting
D. None of the above

Answer: C. The main activity of the FHA is the insuring of residential mortgage loans made by private lenders. It sets standards for construction and underwriting but does not lend money or plan or construct housing.

225. If you purchase a type of insurance called homeowner's warranty, you would do so because

A.   It will cover repairs to certain items, such as heating or air conditioning if they break down within the coverage period
B.   The seller will sometimes pay for it
C.   Both A and B
D.   Neither A nor B

Answer: C. Homeowner's warranty will cover repairs to certain items like air conditioning or heating during the coverage period. The buyer often requests the seller to pay for this, but either party can pay.

226. A type of foreclosure proceeding used in some states that is handled as a civil lawsuit and conducted entirely under the auspices of a court is called

A.   a legal foreclosure
B.   a court-appointed foreclosure
C.   a judicial foreclosure
D.   a civil foreclosure

Answer: C. A type of foreclosure proceeding used in some states that is handled as a civil lawsuit and conducted entirely under the auspices of a court is called a judicial foreclosure.

227. Which of the following is not part of loan servicing?

A. Processing payments, sending statements
B. Managing the escrow account
C. Handling pay-offs and assumptions
D. Sending a monthly statement to the owner

Answer: D. The company you make your loan payments to is "servicing" your loan by processing payments, sending statements, managing the escrow account, providing collection efforts on delinquent loans, making sure insurance and property taxes are made, handling pay-offs and assumptions and other services.

228. A period payment cap applies to

A. any mortgage taken out in the U.S.
B. adjustable rate mortgages
C. fixed-rate loans
D. government loans

Answer: B. The period payment cap applies to an adjustable-rate mortgage where the interest rate and the minimum payment amount fluctuate independently of one another. It is a limit on the amount that payments can increase or decrease during any one adjustment period.

229. The commitment issued by a lender to borrower or other mortgage originator guaranteeing a specified interest rate for a specified period of time at a specific cost is called

A. a rate lock
B. under lock and key
C. a promissory note
D. a deed of trust

Answer: A. A rate lock is a commitment from a lender to the borrower or other mortgage originator guaranteeing a specific rate for a specific time at a specific cost.

230. A fund set aside for replacement of common property in a condominium, PUD, or cooperative project, particularly that which has a short life expectancy, such as carpet or furniture is called

A. a capital improvements fund
B. a replacement reserve fund
C. a savings fund
D. a contingency fund

Answer: B. The fund set aside for replacement of common property in a condominium, PUD or cooperative project is called a replacement reserve fund.

231. The term "servicing" describes

A.   the collection of mortgage payments from borrowers
B.   what the mechanic does to your car
C.   duties of a loan servicer
D.   both A and C

Answer: D. Servicing is the collection of mortgage payments from borrowers and related responsibilities of a loan servicer.

232. A two- to-four family property

A.   consists of a structure that provides living space for two to four families and ownership is evidenced by two to four deeds
B.   consists of a structure that provides living space for two to four families and ownership is evidenced by a single deed
C.   is not a deeded property
D.   is an illegal form of ownership

Answer: B. A two-to-four family property consists of a structure that provides living space for two to four families and ownership is evidenced by a single deed.

1. Many states determine the order of water rights according to which users of the water hold a recorded beneficial use permit. This allocation of water rights is determined by:

A. accretion.
B. riparian theory.
C. littoral theory.
D. the doctrine of prior appropriation.

Answer: D. All terms relate to water rights, with "riparian" -- the right to use water adjacent to one's property -- being the most common in sections of the U.S. where water is abundant. However, in states where water is more scarce, a form of "prior appropriation" applies. Also known as "first in time is first in right," it grants water rights to divert a specific amount of water from a specific source to irrigate a specific piece of property. Those rights are then assigned a priority based on when the right was first used or applied for. In periods of peak demand, they give those whose claim is the oldest the right to get their water first.

2. The right to control one's property includes all of the following EXCEPT:

A. the right to invite people on the property for a political fund-raiser.
B. the right to exclude the utilities meter reader.
C. the right to erect "no trespassing" signs.
D. the right to enjoy pride of ownership.

Answer: B. This right to enter and work on a property is granted to utility companies (water, sewer, gas and electric) as well as telephone and cable companies. Essentially, if a company provides a service and owns the equipment (e.g., phone and cable lines), they are usually granted an easement.

3. Which of the following types of ownership CANNOT be created by operation of law, but must be created by the parties' expressed intent?

A. community property
B. tenancy in common
C. condominium ownership
D. tenancy by the entireties

Answer: D. Tenancy by the entireties is a form of ownership that husbands and wives can choose or create by deciding to do so and declaring it as such in contracts and deeds. Tenancy in common is put in motion by state law. Community Property is a law of ownership that exists in Arizona, California, Idaho, Louisiana, Nevada, New Mexico, Texas, Washington and some other states. Tenancy by the Entireties is an estate that is recognized in some states between husband and wife, who have equal right of possession and enjoyment during their joint lives and with the right of survivorship--that is when one dies, the property goes to the surviving tenant. (In many states, if couples do not specify "Joint Tenancy," this form of ownership will be automatically assumed.) Tenancy in Common is a type of joint ownership by parties NOT married, that allows a person to sell his share or leave it in a will without the consent of the other owners. If a person dies without a will, his share goes to his heirs, not to the other owners.

4. Which of the following is/are considered to be personal property?

A. wood-burning fireplace
B. furnace
C. bathtubs
D. patio furniture

Answer: D. The concept of personal property typically comes into play at the time of sale. Things that are part of the house-- bathroom fixtures, fireplaces, carpeting and such-- go with the sale. (Unless specifically excluded, as can happen in the case of a dining room chandelier or one or two other objects with which the owners have an emotional attachment.) Furniture, rugs, lamps and other portable items that are not "nailed down" constitute personal property and are not included in the sale.

5. The word "improvement" would refer to all of the following EXCEPT:

A. streets.
B. a sanitary sewer system.
C. trade fixtures.
D. the foundation.

Answer: C. The term "trade fixture" refers to an item installed by a tenant in a rented commercial property that he or she removes at the end of the occupancy. More on this topic follows.

6. All of the following are physical characteristics of land EXCEPT:

A. indestructibility.
B. uniqueness.
C. immobility.
D. scarcity.

Answer: D. Scarcity is a fundamental economic concept that holds that the rarer and more desirable something is, the more valuable it will be. For example, professional athletes are highly paid because only the smallest percentage of people have the ability to perform at that level. Land is "scarce" because there is a finite amount available and, as Will Rogers once said, "They ain't making any more of it."

7. Certain items on the premises that are installed by the tenant and are related to the tenant's business are called:

A. fixtures.
B. emblements.
C. trade fixtures.
D. easements.

Answer: C. The term is usually applied to a commercial tenant and refers to items installed in connection with his or her business, such as stoves and refrigerators in a restaurant or display cases in a retail shop.

8. Personal property includes all of the following EXCEPT:

A. chattels.
B. fructus industriales.
C. emblements.
D. fixtures.

Answer: D. "Chattel" is a legal term that means personal property. Emblements and fructus industriales refer to profit from crops that are grown as a result of a person's labor, such as corn, as opposed to those that occur naturally, such as grass or minerals. By the custom of English common law, they are considered personal property. By contrast, a fixture is considered attached to a property and thus part of the structure.

9. A person who has complete control over a parcel of real estate is said to own a:

A. leasehold estate.
B. fee simple estate.
C. life estate.
D. defeasible fee estate.

Answer: B. All the other options have conditions attached. A leasehold estate is, as the name implies, leased property. Similarly, a life estate gives a person ownership or control of a property only for the duration of his or her natural life. "Defeasible estates" give a person or entity control over a property only so long as certain conditions are met or avoided. For example, a community might be deeded a property on the condition that it be used only for building a school, or land willed to a child on the condition it never be used for commercial development. If the community tries to use the property for a recreation complex or the heir tries to sell to a retail developer, control would automatically revert to another party and the deed would become void.

10. A portion of Wendell's building was inadvertently built on Ginny's land. This is called an:

A. accretion.
B. avulsion.
C. encroachment.
D. easement.

Answer: C. The principal attributes of an encroachment are: 1) It is accidental and 2) it involves only part of a structure. Typically, the issue would be resolved by selling Wendell an easement or a lease or, if practical, actually moving the structure.

11. The purchase of a ticket for a professional sporting event gives the bearer what?

A. an easement right to park his car
B. a license to enter and claim a seat for the duration of the game
C. an easement in gross interest in the professional sporting team
D. a license to sell food and beverages at the sporting event

Answer: B. Easements grant access, not use. Commercial licenses, such as those required to sell beverages, souvenirs or services, cover extended periods. Although tickets to sporting events, concerts, shows and the like are technically licenses, they differ from most in their degree of restriction. For example, a concert ticket does not give the bearer the right to sit anywhere he or she chooses or wander backstage to meet the performers.

12. If the owner of the dominant tenement becomes the owner of the servient tenement and merges the two properties, what happens?

A. The easement becomes dormant.
B. The easement is unaffected.
C. The easement is terminated.
D. The properties retain their former status.

Answer: C. "Dominant" and "servient" tenements involve two adjacent properties in which an easement is involved. For example, let's say Bridle Creek Farms and Barnstable Farms are separate parcels divided by a country lane that provides access to the county road system. The lane is owned by Bridle Creek, but the deeds of both properties stipulate that Barnstable Farms shall have unrestricted access for the purpose of accessing county roads. That access is an easement. Thus, if the owner of

Barnstable Farms buys Bridle Creek Farms, the need for the easement disappears.

13. Homeowner Ginny acquired the ownership of land that was deposited by a river running through her property by:

A. reliction.
B. succession.
C. avulsion.
D. accretion.

Answer: D. Accretion means the addition to a parcel of land by sand or soil deposits due to the action of a river or other body of water over time. Avulsion refers to the loss of land as a result of its being washed away by sudden or unexpected action of nature, such as a flash flood that re-routes a river.

14. The rights of the owner of property located along the banks of a river are called:

A. littoral rights.
B. prior appropriation rights.
C. riparian rights.
D. hereditament.

Answer: C. "Littoral" and "prior appropriation" are different kinds of water rights: in the first case, navigation rights to an ocean or other large body of water; in the second, the right to use a water source for irrigation. A hereditament is any inheritable property.

15. The local utility company dug up Frank's garden to install a natural gas line. The company claimed it had a valid easement and proved it through the county records. Frank claimed the easement was not valid because he did not know about it. The easement:

A. Was valid even though the owner did not know about it.
B. Was an appurtenant easement owned by the utility company.
C. Was not valid because it had not been used during the entire time that Frank owned the property.
D. Was not valid because Frank was not informed of its existence when he purchased the property.

Answer: A. Easements grant only access, not ownership, use or occupancy rights. Further, that access is generally for the benefit of the property owner, such as maintaining utilities or sidewalks. As such, they "attach" to a deed or lease and remain in effect, until specifically lifted.

16. Jim and Sandy are next-door neighbors. Sandy tells Jim that he can store his camper in her yard for a few weeks until she needs the space. Sandy did not charge Jim rent for the use of her yard. Sandy has given Jim a(n) what?

A. easement appurtenant
B. easement by necessity
C. estate in land
D. license

Answer: D. Granting the use of property for a defined period for a specific purpose is almost always a form of licensing. Easements grant only access, not ownership, use or occupancy rights. Further, that access is generally for the benefit of the property owner, such as maintaining utilities or sidewalks.

17. Your neighbors use your driveway to reach their garage on their property. Your attorney explains that the ownership of the neighbors' real estate includes an easement appurtenant giving them the driveway right. Your property is the:

A. leasehold interest.
B. dominant tenement.
C. servient tenement.
D. license property.

Answer: C. An "easement appurtenant" allows the holder of one property to benefit from another's. In this case, your property is "servient" because it is the one burdened by the easement while your neighbor's is "dominant" since it is the one that benefits.

18. Quintin owned two acres of land. He sold one acre to Frank and reserved for himself an appurtenant easement over Frank's land for ingress and egress. Frank's land:

A. Is the dominant tenement.
B. Is the servient tenement.
C. Can be cleared of the easement when Quintin sells the withheld acre to a third party.
D. Is subject to an easement in gross.

Answer: B. Frank's land interest is the one burdened by the easement; therefore it is the servient property.

19. Ginny owns 50 acres of land with 500 feet of frontage on a desirable recreational lake. She wishes to subdivide the parcel into salable lots, but she wants to retain control over the lake frontage while allowing lot owners to have access to the lake. Which of the following types of access rights would provide the greatest protection for a prospective purchaser?

A. an easement in gross
B. an appurtenant easement
C. an easement by necessity
D. a license

Answer: B. Appurtenant easements afford the most protection since they are generally a permanent feature of the property. Thus, in the case of sale, the lake access passes to any new owners. By contrast, an "easement in gross" is between two individuals, which would severely limit the attractiveness and value of the property if the original owner wished to sell.

20. Sam and Nancy bought a store building and took title as joint tenants. Nancy died testate. Sam now owns the store:

A. as a joint tenant with rights of survivorship.
B. in severalty.
C. as a tenant in common with Nancy's heirs.
D. in trust.

Answer: B. Joint tenancy means that two parties have an undivided interest in a particular property and, upon the death of one party, full ownership automatically goes to the survivor. Despite the way it sounds, "in severalty" means as sole owner.

21. When real estate under an estate for years is sold, what happens to the lease?

A. It expires with the conveyance.
B. It binds the new owner.
C. It is subject to termination with proper notice.
D. It is valid but unenforceable.

Answer: B. Tenancy for years is the common form of rental agreements and binds all future owners for the term of the lease.

22. Evan lives in an apartment building. The land and structures are owned by a corporation, with one mortgage loan covering the entire property. Like the other residents, Evan owns stock in the corporation and has a lease on his apartment. This type of ownership is called a(n):

A. condominium.
B. planned unit development.
C. time-share.
D. cooperative.

Answer: D. This is the distinguishing characteristic that differentiates cooperative from condominium ownership. Although often confused, a condominium owner holds title to his individual unit. A co-op owner, on the other hand, is technically a renter. It's his stock in the corporation holding title to the property that gives him the right to lease the unit as well as sell that right to another.

23. Tom leases store space to Kim for a restaurant, and Kim installs her ovens, booths, counters, and other equipment. When do these items become real property?

A. when they are installed
B. when Kim defaults on her rental payments
C. when the lease takes effect
D. when the lease expires, if the items are not taken by the tenant

Answer: D. Kim is free to move these fixtures at the end of her lease. However, if she chooses to leave them behind, they are considered a permanent part of the structure (just like a dining room chandelier in a home) and revert to Tom.

24. Jim, Manny and Harry are joint tenants owning a parcel of land. Harry conveys his interest to his long-time friend Wendell. After the conveyance, Jim and Manny:

A. become tenants in common.
B. continue to be joint tenants with Harry.
C. become joint tenants with Wendell.
D. remain joint tenants owning a two-thirds interest.

Answer: D. Because joint tenancy must be declared, Jim and Manny remain joint tenants with a two-thirds interest while Wendell, because of his passive acquisition of his share of the property, becomes a tenant in common with Jim and Manny. The difference between the two forms is that Jim and Manny's share retains the right of survivorship provisions but Wendell's does not.

25. In a gift of a parcel of real estate, one of the two owners was given an undivided 60 percent interest and the other received an undivided 40 percent interest. The two owners hold their interests as what?

A. cooperative owners
B. joint tenants
C. community property owners
D. tenants in common

Answer: D. In order to create joint tenancy, some form of relationship must exist between the parties involved, whether business, spousal or other. Because their interests were acquired as a gift, the parties in this instance become tenants in common, with all the ownership benefits of joint tenancy, but not the survivorship rights.

26. To create a joint tenancy relationship in the ownership of real estate, there must be unities of:

A. grantees, ownership, claim of right, and possession.
B. title, interest, encumbrance, and survivorship.
C. possession, time, interest, and title.
D. ownership, possession, heirs, and title.

Answer: C. This essentially means that all parties to the agreement share equally in all aspects of the property, including the length of time it's been held. That means if one party sells or transfers interest in a joint tenancy relationship, his or her place is taken by another in the same capacity.

27. What is a Schedule of Exceptions on a title policy?

A. encumbrances
B. tax liens
C. list of things not insured in the policy
D. defects

Answer: C. Almost no title insurance policy protects against all conceivable events. As the name suggests, the Schedule of Exceptions is a specific list of items not covered and can include things such as unrecorded mechanic's liens, assessments, water rights and mining claims.

28. When a company furnishes materials for the construction of a house and is subsequently not paid, it may file a(n):

A. deficiency judgment.
B. lis pendens.
C. estoppel certificate.
D. mechanic's lien.

Answer: D. A mechanic's lien is the first, and usually most cost-effective, step for a person providing labor and/or materials to a homeowner to recover monies owed—in large part because of the pressure it puts on the homeowner to settle quickly and without costly court involvement.

29. Which of the following liens does not need to be recorded to be valid?

A. materialman's lien
B. real estate tax lien
C. judgment lien
D. mechanic's lien

Answer: B. The requirement for individuals to record liens is due in part to the necessity of correctly identifying the complainant. For example, not just "Jones Contracting," but the specific Jones Contracting that performed the work and is owed the money. Because they bear the authority of government and are easily identified, liens by taxing authorities do not need to be recorded.

30. The system of ownership of real property in the United States is what?

A. incorporeal
B. allodial
C. inchoate
D. feudal

Answer: B. "Allodial" is the modern form of ownership and is often contrasted with "feudal" in which land is held on the condition of rent or service due the government. For example, a medieval knight held property subject to coming to his baron's service when called. Similarly, the baron's land holdings were conditional on his raising an army and fighting for the king in times of conflict. Failure of any party to "perform as promised" was cause for holdings to be confiscated, often as a preliminary step to more extreme actions

31. mechanic's lien would be properly classified as a(n):

A. equitable lien.

B. voluntary lien.

C. general lien.

D. statutory lien.

Answer: D. A "statutory lien" is one that arises out of specific law (otherwise known as statutes). By contrast, an "equitable lien" has its roots in common law or custom. A "voluntary lien" is one entered with the property owner's knowledge and consent, such as a mortgage. A "general lien" grants a creditor the right to file a claim against all of a debtor's assets, not just a particular property.

32. Under which of the following types of liens can both the real property and the personal property of the debtor be sold to pay the debt?

A. real estate tax lien

B. mechanic's lien

C. judgment lien

D. assessment lien

Answer: C. Most liens are against a specific property, such as a primary residence. Thus, a contractor seeking payment for a new deck cannot have a homeowner's car attached in settlement. A judgment lien, however, is a decision directed by the courts and can apply to whatever assets it deems appropriate.

33. A homeowner owned a house on a lot. The front ten feet of the lot were taken by eminent domain for a sidewalk. Would the homeowner be entitled to compensation?

A. Yes. The land was taken for public use by eminent domain.
B. Yes. He must be paid for the use of the sidewalk.
C. No. He still had use of the house and lot.
D. No. Compensation is not given on land taken for public use.

Answer: A. Governments and municipalities can only seize property (other than in criminal cases) for the public good and through eminent domain, which is a process, not an arbitrary action. Part of that process involves determining fair compensation to the owner.

34. The covenant in a deed which states that the grantor is the owner and has the right to convey the title is called:

A. covenant of further assurance.
B. Yes. He must be paid for the use of the sidewalk.
C. covenant of seisin.
D. covenant against encumbrances.

Answer: C. Another outgrowth of the feudal system, "seisen" derives from the French meaning to "sit upon or own" and gives owners the right to sell or transfer property at will.

35. The recording of a deed:

A. Is all that is required to transfer the title to real estate.
B. Gives constructive notice of the ownership of real property.
C. Insures the interest in a parcel of real estate.
D. Warrants the title to real property.

Answer: B. Recording a deed does not convey, insure or warrant ownership. However, it does protect the owner's interest in a property by serving notice that the recorded owner is the only recognized holder of title. This places a larger burden of proof and process on someone trying to assert a prior ownership interest and/or claiming a deedholder's title is clouded.

36. Which of the following provides a buyer with the best assurance of clear, marketable title?

A. certificate of title
B. title insurance
C. abstract of title
D. general warranty deed

Answer: B. Title insurance provides the best assurance of marketable title.

37. What do liens and easements have in common?

A. Both are encumbrances.
B. Both must be on public record to be valid.
C. Neither can be done without the consent of the owner.
D. Both are money claims against the property.

Answer: A. Liens are, of course, serious in that they indicate the owner has failed to pay a debt secured directly or indirectly by the property. Easements, on the other hand, are generally a practical necessity for most residential properties.

38. The title to real estate passes when a valid deed is:

A. signed and recorded.
B. delivered and accepted.
C. filed and microfilmed.
D. executed and mailed.

Answer: B. Fundamentally, real estate transactions only involve two parties--the buyer and the seller. All that's necessary to create a legal sale is for one party to make an offer the other accepts. Recording, escrow, real estate licensees, mortgage companies and the like facilitate and support the transaction process but are not requirements of a legal sale.

39. The primary purpose of a deed is to:

A. Prove ownership.
B. Transfer title rights.
C. Give constructive notice.
D. Prevent adverse possession.

Answer: B. A deed is the instrument by which ownership of a property is transferred from one person to another, while a title is evidence of that ownership.

40. A special warranty deed differs from a general warranty deed in that the grantor's covenant in the special warranty deed:

A. Applies only to a definite limited time.
B. Covers the time back to the original title.
C. Is implied and is not written in full.
D. Protects all subsequent owners of the property.

Answer: A. The more common deed in most states is the general warranty, because it establishes the ownership trail and validity of title going back to the original recorded ownership (for example, the purchase of Manhattan Island and all subsequent divisions, subdivisions and resales). Under a special warranty deed, an owner transfers property guaranteeing the quality of title only during the period of his or her ownership, leaving subsequent buyers vulnerable to prior claims.

41. Which of the following deeds contains no expressed or implied warranties?

A. a bargain and sale deed
B. a quitclaim deed
C. a warranty deed
D. a grant deed

Answer: B. A "quit claim" deed means what it implies: The seller gives up any claims he or she may have to the property but makes no warranties whatsoever about the possibility of other claims.

42. When the grantor does not wish to convey certain property rights, he or she:

A. must note the exceptions in a separate document.
B. may not do so, since the deed conveys the entire premises.
C. may note the exceptions in the deed of conveyance.
D. must convey the entire premises and have the grantee reconvey the rights to be retained by the grantor.

Answer: C. Most commonly known as "restrictive covenants," such deed restrictions are often used to maintain the consistency of a neighborhood by, for example, stipulating that only traditional home styles of a particular size and painted in traditional colors may be constructed and occupied within the subdivision. These are encumbrances on the property since they limit current and future owners in how they use the property.

43. A partition suit is used for which of the following?

A. determination of party fences
B. to allow construction of party walls
C. to force a division of property without all the owners' consents
D. to change a tenancy by entireties to some other form of ownership

Answer: C. Partition suits are typically pursued when a co-owner of a property wants to sell his or her share and the other owners are opposed. Since it is a legal action involving the courts, it is an expense with often unsatisfactory results.

44. The condemnation of private property for public use is exercised under which government right?

A. taxation

B. escheat
C. manifest destiny
D. eminent domain

Answer: D. As noted previously, eminent domain actions are generally reserved for "public good" projects such as highway expansion. However, there have been recent instances of municipalities using this power to condemn well-kept neighborhoods of middle-class housing to make way for high-end properties that will provide a higher tax base.

45. When a claim is settled by a title insurance company, the company acquires all rights and claims of the insured against any other person who is responsible for the loss. This is known as what?

A. caveat emptor
B. surety bonding
C. subordination
D. subrogation

Answer: D. For example, let's say Amanda Livingstone buys a property and the seller provides a general warranty deed stipulating clear title. However, that turns out not to be the case and a third party provides a valid claim to a share of the property. Since Amada took out title insurance, the title insurance company negotiates and pays a settlement with the claimant on Amanda's behalf. Amanda's right to sue the seller then transfers to the title insurance company, which will take action to recover the amount they paid on Amanda's behalf.

46. Which of the following would be used to clear a defect from the title records?

A. a lis pendens
B. an estoppel certificate
C. a suit to quiet title
D. a writ of attachment

Answer: C. A owner might bring a "quiet title" action to correct a minor mistake in the property description or to remove an easement that's been unused for years. Additionally, they are used when a third party tries to asset some right to the property through a dubious claim. The suit "quiets the mouth" of that person and establishes a clear title.

47. A bill of sale is used to transfer the ownership of what?

A. real property
B. fixtures
C. personal property
D. appurtenances

Answer: C. Personal property differs from "real property" in a number of respects, most importantly its portability. Cars, furniture, clothing, paintings, jewelry, appliances and just about any other non-food item one buys are examples of personal property.

48. A written summary of the history of all conveyances and legal proceedings affecting a specific parcel of real estate is called a(n):

A. affidavit of title.
B. certificate of title.
C. abstract of title.
D. title insurance policy.

Answer: C. An "abstract of title" is a written summary that traces every change of ownership and claim against a property (such as mortgages, liens, and easements). In some cases, the abstract goes back to the last change of title, in others to the first recorded owner. It is part of the title report required by virtually all lenders.

49. When the preliminary title report reveals the existence of an easement on the property, it indicates that the easement is a(n):

A. lien.
B. encumbrance.
C. encroachment.
D. tenement.

Answer: B. Anything that limits a person's use of a property is an encumbrance. Easements limit use in that they generally prohibit any kind of permanent structure on the area in question. For example, if a homeowner wanted to build a swimming pool in an area of his back yard and the local sewer company had an easement for pipes running under that area, he would have to find another location for his pool, even if it was not as desirable.

50. The list of previous owners of conveyance from whom the present real estate owner derives his or her title is known as the:

A. chain of title.
B. certificate of title.
C. title insurance policy.
D. abstract of title.

Answer: A. The "chain" links together the successive owners of a property from the most recent to the original recorded title holder. In addition, it notes other relevant information such as mortgages, judgments, liens, death of title holders, inheritors and so forth.

51. A person agrees to sell a property for $500,000. The buyer gives the seller $150 as valuable consideration for a six-month option. Which of the following statements is true?

A. The $150 is valuable consideration if the seller accepted it.
B. The buyer must have at least 5% down as valuable consideration.
C. The buyer must have at least 20% down.
D. The seller cannot accept money for the option.

Answer: A. "Valuable consideration" is a necessary component of all contracts. It is the benefit one party receives in exchange for granting benefit to the other. Generally it is money in any amount both parties agree to, though it can take other forms such as personal property, work or refraining from an act.

52 . Which of the following activities is a violation of the Federal Fair Housing Act?

A. a nonprofit church that denies access to its retirement home to any person because of race
B. a nonprofit private club that gives preference in renting units to its members at lower rates
C. the owner of a single-family residence selling his/her own home who gives preference to a buyer based on his/her sex

D. discrimination in the sale of a warehouse based on the prospective purchaser's gender

Answer: A. The private club is exempt because its preferential treatment is based on its membership; the home owner is exempt, so long as he is selling his home without a broker; the warehouse is exempt because it's not a housing unit.

53. A Savings & Loan institution would be violating the Federal Fair Housing Act by denying a loan to Mr. and Mrs. Happy Borrower for which of the following reasons?

A. low earnings
B. too old
C. too many loans
D. minority background

Answer: D. Fair Housing and other anti-discrimination legislation doesn't force lenders or others to abandon sound business practices (such as denying loans to unqualified borrowers), merely to be fair and equally accessible to all people.

54. The Civil Rights Act of 1866 prohibits discrimination in housing based on which of the following reasons?

A. race
B. religion
C. sex
D. marital status

Answer: A. Although surprising to many, the original civil rights legislation was passed in 1866--by one vote over the veto of President Andrew Johnson.

55. An agent working as a subagent of the seller would suggest that the buyer hire an inspector from an outside service in all of the following cases EXCEPT:

A. when they smell gas in the basement.
B. when there is a slow drain in the toilet.
C. when a hinge is off the door.
D. when there is sawdust in the kitchen cabinets.

Answer: C. Home inspectors are hired to find significant and often hidden property defects, such as signs of a leaking roof, termites, foundation cracking and so forth. Hinges and other "wear and tear" items are obvious and not among the reasons for hiring an inspector.

56. The federal anti-discriminatory laws apply to which of the following?

A. a broker selling a single-family home
B. a private club not open to the general public
C. office building sales
D. the rental of industrial property

Answer: A. Civil rights laws apply to owners of residential property, rental units, hotels and virtually any other building offering housing or accommodations to the general public.

57. A tenant complained to HUD about his landlord's discriminatory practices in his/her building. A week later the landlord gave the tenant an eviction notice. Under which of the following situations would the Federal Fair Housing Act be violated?

A. when the tenant is two months behind in his/her rent
B. when the landlord evicts the tenant for reporting him to HUD
C. when the tenant has damaged the premises
D. when the tenant is conducting an illegal use on the premises

Answer: B. Anti-discrimination laws do not apply to situations that are in violation of generally accepted policies such as paying rent on time, maintaining the premises and abiding by use agreements.

58. The Federal Fair Housing Act states that a prima facie (at first view) case against a broker for discrimination be established after a complaint has been received because the broker has failed to do which of the following?

A. The broker has failed to display a HUD Equal Opportunity poster.
B. The broker has failed to join an affirmative marketing program.
C. The broker has failed to join the HUD anti-discriminatory task force.
D. The broker has failed to attend mandatory classes on fair housing.

Answer: A. Included among Fair Housing regulations is the requirement that the HUD Equal Opportunity signage be prominently displayed.

59. A broker is discussing a new listing with a prospective Mexican American buyer. The buyer wants to inspect the property immediately, but the owner of said property has instructed the broker, in writing, not to show the house during the owner's three-week absence. The buyer insists on viewing the property. The broker should:

A. Show the property to avoid a violation of the Federal Fair Housing Act.

B. Request the Real Estate Commission arbitrate the problem.
C. Inform the buyer of the seller's instructions.
D. Notify the nearest HUD office.

Answer: C. Following an owner's lawful instructions is not only allowable, but a responsibility of the licensee. However, if the owner instructed the broker to tell minority buyers that he was out of town when he was not in order to avoid selling to a minority, the broker would be in violation of the law if he acted as the owner requested.

60. A three-story apartment complex built in 1965 does not meet with the handicapped access provisions for the 1988 Fair Housing Act. The owner must:

A. Make the ground floor handicapped accessible.
B. Make the 1st and 2nd floors accessible.
C. Make the entire building accessible.
D. The owner doesn't have to comply since it's less than 4 stories.

Answer: A. Because the building was constructed before the 1991 standards went into effect, only the first floor needs to be modified.

61. What type of a listing agreement allows the owner to appoint an exclusive agent to sell his property, but retains the right to sell the property himself?

A. open
B. exclusive right to sell
C. multiple listing
D. exclusive agency

Answer: D. Open listings mean that if the owner or any other broker or salesperson produces the buyer, the broker will lose his or her commission. Exclusive Right to Sell gives the broker his or her commission regardless of who actually sells the property, even if it is the owner. Exclusive Agency allows the seller to appoint an exclusive agent, but retain the right to sell the property himself.

62. Under an Exclusive Right to Sell Listing agreement, if the seller produces a ready, willing and able buyer he:

A. will not have to pay a commission since he produced the buyer.
B. will only have to pay the broker half the commission since he produced the buyer.
C. owes the listing broker a full commission.
D. will not be able to turn the buyer over to the listing agent since the agent has the exclusive right to sell the property.

Answer: C. In contrast to exclusive agency, the exclusive right to sell entitles the broker to his or her commission regardless of who actually sells the property.

63. Which of the following would not terminate an agency relationship?

A. abandonment by the agent
B. revocation by the principal
C. submission by the agent of two offers at the same time
D. fulfillment of the agency purpose

Answer: C. Submitting offers doesn't end the relationship--only the owner's acceptance of one and ultimately closing on the transaction.

64. The buyer of an apartment complex is told that the refrigerator in one of the apartments goes with the sale. After taking title, he discovered that the refrigerator belonged to the tenant. Which is true about this situation?

A. Since the refrigerator was in the apartment, it automatically belongs to the new owner.
B. The refrigerator is the personal property of the tenant. The seller had no right to offer it to the buyer.

C. The refrigerator was plugged into the wall and that makes it real property.
D. The tenant will have to get permission from the new owner to remove the refrigerator.

Answer: B. Plugging in an appliance does not constitute installation. Thus it is personal property that belongs to the tenant.

65. The illegal process of a banker refusing to approve loans for a neighborhood based on the racial composition of the area is:

A. blockbusting.
B. steering.
C. redlining.
D. panic peddling.

Answer: C. Loans may only be approved or denied on the basis of whether a specific individual and property meet established standards. Thus lenders are well within their rights to deny a loan to a particular person because he or she lacks sufficient income or has poor credit. Additionally, a loan for a partially completed home or one that doesn't meet code can also be denied. However, "macro" issues such as race or neighborhood cannot be considered.

66. The illegal practice of directing minorities to areas populated by the same race or religion is called:

A. steering.
B. blockbusting.
C. redlining.
D. panic peddling.

Answer: A. "Steering" is driving people towards particular neighborhoods, and is the correct answer to this question. On the other hand, "blockbusting" is the opposite side of the same coin. Synonymous with "panic peddling," it refers to trying to generate panic selling in a neighborhood dominated by one race or ethnic group by representing that another group is about to start moving in.

67. Carl Chauvinist, the owner of an apartment complex, lives in one unit of a triplex and routinely refuses to rent either of the other two units to a female. Can he do this?

A. Yes. He may do this if he does not use a broker or discriminate in advertising.
B. Yes. He may do this if he doesn't ask the tenant's age.
C. No. Carl can never discriminate on sex.
D. No. Carl must live in a single family home to discriminate.

Answer: A. Although laws vary by state as to number of units that fall under this type of provision, if a person owns and lives in a unit, he or she is entitled to practice a certain measure of discrimination. The view is that a person's dwelling (which includes units such as duplexes and triplexes) enjoys a degree of "sanctity" and the person may choose whom he or she brings into their "home."

68. An aggrieved party with a Fair Housing violation claim has how long to file a complaint with the Department of Housing and Urban Development?

A. 1 month
B. 1 week
C. 1 year
D. 7 years

Answer: C. If the complaint is not filed within one year, a person may still file a civil suit in a Federal Court.

69. Jim Jones, the landlord, rents a property to Tom Smith, a handicapped person. Mr. Smith, with Mr. Jones' permission, modifies the house to suit his needs. When the lease expires, which of the following requirements would not have to be met by Mr. Smith?

A. Mr. Smith must remove the "grab rails" in the bathroom that were installed for his use.
B. Mr. Smith must raise the kitchen cabinets that were lowered for his use.
C. Mr. Smith must repair the walls where the "grab rails" in the bathroom were removed.
D. Mr. Smith must restore the wide doorways, that were installed for him, to the original size.

Answer: D. Since the width of the door will not in any way be detrimental to future tenants, there is not a requirement for the original width of the doors to be replaced by the handicapped tenant. All of the other issues must be restored to original status.

70. All of the following are duties of the property manager EXCEPT:

A. reporting to the owner all notices of building violations.
B. providing upkeep and maintenance on the property.
C. maintaining financial records and accounts.
D. securing tenants of a particular ethnic origin in accordance with the owner's wishes.

Answer: D. Except in certain circumstances regarding the rental of space within one's personal residence or unit, owners, landlords and their agents are not permitted to discriminate against people based on race, gender, creed, handicap and other personal characteristics.

71. A mobility impaired person was renting a unit in an apartment complex. Half the units had been assigned parking spaces near the door; the other half had not. The owner:

A. may charge extra money to the handicapped person for providing the parking space near the door.
B. must take a vote of all tenants to see if they want to allow the handicapped person a parking space.
C. must give a parking space near the door to the handicapped person, if one is available and a need is demonstrated.
D. must allow the handicapped person to live there for a month and if a space becomes available during that time, give the parking space to the handicapped person.

Answer: C. The "equal access" aspects of fair housing legislation do not necessarily mean equal treatment. "Reasonable accommodation" must also be made to meet the needs of handicapped people, including exceptions to standard policies such as convenient parking and guide dogs.

72. A salesperson is involved in a transaction where an individual wishes a six-month lease with an option to buy. What is true about this situation?

A. The individual must go to an attorney since it is too complicated a transaction for a salesperson.
B. This transaction is too complicated for a salesperson. Only a person with a broker's license should handle this transaction.
C. A salesperson could use two standard forms, fill in the blanks and request that his or her broker review the forms before signing.
D. The salesperson should write the purchase offer. A lease for 6 months does not need to be in writing.

Answer: C. Generally speaking, salespeople may complete standard forms so long as they are reviewed by and with the approval of their broker.

73. A void contract is one that is:

A. not in writing.
B. not legally enforceable.
C. rescindable by agreement.
D. voidable by only one of the parties.

Answer: B. In order to be enforceable, real estate contracts must meet the legal requirements for contracts in general. For example, a contract signed by a minor or a "seller" who doesn't own the property in question was never legal to begin with and is thus "void."

74. The essential elements of a contract include all of the following EXCEPT:

A. offer and acceptance.
B. notarized signatures.
C. competent parties.
D. consideration.

Answer: B. A contract sets forth the terms and conditions of a real estate transaction, but does not itself transfer ownership. Thus it does not need to be notarized.

75. If, upon the receipt of an offer to purchase his property under certain conditions, the seller makes a counteroffer, the prospective buyer is:

A. bound by his original offer.
B. bound to accept the counteroffer.
C. bound by whichever offer is lower.
D. relieved of his original offer.

Answer: D. Offers are "one-time-only" events that must be accepted or rejected. Once the seller made a counter-proposal, he rejected the buyer's offer and no contract exists. The buyer is under no obligation to continue and is entitled to have any earnest money that accompanied the offer returned immediately.

76. The amount of earnest money deposit is determined by:

A. the real estate licensing statutes.
B. an agreement between the parties.
C. the broker's office policy on such matters.
D. the acceptable minimum of 5 percent of the purchase price.

Answer: B. Earnest money is a demonstration of sincerity on the part of the purchaser and provides preliminary evidence that he or she is financially capable of completing the transaction. While it should be substantial enough to meet these two criteria, there is no set or customary amount or percentage.

77. If the buyer defaulted some time ago on a written contract to purchase a seller's real estate, the seller can still sue for damages, if he is not prohibited from doing so by the:

A. statute of frauds.
B. law of agency.
C. statute of limitations.

D. broker-attorney accord.

Answer: C. Statutes of limitations exist to keep the legal system from getting bogged down in old disputes and allow for evidence and recollections to remain reasonably fresh. Civil limitations typically range from one to six years, though in some cases up to twenty-five years.

78. A competent and disinterested person who is authorized by another person to act in his or her place and sign a contract of sale is called:

A. an attorney in fact.
B. a substitute grantor.
C. a vendor.
D. an agent.

Answer: A. "Disinterested" means being able to act in an objective manner without any hidden motivation or prospect of gain. For example, a person who made a secret deal to sign a contract contrary to his client's best interests in exchange for an under-the-table payment would not be "disinterested."

79. An option:

A. requires the optionor to complete the transaction.

B. gives the optionee an easement on the property.

C. does not keep the offer open for a specified time.

D. makes the seller liable for a commission.

Answer: A. It is up to the optionor (seller)to finish the transaction. The optionee (buyer) does not have to complete (close) on the property, but would lose whatever option monies that have been deposited.

80. When a prospective buyer makes a written purchase offer that the seller accepts, then the:

A. Buyer may take possession of the real estate.

B. Seller grants the buyer ownership rights.

C. Buyer receives legal title to the property.

D. Buyer receives equitable title to the property.

Answer: D. "Equitable title" means that the prospective buyer has obtained the right to acquire ownership of a property currently owned and occupied by another.

81. H agrees to purchase V's real estate for $230,000 and deposits $6,900 earnest money with Broker L. However, V is unable to clear the title to the property, and H demands the return of his earnest money as provided in the purchase contract. Broker L should:

A. Deduct his commission and return the balance to H.
B. Deduct his commission and give the balance to V.
C. Return the entire amount to H.
D. Give the entire amount to V to dispose of as he decides.

Answer: C. Brokers and salespeople only earn their commission when a transaction closes. Since the transaction was never completed, no commission is owed. Additionally, H is entitled to have all his earnest money returned since it was the seller, not he, who defaulted on the contract.

82. A buyer makes an earnest money deposit of $1,500 on a $15,000 property and then withdraws her offer before the seller can accept it. The broker is responsible for disposing of the earnest money by:

A. turning it over to the seller.
B. deducting the commission and giving the balance to the seller.
C. returning it to the buyer.
D. depositing it in his or her trust account.

Answer: C. A contract only exists when it is both offered by the buyer and accepted by the seller. Since the second part of this requirement was never fulfilled, the buyer is entitled to have his earnest money returned.

83. Broker K arrives to present a purchase offer to Mrs. D, an 80 year old invalid who is not always of sound mind, and finds her son and her daughter-in-law present. In the presence of Broker K, both individuals persistently urge D to accept the offer, even though it is much lower than the price she has been asking for her home. If D accepts the offer, she may later claim that:

A. Broker K should not have brought her such a low offer for her property.
B. She was under undue duress from her son and daughter-in-law, and, therefore, the contract is voidable.
C. Broker K defrauded her by allowing her son and daughter-in-law to see the purchase offer he brought to her.
D. Her consumer protection rights have been usurped by her son and daughter-in-law.

Answer: B. "Duress" is the application of coercion or pressure to influence a person to act in a way contrary to his/her best interests. Further, since voluntary participation is a key condition of any contract, Mrs. D could well be successful in such an action. A voidable contract is one that is able to be voided because Mrs D was under duress or undue influence.

84. The law that requires real estate contracts to be in writing to be enforceable is the:

A. law of descent and distribution.
B. statute of frauds.
C. parole evidence rule.
D. statute of limitations.

Answer: B. Contrary to popular belief, the statute of frauds is not about specific actions defined as fraud, but the requirement in every state that certain documents be in writing, especially those pertaining to real estate. It's called the statute of frauds because it was first enacted in England in 1677 to prevent fraudulent claims of title.

85. A(n) _____ is when an owner takes his property off the market for a definite period of time in exchange for some consideration, but he grants the right to purchase the property within that period for a stated price.

A. option
B. contract of sale
C. right of first refusal
D. installment agreement

Answer: A. It's important to note that options generally give flexibility to only one side of the transaction. For example, let's say Barney is expecting a big promotion in six months and wants to buy Fred's house for $300,000 if it comes through. In exchange for keeping his home off the market for six months and agreeing to sell it to Barney for $300,000 at Barney's option, Barney gives Fred $3,000. The $3,000 is Fred's to keep no matter what. However, Barney is not obligated to buy Fred's house; it's his choice. Further, if he does get the promotion and wants to exercise his option, Fred must sell Barney his home for $300,000, even if market conditions have now made it worth more.

86. A breach of contract is a refusal or a failure to comply with the terms of the contract. If the seller breaches the purchase contract, the buyer may do all of the following EXCEPT:

A. Sue the seller for specific performance.
B. Rescind the contract and recover the earnest money.
C. Sue the seller for damages.
D. Sue the broker for non-performance.

Answer: D. While brokers and salespeople are responsible for bringing people together, they cannot be expected to know every detail of their circumstances or intent. Thus, if a buyer cannot get clear title or a seller is unexpectedly transferred, it is not the broker's fault the transaction failed and he or she bears no responsibility or liability.

87. To assign a contract for the sale of real estate means to:

A. Record the contract with the county recorder's office.
B. Permit another broker to act as agent for the principal.
C. Transfer one's rights under the contract.
D. Allow the seller and the buyer to exchange positions.

Answer: C. Assigning a contract means to transfer it to another.

88. The property manager suspects that the tenants in a property are engaging in illegal drug trafficking. What should the property manager do?

A. Cancel the property management agreement.
B. Observe the property for 30 days and then tell the owner.
C. Notify the owner immediately of the suspicious activity.
D. Don't worry. It's the owner's problem.

Answer: C. The property manager is the owner's agent, but not his "proxy." That is, he must inform the owner but not act on his behalf without authorization. For example, while calling the police to investigate might be appropriate, if the manager's suspicions were groundless and he called the authorities without authorization, the tenants might be able to sue the owner.

89. A zoning change has been announced that will result in the loss of value of the property to a property owner. What should a property manager do?

A. Advise the owner immediately.
B. Terminate the property management agreement.
C. Follow the owner's instructions that were previously given.
D. Keep his/her mouth shut.

Answer: A. Again, the property manager is the owner's "eyes and ears" for protecting the owner's best interests. Anything that can impact the property's value in either a positive or negative way should be communicated immediately.

90. A broker and seller terminate the listing contract. An offer is received in the mail by the broker after the termination of the listing contract. The offer is for full price and includes all of the terms and conditions of the seller. Why is this NOT a valid contract?

A. There is no consideration involved.
B. No acceptance has been given.
C. No earnest money has been enclosed.
D. There is no current listing agreement.

Answer: B. It has not been presented to or accepted by the owner. Remember, contracts aren't valid until both parties agree. However, even though the listing agreement has expired, the offer should be presented. If it's accepted and the transaction closes, the broker will generally be entitled to his or her full commission.

91. Which of the following activities does NOT require a real estate license?

A. Holding a real estate auction.
B. Selling property listed by other brokers or agencies.
C. Showing and selling one's own property.
D. Offering to buy properties on behalf of third parties.

Answer: C. Buying or sell properties for one's own benefit or for the benefit of a family member generally does not require a license. However, only licensed professionals may engage in transactions on behalf of third parties. Additionally, brokers or provisional brokers selling their own properties must disclose that fact to the public.

92. In addition to selling one's own property, which of the following is also exempt from normal licensing requirements?

A. Acting as a guardian.
B. Acting as a trustee.
C. Acting as an attorney-in-fact.
D. Each of the above.

Answer: D. Although often limited in scope (such as the authority to negotiate tax matters or conduct real estate transactions), someone performing any of these duties "becomes" the person he or she is representing. No license is required because that person is now acting, in effect, on his or her own behalf.

93. As long as it is specified as part of his or her duties, is it legal for an unlicensed salaried assistant to solicit listings for the broker?

A. Yes, if it is part of a written job description.
B. No, soliciting listings is the exclusive responsibility of the broker-in-charge.
C. Yes, because she is being paid a salary, not commissions.
D. No, active participation in real estate transactions requires a license.

Answer: D. Tasks such as answering phones or making copies are considered support and don't require any licensing or course work. However, activities such as soliciting listings or providing information about a property are part of the transaction process and may be handled only by licensed real estate professionals.

94. Regarding the North Carolina Real Estate Commission, which of these statements is true?

A. A monthly salary plus expenses is paid to each member.
B. The North Carolina Association of Realtors® appoints the members.
C. The governor appoints members for a three-year term.
D. The Commission consists of seven members, all of whom must be active in real estate.

Answer: C. The governor appoints members to the Commission. Additionally, there are nine, not seven members and, although at least three must be active in real estate, there also must be at least two non-licensed "public members."

95. Which of these is a requirement to hold a real estate license in North Carolina? 1) Be a resident in good standing of the state. 2) Be at least 21 years old.

A. Only #1.
B. Only #2.
C. Neither #1 nor #2.
D. Both #1 and #2.

Answer: C. In North Carolina, the minimum age requirement is 18, not 21. In addition to course-work and exam requirements, one must also be of good character, though not a "resident in good standing."

96. Licensees must notify the Real Estate Commission when which of these events occur?

A. There is a significant change in sales volume.
B. The business tradename has changed within the past ten days.
C. The business trade-name has changed within the past thirty days.
D. The licensee has received more than two traffic violations within the past eighteen months.

Answer: B. Licensees have ten days in which to notify the Commission of any change in their business name, trade-name or address.

97. What is the first point at which a person may begin practicing real estate in North Carolina?

A. When a broker activates his or her license.
B. Upon successful completion of all course and exam work.
C. Upon completion of all education requirements.

D. Upon completion of course work requirements, successfully pass the exam and finish a recognized training program.

Answer: A. In effect, obtaining a provisional brokers license means that a person is now eligible to be hired by a broker. Only provisional brokers operating under the direct supervision of a broker may actually sell real estate.

98. Which of these is required to be a broker-in-charge? 1) An active broker's license for the state of North Carolina. 2) Eight hours of continuing education each year.

A. Only #1.
B. Only #2.
C. Neither #1 nor #2.
D. Both #1 and #2.

Answer: D. Unlike some other states, North Carolina requires Brokers-in-Charge to complete continuing education requirements every year in addition to holding an active broker's license. In addition, beginning July 1, 2006, all brokers-in-charge must complete a four classroom hour Broker-in-Charge Annual Review Course each full license period after being designated a broker-in-charge. This will count as their elective course for the license period. The broker-in-charge must also complete the Real Estate Update continuing education course each license period as well.

99. What is "first substantial contact?"

A. An initial meeting to formalize a client-agency relationship.
B. A flexible standard for establishing client-agency relationships.
C. A new agent's first listing agreement or sales contract.
D. The point at which buyers or sellers must be given the North Carolina consumers' real estate disclosure document.

Answer: D. Although answers 1 and 2 answer are both partially correct, the real purpose of "first substantial contact" is to give prospective clients the information they need to fully understand the roles, responsibilities and loyalties of real estate agents in different kinds of relationships. This information must be provided before any client-agency agreements are presented.

100. What is the definition of "dual agency" in North Carolina?

A. One firm represents both the buyer and the seller equally.
B. One firm represents the seller and another represents the buyer in the same transaction.
C. One firm represents both the buyer and the seller, but owes primary loyalty to seller.

D. One firm represents both the buyer and the seller, but owes primary loyalty to the buyer.

Answer: A. Dual agency is legal in North Carolina, but requires a written agreement signed by all parties that includes compensation details. Further, licensees must represent the interests both parties in the transaction equally.

101. What is "designated agency" in North Carolina?

A. An alternative to dual agency.
B. A form of dual agency.
C. A minimum standard for client representation.
D. A form of representation that every company in NC must practice.

Answer: B. Designated agency occurs when firms that practice dual agency assign one agent to the seller and another to the buyer in an effort to better represent the interests of each party.

102. Who may practice designated agency?

A. Only one firm.
B. Only two firms involved in the same transaction.
C. Only brokers.
D. Only brokers or salespeople from separate firms.

Answer: A. By definition, designated agency occurs only when one firm represents both buyer and seller in the same transaction. Further, only firms that practice dual agency have the option of designated agency and it is the broker-in-charge who makes the decision.

103. Sally Lennox, a provisional broker working under the guidance of XYZ Real Estate Company, and with the owner's knowledge, deliberately fails to disclose that there is a dispute regarding title to the property. Who, if anyone, is liable in this situation?

A. No one is liable, since the dispute has not yet been resolved.
B. No one is liable since it's the buyer's responsibility to verify all representations, including title.
C. Only Sally is liable for her own actions.
D. Sally, the owner of the property, and the broker of XYZ Real Estate Company can all be held liable for Sally's lack of disclosure.

Answer: D. As a provisional broker, Sally represents not only herself, but also her firm, (The Broker) and the owner of the property. All can be held liable for any misrepresentations she may make.

104. Which of the following is NOT a responsibility of a broker in North Carolina?

A. Disclosing property defects to the buyer.
B. Disclosing the seller's reasons for selling.
C. Accounting for all funds in the transaction.
D. Loyalty to his or her client.

Answer: B. A broker owes loyalty and confidentiality to his or her client... full disclosure to buyers... and a complete accounting of all funds to both parties. In this case, the seller is the broker's client and disclosing his or her reasons for selling are not only irrelevant to buyers, but violate the owner's right to confidentiality.

105. Bill Timmons has a listing agreement to sell Paula Robinson's home. So far, Paula has turned down all offers, including those Bill thought were good. A new offer comes in the Friday before a weekend open house that's less than 70% of the asking price. Bill is certain it wont be accepted. What should he do?

A. Let Paula know he has a low offer, but deliver it to her anyway as soon as possible.
B. Tell the buyer it won't be accepted and refuse the offer.
C. Accept the offer, but don't present it.

D. Accept the offer, but hold it until after the open house to see if a better one comes along.

Answer: A. All offers must be presented as quickly as possible. Remember, what constitutes a "good offer" in the client's mind is sometimes more than price alone and agents must be careful not to make assumptions.

106. In which of these capacities may an agent represent a client?

A. As a buyer's agent.
B. As a seller's subagent.
C. As a dual agent.
D. Any of these relationships is acceptable.

Answer: D. As long as all other conditions of law and regulations are met, a licensee may represent, and be compensated, in whatever manner all parties agree to in writing.

107. When may a provisional broker represent both the buyer and the seller in the same transaction?

A. Never.
B. If the provisional broker's broker approves.
C. If the provisional broker informs both parties.

D. None of these situations are acceptable.

Answer: D. If a provisional broker represents both sides of a transaction, he or she is acting as a dual agent and may do so only with the parties informed written consent.

108. Before a person can receive compensation in a real estate transaction, he or she must have which of these credentials?

A. An MLS membership.
B. An agency-exclusive agreement.
C. An active license.
D. An active or inactive license and certificates of completion for all course and examination requirements.

Answer: C. Although inactive and expired licenses can often be renewed quickly and easily, agents cannot participate in real estate transactions in any way without an active license.

109. Phil Patterson is the broker-in-charge of Patterson-Stark Realty, a firm that practices dual agency. One of his agents, Barb, is working with a client as a buyer's agent. Another P&S agent, Rebecca, has one of the company's listings that Barb's client is interested in. How should they proceed to complete a transaction?

A. They cannot proceed because it would create conflicts of interest and confidentiality.

B. The listing relationship takes precedence, so Phil and Rebecca can only represent the seller and Barb can only represent the buyer.

C. If all parties agree, each can function as a dual agent.

D. As the listing firm, Phil, Rebecca and Barb must represent the seller.

Answer: C. Since the firm practices dual agency and discloses that fact Phil, Rebecca and Barb can all function as dual agents. However, before proceeding they need written agreement from both buyer and seller and need to ensure both parties are equally represented and that no confidential information is improperly shared.

110. Which of these is required to practice designated agency? 1) The firm has a policy of dual agency. 2) The firm has a policy of designated agency. 3) There are at least two licensees in the firm.

A. #1 only.

B. #2 only.

C. #1 and #2.

D. #1, #2 and #3.

Answer: D. All are required. Remember, a firm can't practice designated agency if it does not first practice dual agency. And, since designated agency means that the seller is represented by one person within the firm and the buyer by another, there must be at least two licensees on staff.

111. At what point should associates at Bay Head Realty discuss the possibility of dual agency?

A. When they meet a fellow associate they'd like to partner with.
B. At the point of first substantial contact with a prospective client.
C. When one associate agrees to show some properties to a prospective client he met at an open house and who, as it turns out is also working with another agent in the firm.
D. As soon as a new client signs an agreement.

Answer: B. The state requires that discussing the possibility of dual agency, when appropriate, and presenting prospective clients with the North Carolina real estate brochure must be done at "first substantial contact" and always before any agreements are presented.

112. What is the rule describing brokers and trust accounts?

A. Brokers may have trust accounts if and as needed.

B. Firms, not brokers, hold trust accounts.

C. A broker must have a trust account for every client.

D. Brokers must always have a trust account.

Answer: A. A broker is only required to have a trust account if he or she handles client monies directly. A broker may also have multiple trust accounts if needed.

113. If a dispute over monies in a trust account arises between a buyer and seller, what action must a broker take?

A. Hold the monies in the trust account until the parties reach agreement.

B. Turn the monies over to an attorney.

C. Return all monies to the buyer.

D. Split the monies between the buyer and seller.

Answer: A. The broker holds the monies and pays particularly close attention to accounting for all funds. However, he or she may disburse funds if so ordered by a court or if one of the parties abandons their claim.

114. Which of the following is NOT considered trust money?

A. Earnest money.

B. Broker funds for service charges.

C. Down payments.

D. Funds for final settlement.

Answer: B. The purpose of trust accounts is to hold funds paid by clients towards the settlement of real estate transactions separate from general funds. They are monies that belong to clients, such as down payments, and should never be commingled with accounts used to pay commissions, salaries, office expenses and the like.

115. Are interest-bearing trust accounts permissible?

A. No, any interest that accrues in a trust account goes to the state to fund real estate programs and studies.

B. Yes, and the interest is split between the buyer and seller as well as the broker to cover administrative expenses.

C. Yes, and the interest is split between the seller and broker.

D. Yes, in certain conditions.

Answer: D. Generally, trust monies are held in non-interest bearing accounts. For the money to earn interest, both buyer and seller must agree the account will be interest bearing and who will earn the interest or how it will be divided. Such agreements should be incorporated into the purchase contract and may require an attorney's assistance to prepare.

116. What is the maximum amount of personal funds a provisional broker may keep in a trust account

A. 100
B. 300
C. Enough to cover service charges.
D. None of the above.

Answer: D. Trick question -- only brokers, not provisional brokers have trust accounts. The intent here is to remind you to read carefully and think about your answers. Although the state exam will not have trick questions, the practice of real estate requires comprehensive knowledge and attention to detail and you will be expected to understand subtle differences and distinctions.

117. What is the deadline for depositing monies into a trust account?

A. The same day they are received.
B. Within three banking days of receipt.
C. As stipulated in the contract.
D. It varies with the type of deposit (earnest money, downpayment, etc.).

Answer: B. The rules stipulate three banking days. Saturdays, Sundays and official holidays are not considered banking days.

118. When may a licensee pay a referral fee?

A. If it is $50 or less.
B. If there is a written agreement between the parties.
C. If it is to a licensee.
D. Never.

Answer: C. Referral fees may be paid only to licensed real estate professionals and must go through the employing broker.

119. When it comes to financing theory, what kind of state is North Carolina?

A. A title theory state.
B. A lien theory state.
C. Both 1 and 2.
D. Neither 1 nor 2.

Answer: A. North Carolina is a "title theory" state, which means that the lender has title to the property and the owner has an equitable interest. By contrast, a "lien theory" state grants legal title to the borrower while granting the mortgage holder a lien against the property.

120. Rita Spenser is a provisional broker completing a transaction with her seller when she discovers an error on the closing statement. Who is responsible for ensuring the accuracy of closing statements?

A. Rita, as the provisional broker, is responsible.
B. Rita's broker is responsible.
C. The title company.
D. The attorney.

Answer: B. Although Rita should double-check all documents for accuracy, it is the broker who is responsible for the accuracy of agreements, offers, contacts, closing statements and other documents.

121. Bob is a recent college graduate planning on a career in real estate. Although not yet licensed, he proceeds to show a property for the experience, even though it's a violation of real estate law. Who is subject to disciplinary action?

A. Bob.
B. The principal of the firm.
C. Bob's broker.
D. No one, since Bob is not yet licensed and thus exempt from the rules.

Answer: C. Brokers are responsible for ensuring the legal and ethical conduct of all persons under their supervision, including both licensed provisional brokers and unlicensed assistants.

122. There is strong evidence a licensee embezzled from his firm. What action may the Real Estate Commission take?

A. None, unless the embezzlement was from a trust account and directly related to real estate transactions.
B. If found guilty, he can be fined by the Commission.
C. He can be prosecuted by the Commission and, if found guilty, is subject to criminal penalties including possible jail time.
D. He can be prosecuted by the Commission and, if found guilty, is subject to noncriminal licensure penalties.

Answer: D. The Real Estate Commission's responsibilities include investigating, coordinating and prosecuting charges against licensees. However, they have no criminal authority and cannot sentence people to jail. That does not mean, of course, that other authorities such as the attorney general cannot proceed criminally against licensees.

123. An unhappy seller took a licensee to court which found in the seller's favor. Which of the following would NOT occur as a result?

A. The licensee could be fined.

B. The court could recommend disciplinary action against the licensee to the chairman of the Real Estate Commission.

C. The court could revoke his or her license.

D. The seller could file an additional complaint with the Real Estate Commission.

Answer: C. The courts decide issues of law, while the Commission regulates the conduct of real estate practioners. Thus the court cannot suspend or revoke licenses in North Carolina, though it can recommend such action to the Commission.

124. Vicky is a real estate licensee whose friend Thomas is a home inspector with an excellent reputation. When Vicky has a buyer interested in a property, she sends them to Thomas, who pays her brokerage a $50 referral fee. Is this a legal practice?

A. Under no circumstances.

B. Yes, with the permission of Vicky's broker, and if the buyer knows of and agrees to the arrangement.

C. Yes, if the money is paid to Vicky through the broker-in-charge.

D. Yes, because small amounts of $50 or less are viewed as "honorariums," not fees or commissions.

Answer: B. Real Estate License Laws require that all elements in a transaction be open and above-board. There can be no hidden deals or secret transactions between any parties. While the Real Estate Settlement Procedures Act does prohibits licensees from receiving "Kickbacks" from mortgage lenders for referrals, there is not any law that prohibits licensees from receiving referral fees from service providers with full disclosure to all parties.

125. Violations of license law tend to be which of the following?

A. Misdemeanors.
B. Felonies.
C. Civil violations that result in loss of license.
D. Civil violations that result in license suspension.

Answer: A. Violations of license law are serious issues, but do not always result in the loss or suspension of a license. Because of past abuses, some time-share issues are classed as felonies, which is a criminal offense.

126. Can Lance, a successful provisional broker ambitious to move to the "next level," place a series of ads in the newspaper?

A. Yes, if his broker approves and the ads carry the name of the firm or broker in addition to Lance's.

B. Yes, if the ads only feature Lance's name and don't attempt to "borrow equity" by including the firm's name.

C. No, only firms can place ads.

D. No, other than classifieds, newspapers only accept ads from recognized advertising agencies.

Answer: A. Provisional brokers are free to advertise or promote their own services so long as the name of the firm or broker is also prominently featured.

127. Provisional broker Jackie Revson-Smith receives an earnest money deposit on a major property. What must she do with the check?

A. Deposit it into a trust account within three banking days.

B. Give it to her broker as soon as possible.

C. Present it to the seller within twenty-four hours.

D. Give it to the closing attorney to hold.

Answer: B. Only a broker can hold a trust account and funds must be deposited no later than three banking days from receipt.

128. Brokers-in-charge are responsible for all of the following, EXCEPT:

A. Other brokers associated with his or her office.
B. Part-time provisional brokers.
C. Unlicensed support staff.
D. Trust accounts.

Answer: A. Brokers-in-charge are responsible for all people and activities in their office that are subject to real estate license regulations, except those of other brokers.

129. What actions are required of agents regarding "material facts?"

A. They are deemed confidential between the agent and client and should be protected.
B. They should generally be disclosed to the public although in some instances they may be considered minor or confidential and need not be disclosed.
C. Must always be disclosed.
D. Should be disclosed to serious buyers.

Answer: C. Material facts -- those dealing with a property's physical structure or the ability of parties to perform as promised -- must always be disclosed when the agent knows or should have known about them.

130. Sheila Rittenhouse knows that a property she hopes to sell is in foreclosure but fails to disclose the fact to potential buyers. Since she also knows this is a material fact, what violation is she guilty of?

A. Negligent omission.
B. Willful omission.
C. Negligent misrepresentation.
D. Willful misrepresentation.

Answer: B. Because Sheila knew the information, knew it was material and yet deliberately withheld it, she is guilty of "willful omission." If she had not known the property was in foreclosure or that it was a material fact, she would have been guilty of negligent omission because that's information she should have known. Misrepresentation is the opposite side of the same coin and means the same thing as far as regulations and the law are concerned.

131. The widening of a highway adjacent to a large subdivision has been proposed. There is a 20-foot buffer of mature trees sheltering the subdivision from the highway that is unlikely to be affected. Is this a material fact that needs to be disclosed.

A. No, since the subdivision is unlikely to be affected.

B. Yes, but only if the proposal passes.

C. No, it is not material since it does not pertain to the actual property or the ability of parties to perform as promised.

D. Yes, it must be disclosed.

Answer: D. Even the possibility of widening a road is considered a material fact in North Carolina. Although though it may not physically affect a property other factors such as noise, traffic congestion or the perception of desirability can have a direct and "material" impact on value.

132. Peggy buys her new home through Fred Priori an agent for Eastern Shore Realty. Fred assures Peggy her utility bills will be low since the house is newly built, although he has no actual knowledge of the property's utility costs. Peggy's bills turn out to be much higher than average because of poor construction and materials. Is Fred guilty of any violation?

A. Yes, willful omission.

B. Yes, willful misrepresentation.

C. No, Fred made a reasonable assumption that simply turned out to be incorrect.

D. No, because Fred was not representing the builder.

Answer: B. Fred made an assertion without any foundation in fact. He should have told her he didn't know what the costs would be and suggested asking the builder to provide documentation of actual utility costs, or having the property professionally inspected and/or other courses of action to obtain reliable opinions of construction quality, materials and likely energy costs.

133. John Martin assures real estate provisional broker, Alison Jacoby, that the home he's selling has hardwood floors throughout. This appears to be true, since it is exposed in all rooms but two of the bedrooms which have wall-to-wall carpeting. Alison passes these assurances on to buyers who later discover that one of the bedrooms does not have hardwood. What, if anything, is Allison guilty of.

A. She's not guilty of anything since she made a good faith effort to discover the truth and relied on the owner's assurance.
B. She's guilty of willful omission.
C. She's guilty of negligent misrepresentation.
D. She's guilty of willful misrepresentation.

Answer: C. Alison is guilty of negligent misrepresentation because she made a false assertion based on facts she should have verified. She could have avoided the violation by lifting a corner of the carpet to inspect the flooring or making a written disclosure to the buyers such as, although the seller believes hardwood is under the carpet, she does Not know and cannot guarantee that to be true.

134. A buyer enthusiastically tells a provisional broker that his reason for purchasing a particular property is its peace and quiet. The provisional broker knows construction will soon start on a major shopping center immediately behind the property but says nothing because the buyer didn't ask about future development or surrounding properties. What, if anything, is the provisional broker guilty of?

A. Nothing, the buyer didn't ask.
B. He is guilty of negligent misrepresentation.
C. He's guilty of willful omission.
D. He's guilty of willful misrepresentation.

Answer: C. Willful omission because he deliberately withheld a material fact. The new shopping center is "material" not only because it is defined as such by the state, but because it will have a direct impact on the property and the new owner's ability to enjoy it as he expects.

135. When a real estate firm practices dual agency, which of these statements is true? 1) It must make full disclosure to all parties when an offer is written. 2) Dual agency must be explained to all parties at the first substantial contact.

A. Only #1 is true.

B. Only #2 is true.
C. Both #1 and #2 are true.
D. Neither #1 or #2 is true.

Answer: C. An explanation of the dual agency concept along with full disclosure, must be made as soon as possible and is reaffirmed at the time agreements, offers and contracts are prepared.

136. Which of these can define "first substantial contact?" 1) A person calls a real estate company to ask about a listed property. 2) A person attends an open house and speaks with an agent.

A. Only #1.
B. Only #2
C. Both #1 and #2.
D. Neither #1 or #2.

Answer: C. "Substantial contact" can be defined as any conversation or meeting about the possible sale or purchase of property, at which point all relevant disclosures should be made.

137. Which of these are relevant disclosures that must be addressed at time of first substantial contact? 1) The concept of agency is discussed and disclosed to members of the

general public. 2) The agent's duties and responsibilities to clients are discussed and disclosed to members of the general public. 2) The agents duties and responibilities to clients are discussed and disclosed to members of the public.

A. Only #1.
B. Only #2.
C. Both #1 and #2.
D. Neither #1 or #2.

Answer: C. Agents must disclose both the concept of agency as well as their roles, representations and loyalties in various kinds of agent-client relationships.

138. What is the violation when a broker should know that a statement about a material fact is false, but unintentionally misinforms a party in a real estate transaction?

A. Negligent misrepresentation.
B. Negligent omission.
C. Willful misrepresentation.
D. Willful omission.

Answer: A. Misrepresentation occurs when an agent makes an statement about a property that is false, such as saying the foundation is sound when it is not. It is willful when the agent knows the statement to be false and negligent when he or she doesn't know it's false but should have,

139. What is the violation when a broker has information about a property that could impact the decision of a party in a real estate transaction but fails to disclose it?

A. Negligent misrepresentation.
B. Negligent omission.
C. Willful misrepresentation.
D. Willful omission.

Answer: D. Willful omission occurs when an agent deliberately fails to disclose information that could have an impact on a transaction. Negligent omission occurs when an agent does not, but should have, known about the information.

140. Which of these statements about the Residential Property Disclosure Statement is true? 1) All sellers must provide the form to potential buyers. 2) Non-licensed owners selling their own property are exempt from this law.

A. Only #1.
B. Only #2.
C. Both #1 and #2.
D. Neither #1 or #2.

Answer: A. The law applies to all parties selling a property that has been lived in. Unlike some other provisions of real estate law that do not apply to individuals selling their own property, there is no exemption for "FSBOs."

141. If the Residential Property Disclosure Statement is not delivered to a buyer before or at the time of offer, the buyer may cancel the offer under which of these circumstances?

A. If the seller does not give the buyer a copy of the form by the time he/she makes an offer to purchase the property.
B. If the buyer personally delivers his/her decision to cancel to the owner or the owner's agent within three calendar days following receipt of the Statement.
C. If the buyer personally delivers his/her decision to cancel to the owner or the owner's agent within three calendar days following receipt of the Statement, or the date of the contract, whichever occurs first.
D. All apply.

Answer: D. Failure to deliver the Disclosure Statement allows buyers the right to cancel their offer at almost any time.

142. If the Disclosure Statement is properly delivered, when may potential buyers still cancel a contract? 1) If properly

informed by the Disclosure Statement, buyers may not cancel any resulting contracts. 2) Under certain circumstances a buyer may still cancel a contract.

A. Only #1.
B. Only #2.
C. Both #1 and #2.
D. Neither #1 or #2.

Answer: A. So long as proper disclosures are made, all contracts are binding on buyer and seller and may not be cancelled.

143. Jerome Billings tells a buyer he represents that a property is served by city water. He believes this is true because several nearby homes he sold did have city water service, although this property does not. Is he guilty of any violation?

A. No, he had reasonable grounds for believing the statement was truc and did not intend to misrepresent the facts.
B. Yes, although unintentional, he is still guilty of fraudulent misrepresentation.
C. Yes, he is guilty of willful misrepresentation because water service is a matter of record he had a fiduciary responsibility to verify.
D. Yes, he is guilt of negligent misrepresentation.

Answer: D. Jerome believed his statement was accurate and did not intend to misrepresent either by a false statement or deliberate omission. Although still a significant violation, it is not a fraudulent or deliberate misrepresentation.

144. Which of these provisions must be included in North Carolina listing agreements? 1) A defined period of time for which they are active. 2) An automatic right of renewal.

A. #1 only.
B. #2 only.
C. Both #1 and #2.
D. Neither #1 or #2.

Answer: A. There is no "passive" or automatic renewal provision in North Carolina listing agreements; they must be "actively" extended by both parties.

145. What is another name for a "quitclaim deed?"

A. A "limited warranty" deed.
B. A non-warranty deed.
C. A special warranty deed.
D. A "sweetheart sale" deed.

Answer: B. A quitclaim deed transfers ownership or share of ownership to another party but does not guarantee anything about what is being transferred, including the ownership interest. For example, one party in a divorce may sign a quitclaim deed transferring whatever right they may have to the other.

146. A North Carolina sales contract is viewed to be which of the following? 1) Bilateral. 2) Unilateral.

A. Only #1.
B. Only #2.
C. Both #1 and #2.
D. Neither #1 or #2.

Answer: A. Bilateral means contracts are entered into by and are equally binding upon both parties to a real estate transaction. Unilateral would mean only party could amend, cancel, change or otherwise modify the contract without the other party's agreement.

147. What is the name of the clause in a listing agreement granting brokers a protection period beyond the expiration date? 1) An override clause. 2) An extender clause.

A. Only #1.

B. Only #2.
C. Both #1 and #2.
D. Neither #1 or #2.

Answer: C. Both terms are used. They refer to the provision that entitles a broker to his or her commission if a party they brought to the table should enter into an agreement within a reasonable time after the listing expires.

148. What does "parol evidence" mean? 1) Oral agreements can be part of a contract. 2) Hand-written notes and addendums to a contract take precedence over printed portions.

A. Only #1.
B. Only #2.
C. Both #1 and #2.
D. Neither #1 or #2.

Answer: B. Parol evidence means evidence of oral agreements purporting to explain, change or contradict written portions of a contract. Parol evidence is NOT accepted in North Carolina. However, handwritten changes and addendums signed or initialed by both parties due take precedence over printed portions.

149. According to the North Carolina Statute of Fraud, which of these real estate agreements must be in writing? 1) Installment land contracts. 2) Sales contracts. 3) Property management agreements. 4) Lease or rental agreements of more than one year.

A. Only #1.
B. Both #1 and #2.
C. All of the above.
D. None of the above.

Answer: B. Deeds, sales contracts, mortgages and other such agreements transferring ownership or a sale of ownership must be in writing. A lease agreement longer than three years must be in writing to be enforceable. Property management agreements have nothing to do with the conveyance, ownership or occupation of property and are primarily covered under different statutes.

150. Which, if any, of these forms of buyer agency are allowable in North Carolina?

A. Non-exclusive buyer agency.
B. Exclusive buyer agency.
C. 24-hour buyer agency.
D. All of the above.

Answer: D. As long as all other conditions of buyer agency are met and the agreement is in writing, the parties may agree to whatever terms they choose.

1. Which of the following activities does NOT require a real estate license?

A. Holding a real estate auction.
B. Selling property listed by other brokers or agencies.
C. Showing and selling one's own property.
D. Offering to buy properties on behalf of third parties.

Answer: C. Buying or sell properties for one's own benefit or for the benefit of a family member generally does not require a license. However, only licensed professionals may engage in transactions on behalf of third parties. Additionally, brokers or provisional brokers selling their own properties must disclose that fact to the public.

2. In addition to selling one's own property, which of the following is also exempt from normal licensing requirements?

A. Acting as a guardian.
B. Acting as a trustee.
C. Acting as an attorney-in-fact.
D. Each of the above.

Answer: D. Although often limited in scope (such as the authority to negotiate tax matters or conduct real estate transactions), someone performing any of these duties "becomes" the person he or she is representing. No license is required because that person is now acting, in effect, on his or her own behalf.

3. As long as it is specified as part of his or her duties, is it legal for an unlicensed salaried assistant to solicit listings for the broker?

A. Yes, if it is part of a written job description.
B. No, soliciting listings is the exclusive responsibility of the broker-in-charge.
C. Yes, because she is being paid a salary, not commissions.
D. No, active participation in real estate transactions requires a license.

Answer: D. Tasks such as answering phones or making copies are considered support and don't require any licensing or course work. However, activities such as soliciting listings or providing information about a property are part of the transaction process and may be handled only by licensed real estate professionals.

4. Regarding the North Carolina Real Estate Commission, which of these statements is true?

A. A monthly salary plus expenses is paid to each member.
B. The North Carolina Association of Realtors® appoints the members.
C. The governor appoints members for a three-year term.
D. The Commission consists of seven members, all of whom must be active in real estate.

Answer: C. The governor appoints members to the Commission. Additionally, there are nine, not seven members and, although at least three must be active in real estate, there also must be at least two non-licensed "public members."

5. Which of these is a requirement to hold a real estate license in North Carolina? 1) Be a resident in good standing of the state. 2) Be at least 21 years old.

A. Only #1.
B. Only #2.
C. Neither #1 nor #2.
D. Both #1 and #2.

Answer: C. In North Carolina, the minimum age requirement is 18, not 21. In addition to course-work and exam requirements, one must also be of good character, though not a "resident in good standing."

6. Licensees must notify the Real Estate Commission when which of these events occur?

A. There is a significant change in sales volume.
B. The business tradename has changed within the past ten days.
C. The business trade-name has changed within the past thirty days.
D. The licensee has received more than two traffic violations within the past eighteen months.

Answer: B. Licensees have ten days in which to notify the Commission of any change in their business name, trade-name or address.

7. What is the first point at which a person may begin practicing real estate in North Carolina?

A. When a broker activates his or her license.
B. Upon successful completion of all course and exam work.
C. Upon completion of all education requirements.
D. Upon completion of course work requirements, successfully pass the exam and finish a recognized training program.

Answer: A. In effect, obtaining a provisional brokers license means that a person is now eligible to be hired by a broker. Only provisional brokers operating under the direct supervision of a broker may actually sell real estate.

8. Which of these is required to be a broker-in-charge? 1) An active broker's license for the state of North Carolina. 2) Eight hours of continuing education each year.

A. Only #1.
B. Only #2.
C. Neither #1 nor #2.
D. Both #1 and #2.

Answer: D. Unlike some other states, North Carolina requires Brokers-in-Charge to complete continuing education requirements every year in addition to holding an active broker's license. In addition, beginning July 1, 2006, all brokers-in-charge must complete a four classroom hour Broker-in-Charge Annual Review Course each full license period after being designated a broker-in-charge. This will count as their elective course for the license period. The broker-in-charge must also complete the Real Estate Update continuing education course each license period as well.

9. What is "first substantial contact?"

A. An initial meeting to formalize a client-agency relationship.

B. A flexible standard for establishing client-agency relationships.

C. A new agent's first listing agreement or sales contract.

D. The point at which buyers or sellers must be given the North Carolina consumers' real estate disclosure document.

Answer: D. Although answers 1 and 2 answer are both partially correct, the real purpose of "first substantial contact" is to give prospective clients the information they need to fully understand the roles, responsibilities and loyalties of real estate agents in different kinds of relationships. This information must be provided before any client-agency agreements are presented.

10. What is the definition of "dual agency" in North Carolina?

A. One firm represents both the buyer and the seller equally.

B. One firm represents the seller and another represents the buyer in the same transaction.

C. One firm represents both the buyer and the seller, but owes primary loyalty to seller.

D. One firm represents both the buyer and the seller, but owes primary loyalty to the buyer.

Answer: A. Dual agency is legal in North Carolina, but requires a written agreement signed by all parties that includes compensation details. Further, licensees must represent the interests both parties in the transaction equally.

11. What is "designated agency" in North Carolina?

A. An alternative to dual agency.
B. A form of dual agency.
C. A minimum standard for client representation.
D. A form of representation that every company in NC must practice.

Answer: B. Designated agency occurs when firms that practice dual agency assign one agent to the seller and another to the buyer in an effort to better represent the interests of each party.

12. Who may practice designated agency?

A. Only one firm representing the buyer and seller in the same transaction.
B. Only two firms involved in the same transaction.
C. Only brokers.
D. Designated agency can be practiced by firms who do not practice dual agency in North Carolina.

Answer: A. By definition, designated agency occurs only when one firm represents both buyer and seller in the same transaction. Further, only firms that practice dual agency have the option of designated agency and it is the broker-in-charge who makes the decision.

13. Sally Lennox, a provisional broker working under the guidance of XYZ Real Estate Company, and with the owner's knowledge, deliberately fails to disclose that there is a dispute regarding title to the property. Who, if anyone, is liable in this situation?

A. No one is liable, since the dispute has not yet been resolved.
B. No one is liable since it's the buyer's responsibility to verify all representations, including title.
C. Only Sally is liable for her own actions.
D. Sally, the owner of the property, and the broker of XYZ Real Estate Company can all be held liable for Sally's lack of disclosure.

Answer: D. As a provisional broker, Sally represents not only herself, but also her firm, (The Broker) and the owner of the property. All can be held liable for any misrepresentations she may make.

14. Which of the following is NOT a responsibility of a broker in North Carolina?

A. Disclosing property defects to the buyer.

B. Disclosing the seller's reasons for selling.

C. Accounting for all funds in the transaction.

D. Accounting for all funds belonging to both parties to a transaction.

Answer: B. A broker owes loyalty and confidentiality to his or her client... full disclosure to buyers... and a complete accounting of all funds to both parties. In this case, the seller is the broker's client and disclosing his or her reasons for selling are not only irrelevant to buyers, but violate the owner's right to confidentiality.

15. Bill Timmons has a listing agreement to sell Paula Robinson's home. So far, Paula has turned down all offers, including those Bill thought were good. A new offer comes in the Friday before a weekend open house that's less than 70% of the asking price. Bill is certain it won't be accepted. What should he do?

A. Let Paula know he has a low offer, but deliver it to her anyway as soon as possible.

B. Tell the buyer it won't be accepted and refuse the offer.

C. Accept the offer, but don't present it.

D. Bill is a knowledgeable licensee, and is fully aware of what Paula will or will not accept. Bill should sit down with the buyer and negotiate for a higher price even at the risk of losing the sale for Paula.

Answer: A. All offers must be presented as quickly as possible. Remember, what constitutes a "good offer" in the client's mind is sometimes more than price alone and agents must be careful not to make assumptions.

16. In which of these capacities may an agent represent a client?

A. As a buyer's agent.
B. As a seller's subagent.
C. As a dual agent.
D. Any of these relationships is acceptable.

Answer: D. As long as all other conditions of law and regulations are met, a licensee may represent, and be compensated, in whatever manner all parties agree to in writing.

17. When may a provisional broker represent both the buyer and the seller in the same transaction?

A. Never.
B. If the provisional broker's broker approves.
C. If the provisional broker informs both parties.

D. None of these situations are acceptable.

Answer: D. If a provisional broker represents both sides of a transaction, he or she is acting as a dual agent and may do so only with the parties informed written consent.

18. Before a person can receive compensation in a real estate transaction, he or she must have which of these credentials?

A. An MLS membership.
B. An agency-exclusive agreement.
C. An active license.
D. An active or inactive license and certificates of completion for all course and examination requirements.

Answer: C. Although inactive and expired licenses can often be renewed quickly and easily, agents cannot participate in real estate transactions in any way without an active license.

19. Phil Patterson is the broker-in-charge of Patterson-Stark Realty, a firm that practices dual agency. One of his agents, Barb, is working with a client as a buyer's agent. Another P&S agent, Rebecca, has one of the company's listings that Barb's client is interested in. How should they proceed to complete a transaction?

A. They cannot proceed because it would create conflicts of interest and confidentiality.
B. The listing relationship takes precedence, so Phil and Rebecca can only represent the seller and Barb can only represent the buyer.
C. If all parties agree, each can function as a dual agent.
D. As the listing firm, Phil, Rebecca and Barb must represent the seller.

Answer: C. Since the firm practices dual agency and discloses that fact Phil, Rebecca and Barb can all function as dual agents. However, before proceeding they need written agreement from both buyer and seller and need to ensure both parties are equally represented and that no confidential information is improperly shared.

20. Which of these is required to practice designated agency? 1) The firm has a policy of dual agency. 2) The firm has a policy of designated agency. 3) There are at least two licensees in the firm.

A. #1 only.
B. #2 only.
C. #1 and #2.
D. #1, #2 and #3.

Answer: D. All are required. Remember, a firm can't practice designated agency if it does not first practice dual agency. And, since designated agency means that the seller is represented by one person within the firm and the buyer by another, there must be at least two licensees on staff.

21. At what point should associates at Bay Head Realty discuss the possibility of dual agency?

A. When they meet a fellow associate they'd like to partner with.
B. At the point of first substantial contact with a prospective client.
C. When one associate agrees to show some properties to a prospective client he met at an open house and who, as it turns out is also working with another agent in the firm.
D. As soon as a new client signs an agreement.

Answer: B. The state requires that discussing the possibility of dual agency, when appropriate, and presenting prospective clients with the North Carolina real estate brochure must be done at "first substantial contact" and always before any agreements are presented.

22. What is the rule describing brokers and trust accounts?

A. Brokers may have trust accounts if and as needed.

B. Firms, not brokers, hold trust accounts.

C. A broker must have a trust account for every client.

D. Brokers must always have a trust account.

Answer: A. A broker is only required to have a trust account if he or she handles client monies directly. A broker may also have multiple trust accounts if needed.

23. If a dispute over monies in a trust account arises between a buyer and seller, what action must a broker take?

A. Hold the monies in the trust account until the parties reach agreement.

B. Turn the monies over to an attorney.

C. Return all monies to the buyer.

D. Split the monies between the buyer and seller.

Answer: A. The broker holds the monies and pays particularly close attention to accounting for all funds. However, he or she may disburse funds if so ordered by a court or if one of the parties abandons their claim.

24. Which of the following is NOT considered trust money?

A. Earnest money.

B. Broker funds for service charges.

C. Down payments.
D. Funds for final settlement.

Answer: B. The purpose of trust accounts is to hold funds paid by clients towards the settlement of real estate transactions separate from general funds. They are monies that belong to clients, such as down payments, and should never be commingled with accounts used to pay commissions, salaries, office expenses and the like.

25. Are interest-bearing trust accounts permissible?

A. No, any interest that accrues in a trust account goes to the state to fund real estate programs and studies.
B. Yes, and the interest is split between the buyer and seller as well as the broker to cover administrative expenses.
C. Yes, and the interest is split between the seller and broker.
D. Yes, in certain conditions.

Answer: D. Generally, trust monies are held in non-interest bearing accounts. For the money to earn interest, both buyer and seller must agree the account will be interest bearing and who will earn the interest or how it will be divided. Such agreements should be incorporated into the purchase contract and may require an attorney's assistance to prepare.

26. What is the maximum amount of personal funds a provisional broker may keep in a trust account?

A. $100.00
B. $300.00
C. Enough to cover service charges.
D. None of the above.

Answer: D. Trick question -- only brokers, not provisional brokers have trust accounts. The intent here is to remind you to read carefully and think about your answers. Although the state exam will not have trick questions, the practice of real estate requires comprehensive knowledge and attention to detail and you will be expected to understand subtle differences and distinctions.

27. What is the deadline for depositing monies into a trust account?

A. The same day they are received.
B. Within three banking days of receipt.
C. As stipulated in the contract.
D. It varies with the type of deposit (earnest money, downpayment, etc.).

Answer: B. The rules stipulate three banking days. Saturdays, Sundays and official holidays are not considered banking days.

28. When may a licensee pay a referral fee?

A. If it is $50 or less.
B. If there is a written agreement between the parties.
C. If it is to a licensee.
D. Never.

Answer: C. Referral fees may be paid only to licensed real estate professionals and must go through the employing broker.

29. When it comes to financing theory, what kind of state is North Carolina?

A. A title theory state.
B. A lien theory state.
C. Both 1 and 2.
D. Neither 1 nor 2.

Answer: A. North Carolina is a "title theory" state, which means that the lender has title to the property and the owner has an equitable interest. By contrast, a "lien theory" state grants legal title to the borrower while granting the mortgage holder a lien against the property.

30. Rita Spenser is a provisional broker completing a transaction with her seller when she discovers an error on the closing statement. Who is responsible for ensuring the accuracy of closing statements?

A. Rita, as the provisional broker, is responsible.
B. Rita's broker is responsible.
C. The title company.
D. The attorney.

Answer: B. Although Rita should double-check all documents for accuracy, it is the broker who is responsible for the accuracy of agreements, offers, contacts, closing statements and other documents.

31. Bob is a recent college graduate planning on a career in real estate. Bob is working as an unlicensed assistant in a real estate office while he is studying for his real estate exam. Although not yet licensed, he proceeds to show a property for the experience even though it's a violation of real estate law. Who is subject to disciplinary action?

A. Bob.
B. The principal of the firm.
C. Bob's broker.
D. No one, since Bob is not yet licensed and thus exempt from the rules.

Answer: C. Brokers are responsible for ensuring the legal and ethical conduct of all persons under their supervision, including both licensed provisional brokers and unlicensed assistants.

32. There is strong evidence a licensee embezzled from his firm. What action may the Real Estate Commission take?

A. None, unless the embezzlement was from a trust account and directly related to real estate transactions.
B. If found guilty, he can be fined by the Commission.
C. He can be prosecuted by the Commission and, if found guilty, is subject to criminal penalties including possible jail time.
D. He can be prosecuted by the Commission and, if found guilty, is subject to noncriminal
licensure penalties.

Answer: D. The Real Estate Commission's responsibilities include investigating, coordinating and prosecuting charges against licensees. However, they have no criminal authority and cannot sentence people to jail. That does not mean, of course, that other authorities such as the attorney general cannot proceed criminally against licensees.

33. An unhappy seller took a licensee to court which found in the seller's favor. Which of the following would NOT occur as a result?

A. The licensee could be fined.
B. The court could recommend disciplinary action against the licensee to the chairman of the Real Estate Commission.
C. The court could revoke his or her license.
D. The seller could file an additional complaint with the Real Estate Commission.

Answer: C. The courts decide issues of law, while the Commission regulates the conduct of real estate practioners. Thus the court cannot suspend or revoke licenses in North Carolina, though it can recommend such action to the Commission.

34. Vicky is a real estate licensee whose friend Thomas is a home inspector with an excellent reputation. When Vicky has a buyer interested in a property, she sends them to Thomas, who pays her brokerage a $50 referral fee. Is this a legal practice?

A. Under no circumstances.
B. Yes, with the permission of Vicky's broker, and if the buyer knows of and agrees to the arrangement.

C. Yes, if the money is paid to Vicky through the broker-in-charge.

D. Yes, because small amounts of $50 or less are viewed as "honorariums," not fees or commissions.

Answer: B. Real Estate License Laws require that all elements in a transaction be open and above-board. There can be no hidden deals or secret transactions between any parties. While the Real Estate Settlement Procedures Act does prohibits licensees from receiving "Kickbacks" from mortgage lenders for referrals, there is not any law that prohibits licensees from receiving referral fees from service providers with full disclosure to all parties.

35. Violations of license law tend to be which of the following?

A. Misdemeanors.
B. Felonies.
C. Civil violations that result in loss of license.
D. Civil violations that result in license suspension.

Answer: A. Violations of license law are serious issues, but do not always result in the loss or suspension of a license. Because of past abuses, some time-share issues are classed as felonies, which is a criminal offense.

36. Can Lance, a successful provisional broker ambitious to move to the "next level," place a series of ads in the newspaper?

A. Yes, if his broker approves and the ads carry the name of the firm or broker in addition to Lance's.
B. Yes, if the ads only feature Lance's name and don't attempt to "borrow equity" by including the firm's name.
C. No, only firms can place ads.
D. No, other than classifieds, newspapers only accept ads from recognized advertising agencies.

Answer: A. Provisional brokers are free to advertise or promote their own services so long as the name of the firm or broker is also prominently featured.

37. Provisional broker Jackie Revson-Smith receives an earnest money deposit on a major property. What must she do with the check?

A. Deposit it into a trust account within three banking days.
B. Give it to her broker as soon as possible.
C. Present it to the seller within twenty-four hours.
D. Give it to the closing attorney to hold.

Answer: B. Only a broker can hold a trust account and funds must be deposited no later than three banking days from receipt.

38. Brokers-in-charge are responsible for all of the following, EXCEPT:

A. Other brokers associated with his or her office.
B. Part-time provisional brokers.
C. Unlicensed support staff.
D. Trust accounts.

Answer: A. Brokers-in-charge are responsible for all people and activities in their office that are subject to real estate license regulations, except those of other brokers.

39. What actions are required of agents regarding "material facts?"

A. They are deemed confidential between the agent and client and should be protected.
B. They should generally be disclosed to the public although in some instances they may be considered minor or confidential and need not be disclosed.
C. Must always be disclosed.
D. Should be disclosed to serious buyers.

Answer: C. Material facts -- those dealing with a property's physical structure or the ability of parties to perform as promised -- must always be disclosed when the agent knows or should have known about them.

40. Sheila Rittenhouse knows that a property she hopes to sell is in foreclosure but fails to disclose the fact to potential buyers. Since she also knows this is a material fact, what violation is she guilty of?

A. Negligent omission.
B. Willful omission.
C. Negligent misrepresentation.
D. Willful misrepresentation.

Answer: B. Because Sheila knew the information, knew it was material and yet deliberately withheld it, she is guilty of "willful omission." If she had not known the property was in foreclosure or that it was a material fact, she would have been guilty of negligent omission because that's information she should have known. Misrepresentation is the opposite side of the same coin and means the same thing as far as regulations and the law are concerned.

41. The widening of a highway adjacent to a large subdivision has been proposed. There is a 20-foot buffer of

mature trees sheltering the subdivision from the highway that is unlikely to be affected. Is this a material fact that needs to be disclosed.

A. No, since the subdivision is unlikely to be affected.
B. Yes, but only if the proposal passes.
C. No, it is not material since it does not pertain to the actual property or the ability of parties to perform as promised.
D. Yes, it must be disclosed.

Answer: D. Even the possibility of widening a road is considered a material fact in North Carolina. Although though it may not physically affect a property other factors such as noise, traffic congestion or the perception of desirability can have a direct and "material" impact on value.

42. Peggy buys her new home through Fred Priori an agent for Eastern Shore Realty. Fred assures Peggy her utility bills will be low since the house is newly built, although he has no actual knowledge of the property's utility costs. Peggy's bills turn out to be much higher than average because of poor construction and materials. Is Fred guilty of any violation?

A. Yes, willful omission.
B. Yes, willful misrepresentation.
C. No, Fred made a reasonable assumption that simply turned out to be incorrect.

D. No, because Fred was not representing the builder.

Answer: B. Fred made an assertion without any foundation in fact. He should have told her he didn't know what the costs would be and suggested asking the builder to provide documentation of actual utility costs, or having the property professionally inspected and/or other courses of action to obtain reliable opinions of construction quality, materials and likely energy costs.

43. John Martin assures real estate provisional broker, Alison Jacoby, that the home he's selling has hardwood floors throughout. This appears to be true, since it is exposed in all rooms but two of the bedrooms which have wall-to-wall. Alison passes these assurances on to the buyers who later discover that one of the bedrooms does not have hardwood. What, if anything is Alison guilty of?

A. She's not guilty of anything since she made a good faith effort to discover the truth and relied on the owner's assurance.
B. She's guilty of willful omission.
C. She's guilty of negligent misrepresentation.
D. She's guilty of willful misrepresentation.

Answer: C. Alison is guilty of negligent misrepresentation because she made a false assertion based on facts she should have verified. She could have avoided the violation by lifting a corner of the carpet to inspect the flooring or making a written disclosure to the buyers such as, although the seller believes hardwood is under the carpet, she does not know and cannot guarantee that to be true.

44. A buyer enthusiastically tells a provisional broker that his reason for purchasing a particular property is its peace and quiet. The provisional broker knows construction will soon start on a major shopping center immediately behind the property but says nothing because the buyer didn't ask about future development or surrounding properties. What, if anything, is the provisional broker guilty of?

A. Nothing, the buyer didn't ask.
B. He is guilty of negligent misrepresentation.
C. He's guilty of willful omission.
D. He's guilty of willful misrepresentation.

Answer: C. Willful omission because he deliberately withheld a material fact. The new shopping center is "material" not only because it is defined as such by the state, but because it will have a direct impact on the property and the new owner's ability to enjoy it as he expects.

45. When a real estate firm practices dual agency, which of these statements is true? 1) It must make full disclosure to

all parties when an offer is written. 2) Dual agency must be explained to all parties at the first substantial contact.

A. Only #1 is true.
B. Only #2 is true.
C. Both #1 and #2 are true.
D. Neither #1 or #2 is true.

Answer: C. An explanation of the dual agency concept along with full disclosure, must be made as soon as possible and is reaffirmed at the time agreements, offers and contracts are prepared.

46. Which of these can define "first substantial contact?" 1) A person calls a real estate company to ask about a listed property. 2) A person attends an open house and speaks with an agent.

A. Only #1.
B. Only #2
C. Both #1 and #2.
D. Neither #1 or #2.

Answer: C. "Substantial contact" can be defined as any conversation or meeting about the possible sale or purchase of property, at which point all relevant disclosures should be made.

47. Which of these are relevant disclosures that must be addressed at time of first substantial contact? 1) The concept of agency is discussed and disclosed to members of the general public. 2) The agent's duties and responsibilities to clients are discussed and disclosed to members of the public.

A. Only #1.
B. Only #2.
C. Both #1 and #2.
D. Neither #1 or #2.

Answer: C. Agents must disclose both the concept of agency as well as their roles, representations and loyalties in various kinds of agent-client relationships.

48. What is the violation when a broker should know that a statement about a material fact is false, but unintentionally misinforms a party in a real estate transaction?

A. Negligent misrepresentation.
B. Negligent omission.
C. Willful misrepresentation.
D. Willful omission.

Answer: A. Misrepresentation occurs when an agent makes an statement about a property that is false, such as saying the foundation is sound when it is not. It is willful when the agent knows the statement to be false and negligent when he or she doesn't know it's false but should have,

49. What is the violation when a broker has information about a property that could impact the decision of a party in a real estate transaction but fails to disclose it?

A. Negligent misrepresentation.
B. Negligent omission.
C. Willful misrepresentation.
D. Willful omission.

Answer: D. Willful omission occurs when an agent deliberately fails to disclose information that could have an impact on a transaction. Negligent omission occurs when an agent does not, but should have, known about the information.

50. Which of these statements about the Residential Property Disclosure Statement is true? 1) All sellers must provide the form to potential buyers. 2) Non-licensed owners selling their own property are exempt from this law.

A. Only #1.
B. Only #2.
C. Both #1 and #2.

D. Neither #1 or #2.

Answer: A. The law applies to all parties selling a property that has been lived in. Unlike some other provisions of real estate law that do not apply to individuals selling their own property, there is no exemption for "FSBOs."

51. If the Residential Property Disclosure Statement is not delivered to a buyer before or at the time of offer, the buyer may cancel the offer under which of these circumstances?

A. If the seller does not give the buyer a copy of the form by the time he/she makes an offer to purchase the property.
B. If the buyer personally delivers his/her decision to cancel to the owner or the owner's agent within three calendar days following receipt of the Statement.
C. If the buyer personally delivers his/her decision to cancel to the owner or the owner's agent within three calendar days following receipt of the Statement, or the date of the contract, whichever occurs first.
D. All apply.

Answer: D. Failure to deliver the Disclosure Statement allows buyers the right to cancel their offer at almost any time.

52. If the Disclosure Statement is properly delivered, when may potential buyers still cancel a contract? 1) If properly informed by the Disclosure Statement, buyers may not cancel any resulting contracts. 2) Under certain circumstances a buyer may still cancel a contract.

A. Only #1.
B. Only #2.
C. Both #1 and #2.
D. Neither #1 or #2.

Answer: A. So long as proper disclosures are made, all contracts are binding on buyer and seller and may not be cancelled.

53. Jerome Billings tells a buyer he represents that a property is served by city water. He believes this is true because several nearby homes he sold did have city water service, although this property does not. Is he guilty of any violation?

A. No, he had reasonable grounds for believing the statement was true and did not intend to misrepresent the facts.
B. Yes, although unintentional, he is still guilty of fraudulent misrepresentation.

C. Yes, he is guilty of willful misrepresentation because water service is a matter of record he had a fiduciary responsibility to verify.

D. Yes, he is guilt of negligent misrepresentation.

Answer: D. Jerome believed his statement was accurate and did not intend to misrepresent either by a false statement or deliberate omission. Although still a significant violation, it is not a fraudulent or deliberate misrepresentation.

54. Which of these provisions must be included in North Carolina listing agreements? 1) A defined period of time for which they are active. 2) An automatic right of renewal.

A. #1 only.
B. #2 only.
C. Both #1 and #2.
D. Neither #1 or #2.

Answer: A. There is no "passive" or automatic renewal provision in North Carolina listing agreements; they must be "actively" extended by both parties.

55. What is another name for a "quitclaim deed?"

A. A "limited warranty" deed.

B. A non-warranty deed.

C. A special warranty deed.

D. A "sweetheart sale" deed.

Answer: B. A quitclaim deed transfers ownership or share of ownership to another party but does not guarantee anything about what is being transferred, including the ownership interest. For example, one party in a divorce may sign a quitclaim deed transferring whatever right they may have to the other.

56. A North Carolina sales contract is viewed to be which of the following? 1) Bilateral. 2) Unilateral.

A. Only #1.

B. Only #2.

C. Both #1 and #2.

D. Neither #1 or #2.

Answer: A. Bilateral means contracts are entered into by and are equally binding upon both parties to a real estate transaction. Unilateral would mean only party could amend, cancel, change or otherwise modify the contract without the other party's agreement.

57. What is the name of the clause in a listing agreement granting brokers a protection period beyond the expiration date? 1) An override clause. 2) An extender clause.

A. Only #1.
B. Only #2.
C. Both #1 and #2.
D. Neither #1 or #2.

Answer: C. Both terms are used. They refer to the provision that entitles a broker to his or her commission if a party they brought to the table should enter into an agreement within a reasonable time after the listing expires.

58. What does "parol evidence" mean? 1) Oral agreements can be part of a contract. 2) Hand-written notes and addendums to a contract take precedence over printed portions.

A. Only #1.
B. Only #2.
C. Both #1 and #2.
D. Neither #1 or #2.

Answer: B. Parol evidence means evidence of oral agreements purporting to explain, change or contradict written portions of a contract. Parol evidence is NOT accepted in North Carolina.

However, handwritten changes and addendums signed or initialed by both parties due take precedence over printed portions.

59. According to the North Carolina Statute of Fraud, which of these real estate agreements must be in writing? 1) Installment land contracts. 2) Sales contracts. 3) Property management agreements. 4) Lease or rental agreements of more than one year.

A. Only #1.
B. Both #1 and #2.
C. All of the above.
D. None of the above.

Answer: B. Deeds, sales contracts, mortgages and other such agreements transferring ownership or a sale of ownership must be in writing. A lease agreement longer than three years must be in writing to be enforceable. Property management agreements have nothing to do with the conveyance, ownership or occupation of property and are primarily covered under different statutes.

60. Which, if any, of these forms of buyer agency are allowable in North Carolina?

A. Non-exclusive buyer agency.
B. Exclusive buyer agency.
C. 24-hour buyer agency.
D. All of the above.

Answer: D. As long as all other conditions of buyer agency are met and the agreement is in writing, the parties may agree to whatever terms they choose.

61. Melissa is listing a house for sale and needs to know its square footage. Which of these methods is acceptable?

A. Consulting tax records.
B. Consulting previous sales or listing agreements.
C. Measuring the house herself.
D. All of the above.

Answer: C. If Nancy uses any other method, and the number turns out to be inaccurate, the Real Estate Commission will not consider that she used appropriate effort and can discipline her.

62. Melissa's new listing is a standard two-story home. In calculating square footage, she can measure the outside of the house and deduct which of the following?

A. Closets.

B. Stairs.
C. Any space with standing headroom of less than five feet.
D. All of the above.

Answer: C. In North Carolina, any space that is heated, finished, useable and directly accessible from the living area may be included in square-footage calculations.

63. Which of these characteristics must be present to include a space in square footage calculations.

A. It must be heated and cooled by a conventional HVAC system.
B. It must be intended to be used as a living area.
C. It must be finished.
D. All of the above.

Answer: D. Unheated rooms such as screened porches or those heated with a space heater should not be included in square-footage calculations. However, they can be described separately in ways such as, "2250 square feet plus a 10x12 screened porch off the family room."

64. Melissa's partner, Terri, has another listing that includes a 600 square-foot guest house at the rear of the property.

According to the Real Estate Commission's guidelines, how should it be reported?

A. It may be listed as additional space, but not included as part of the primary home's square footage.
B. It can be included in the main home's square footage as long if qualified by expressions such as, "3,700 square feet of total living area."
C. It should not be combined with the main house in any way.
D. Any of these options is allowable.

Answer: A. Any additional spaces, including guest houses, porches, patios, decks and the like may be included in property descriptions so long as they are not used as part of the home's square footage calculation.

65. Mark and Phyllis want to list their home. It has a huge bonus room over the garage they want to include as part of the square footage. Under what conditions may they do so?

A. A minimum percentage of its total space must have a ceiling height of at least seven feet.
B. Walls, floors and ceilings must all be finished and the room must be directly accessible from inside the home.
C. It must have a conventional heating system.
D. All of the above.

Answer: D. The square footage guidelines that apply to the rest of the home must be used for bonus rooms as well. They must be heated, finished, and accessible. "Dead space" -- such as dormered areas where the ceiling slopes to a height of less than five feet -- must be excluded.

66. Which, if either, of these elements MUST be in every buyer agency agreement? 1) A written termination date. 2) A clause stating the agent will not discriminate.

A. Only #1.
B. Only #2.
C. Both #1 and #2.
D. Neither #1 or #2.

Answer: C. Anti-discrimination clauses must be in every agreement. Moreover buyer agency agreements must be for a determined period of time... although it may be for whatever the parties agree, from an hour or less to a year or more.

67. Rob wants to cancel his contract to buy Peter's property. Assuming all other conditions are met, to whom must Rob give written notice? 1) The owner's agent. 2) The owner.

A. Only #1.
B. Only #2.

C. Either #1 or #2.
D. Neither #1 or #2.

Answer: C. Either the owner or his or her agent is acceptable.

68. Which type of listing agreement provides the most protection for brokers?

A. An open listing.
B. An exclusive right-to-sell listing.
C. An exclusive agency listing.
D. A net listing.

Answer: B. The exclusive right-to-sell agreement entitles the broker to his or her commission regardless of who actually sells the property. Under exclusive-agency listings, owners can sell property directly and not owe a commission.

69. When are licensees allowed to draft simple paragraphs and addendums to contracts for their clients?

A. Never.
B. When asked to do so and all parties initial the change or addendum.
C. At the request of their broker-in-charge.
D. With the approval of their broker-in-charge.

Answer: A. No matter how seemingly simple or basic, legal language impacting a third party can only be created by an attorney in North Carolina.

70. Nate is using an attorney-approved preprinted offer/sales contract for his client. Which of the following should NOT be included in the agreement's language?

A. Agency disclosures to the other side of the transaction.
B. How the buyer intends to use the property.
C. How the agent is to be compensated.
D. Who is responsible for paying closing costs.

Answer: C. There are nineteen items that must be included in any offers to customers or clients. However, agents compensation is part of the separate agency agreement and is specifically excluded.

71. Deborah sees a property she likes and makes an offer with a $2,500 earnest money binder. The owner makes a counter offer, but Deborah then sees another property she likes better. Which of these situations apply?

A. Deborah is entitled to have her money returned immediately.

B. The seller is entitled to the binder, since Deborah backed out of the agreement.

C. The seller can decide to accept Deborah's first offer and thus create a binding contract.

D. The broker is entitled to hold Deborah's money for thirty days as a "contingency contract."

Answer: A. Offers are "one-time-only" events that must be accepted or rejected. Once the seller made a counter-proposal, he rejected Deborah's offer and no contract exists. She is under no obligation to continue and is entitled to have her earnest money returned immediately.

72. A property is going to closing with delinquent property taxes. What is the correct entry on the closing documents?

A. Debit seller and credit buyer the entire amount.

B. Debit seller the entire amount.

C. Prorate the entire amount between seller and buyer.

D. Deduct taxes owed from purchase price.

Answer: B. Property taxes are owed by the owner of the property through the date of possession and are entirely his or her responsibility.

73. How would an attorney's closing fee of $450 typically be entered on the closing statement?

A. Buyer is debited $450.
B. Seller is debited $450.
C. Debit seller and buyer $225 each.
D. Debit buyer $450 and seller $450.

Answer: A. The attorney's fee for closing is typically paid by the buyer, although other arrangements can be negotiated and incorporated into the sales contract.

74. Jake and Nancy Lopresso have annual association dues of $600 and they paid the entire year in advance on January 2. They've sold their home and will close on April 30. How will this fee be reflected on the closing statement?

A. The seller will be credited $400 and the buyer debited $400.
B. The seller will be debited $200 and the buyer credited $400.
C. The seller will be credited $600 and the buyer debited $600.
D. The seller will be debited $600 and the buyer credited $600.

Answer: A. The buyer owes the seller $400 because $600 divided by $12 months is $50 per month. The sellers paid the entire year in advance, but transferred ownership after four months. Thus the buyer owes the sellers eight months x $50 a month or $400.

75. A homeowner is allowing the buyers to assume his existing mortgage of $65,000 at 8%. Payments are due on the first of the month, but closing is on August 10th. What portion of the August interest will be owed by the buyer and what portion by the seller at closing to the nearest dollar?

A. The seller will be credited $144 and the buyer debited $144.
B. The seller will be credited $289 and the buyer debited $289.
C. The seller will be debited $144 and the buyer credited $144.
D. The seller will be debited $289 and the buyer credited $289.

Answer: C. $65,000 at 8% interest is $14.24 per day in interest. (8% x $65,000 divided by 365 days.) Since the owner will have occupied the home for ten days in August, he will owe the buyer $144.

76. Bill and Joan Wellbridge are selling their home for $125,000 and the buyers are assuming their existing $67,215 mortgage. How will the loan assumption amount be entered in the closing statement?

A. The seller will be credited $57,785 and the buyer will be debited $57,785.
B. The seller will be debited $67,215 and the buyer credited $67,215.

C. The seller will be debited $57,785 and the buyer credited $57,785.

D. The seller will be credited $67,215 and the buyer debited $67,215.

Answer: B. Since the seller is transferring the existing loan to the buyer, it is treated as money coming in to the buyer and appears as a credit towards the total purchase price.

77. Rick is selling one of the rental properties he owns. It brings $570 a month in rent, which is paid on the first of every month and closing is on the 10th of the month. How would the entries read?

A. Debit the seller $380 and credit the buyer $380.
B. Credit the seller $190 and debit the buyer $190.
C. Debit the seller $190 and credit the buyer $190.
D. Credit the seller $380 and debit the buyer $380.

Answer: A. $570 divided by 30 days equals $19 a day in rent. The seller is entitled to 10 days of rent, or $190. However, he has collected the entire amount and thus owes the buyer $570 minus $190 or $380.

78. Rick has also agreed to sell another income property that rents for $1,200 a month. Rent is due on the 1st of the month

and Rick is closing on the 7th, but has not yet collected that month's rent. How will the closing entries read in this situation?

A. The seller will be debited $280 and the buyer credited $280.
B. The buyer will be credited $920 and the seller debited 280.
C. The buyer will be debited $920 and the seller credited $920.
D. The seller will be credited $280 and the buyer debited $280.

Answer: D. Dividing $1,200 by 30 days equals a daily rent of $40. Because Rick owned the property for the first 7 days he is entitled to $280 from the buyer, which will be debited from his side of the ledger at closing. The buyer is then entitled to collect the entire $1,200 from the renter at closing.

79. A buyer made an EMD (earnest money deposit) of $2,500 on a house he's now closing on. How will the EMD entry read on the closing document?

A. The buyer will be debited $2,500.
B. The Seller will be debited $2,500.
C. The seller will be credited $2,500.
D. The buyer will be credited $2,500.

Answer: D. An EMD is money a buyer has already paid towards the purchase price and is credited to his or her account at closing.

80. The buyers of an existing home have secured an 80% loan on the $95,000 property. How will the entries for the loan read in the closing documents?

A. Credit buyer $76,000 and debit the seller $19,000.
B. Credit the buyer $76,000
C. Credit the buyer $76,000 and debit the seller $76,0000.
D. Debit the buyer $76,000.

Answer: B. $76,000 represents the amount coming in from the mortgage lender (80% of $95,000) and has nothing to do with the seller. The entire amount is credited to the buyers account.

81. A couple is selling their house for $137,500 on which they have a mortgage balance of $79,315. How will this portion of the transaction be entered on the closing documents?

A. Debit the seller $79,315 and credit the buyer $79,315.
B. Credit the seller $58,185.
C. Debit the seller $79,315.
D. Credit the seller $79,315.

Answer: C. Any remaining mortgage balance is due to the lender at time of sale and is debited from the sales price and seller's account at closing.

82. To help a young couple purchase their home, sellers are giving the buyers a $25,000 purchase money mortgage (PMM). What are the entries?

A. Debit the sellers $25,000 and credit that amount to the buyers.
B. Debit the sellers $25,000.
C. Credit the buyers $25,000.
D. None of the above.

Answer: A. In this transaction, the seller becomes a lender to the buyers and gives them cash towards the purchase price in exchange for a mortgage on the property.

83. The obligations of an apartment lessor and lesee are governed by which state law?

A. The North Carolina Landlord and Tenant Act.
B. The North Carolina Fair Housing Statute.
C. The North Carolina Apartment and Renters Act.
D. The North Carolina Residential Agreements Act.

Answer: D. The other acts and statutes are fictitious; they do not exist.

84. Which of these is a provision of the North Carolina Residential Rental Agreements Act?

A. A fair and equitable security deposit must be charged before a lease is considered valid.
B. Tenants have the right to withhold rent if heat or other basic services are unavailable for more than three days.
C. Landlords must provide and maintain premises that are fit and habitable.
D. Leases in shopping centers may be cancelled by tenants if business is poor.

Answer: C. The primary purpose of the Resident Agreements Act is to help ensure only habitable units are rented in North Carolina. As an agent, it's also important to know that tenants do not have the right to withhold rent except by court order. And, of course, leased space in a shopping center is commercial and not covered under residential statutes.

85. Which act requires tenants to properly maintain his or her dwelling unit?

A. The North Carolina Tenants Responsibilities Act.
B. The North Carolina Residential Rental Agreements Act.
C. The Fair Housing Opportunity Act.
D. The Joint Tenants and Landlords Responsibilities Statutes.

Answer: B. The Residential Rental Agreements Act spells out responsibilities of both landlords and tenants. The primary obligation of tenants, beyond timely payment of rent, is maintaining their dwelling units in good order, including keeping them clean, safe and properly disposing of all garbage and other waste.

86. How does the sale of a property with long-term lease agreements affect existing tenants?

A. The tenants must negotiate new leases with the new owner(s).
B. The new owners may terminate existing leases with three months notice.
C. It has no effect on the current tenants.
D. The tenants may terminate their leases with three months notice to the new owners.

Answer: C. Purchasers of rental properties must honor all rights of existing tenants. Accordingly, it's important they thoroughly investigate tenant rights of any income property they're considering and remember that leases running longer than three years do not have to be recorded for tenant rights to be protected against third parties.

87. Which of the following statements is NOT TRUE of the Tenant Security Deposit Act?

A. Landlords must make requested repairs within thirty days.
B. Security deposits cannot exceed two months' rent.
C. Security deposits belong to the renter but are under control of the landlord.
D. Landlords must return deposits within a specified period of time after a tenant vacates a unit or specify reasons why all or any portion of the deposit is being withheld.

Answer: A. Landlords are not required to make any requested repairs. With respect to the other answers, security deposits belong to tenants and landlords must explain reasons for withholding any portion within a specific time period or forfeit their rights.

88. Which of the following is NOT TRUE about the ways in which a security deposit may be handled?

A. A real estate agent may place the deposit in a trust account.
B. A landlord may place the deposit in a trust account.
C. A landlord may use the deposit to obtain a bond as a guarantee.
D. A real estate agent may use the deposit to obtain a bond as a guarantee.

Answer: D. A real estate agent does not have an "enduring" relationship with a tenant; it ends once they've helped them find a property. So, while landlords have additional options, real estate agents may only place a security deposit into a trust account.

89. Which of the following are considered "ordinary wear and tear" when a tenant moves out at the end of his lease and gives proper notice? 1) Windows need cleaning. 2) Walls have crayon marks. 3) Plumbing fixtures leak. 4) Drapes or blinds are worn.

A. All are normal wear and tear.
B. Only #1, #3 and #4.
C. Only #3 and #4.
D. None.

Answer: B. Over time, plumbing will leak, furnishings become worn and rental units need to be cleaned for new occupants. These are all the landlord's responsibility. However, crayon marks can be considered damage and deducted from the security deposit.

90. Jim moves out of his apartment before the lease expires, but leaves it in excellent condition. The landlord is able to

**find a new tenant in only three days. How much of Jim's
security deposit may he keep?**

A. Only that amount equal to lost rent and the cost of securing a
new tenant.
B. Only that portion equal to lost rent.
C. All of it.
D. None of it.

Answer: A. The point of a security deposit is to cover landlord
expenses in case of damage, nonpayment of rent, a breach of the
lease or certain other circumstances. However, there is no
"punitive" intent and the landlord cannot keep more than what's
necessary to cover actual expenses or losses.

**91. Rachel Prentiss owns a beach-front property she rents
out. What are her responsibilities under the North Carolina
Vacation Rental Act?**

A. Provide a fit and habitable premises.
B. Place all deposits and other monies received in advance in a
trust or escrow account.
C. Have written rental agreements.
D. All of the above.

Answer: D. Passed in January 2000, the Vacation Rental Act
has many additional provisions to help ensure positive rental

experiences for vacationers and protect North Carolina's reputation as a desirable tourist destination.

92. Which of the following is NOT an example of ordinary wear and tear?

A. Paint that's peeling.
B. Plumbing fixtures leak.
C. Broken plumbing fixtures.
D. Carpet that needs cleaning.

Answer: C. Assuming that plumbing fixtures were undamaged when the tenant moved in (or promised repairs were made), a broken fixture is considered damage which can be paid for from a tenant's security deposit.

93. What is the definition of a time-share?

A. Five or more time periods of use.
B. Five or more separate periods of use over five or more years.
C. Beachfront property rented out to different tenants over five or more years.
D. Vacation property intended for rental for five years or less.

Answer: B. Time-shares can be beach-front, resort, mountain or other leisure destination and their sale and development are subject to strict statutes.

94. Which of the following is required to develop a time-share in North Carolina?

A. A certificate of registration and a project broker.
B. A certificate of registration from the state.
C. A project broker.
D. A real estate license.

Answer: A. Although a developer does not need to be licensed by the Real Estate Commission, he or she does need a broker to handle sales as well as appropriate registrations.

95. Which is true regarding time-share developers and registration certificates?

A. It is the project broker's responsibility to obtain registrations.
B. Registrations must be obtained before 10% of the units are committed.
C. Registrations must be obtained by developers before any units are offered for sale or they are guilty of a felony.
D. #1 and #2 are both true.

Answer: C. Because of past time-share abuses here and in many other states, North Carolina has put strict statutes into place with criminal penalties for certain violations.

96. Who is responsible for recording the instruments conveying ownership in timeshare units?

A. The developer.
B. The registrar.
C. The project broker.
D. Either the developer or the project broker.

Answer: B. Additionally, the registrar does not need to hold a real estate license if he or she does not engage in the sales process.

97. Every purchaser of a time-share unit is entitled to which of the following?

A. A guarantee that they will be able to trade weeks with other owners.
B. A free weekend to evaluate the property.
C. A three-day right of rescission to make certain they want to complete the transaction.
D. None of the above.

Answer: D. The right of recession period is five days, not three. They must be given accurate information on any exchange program, but not a guarantee per se. In addition, they must receive a complete public offering statement.

98. How long must a purchaser's monies be kept in a time-share escrow account?

A. At least five days.
B. At least seven days.
C. At least ten days.
D. At least thirty days.

Answer: C. Although purchasers have a five-day right of rescission, the state requires their funds be kept in escrow for ten days to ensure the money will be available if the purchaser elects to send their rescission by regular mail.

99. Time-share project brokers who violate provisions of G.S. 93A are subject to disciplinary action by which of the following?

A. The SEC.
B. The Justice Department.
C. The attorney general.
D. The Real Estate Commission.

Answer: D. Time-share regulations and the statutes of G.S. 93A are under the jurisdiction of the North Carolina Real Estate Commission. It goes without saying, of course, that project brokers can also break the rules of other statutes and regulatory bodies and be subject to additional penalties beyond those the Commission may impose.

100. Which of the following is NOT an obligation of developers under the North Carolina Condominium Act of 1986?

A. Give prospective buyers the right of rescission.
B. Arrange financing for prospective buyers.
C. Give buyers a set of bylaws.
D. File a plan of the property or plat map.

Answer: B. Developers do not have to provide or find financing for buyers. All the other choices, among many others, are required of developers.

101. Which of the following IS an obligation of the seller of a condominium who is not the developer and owns a unit built after 1986?

A. Provide dues and assessments information to the buyer.

B. Provide the buyer with the original or updated plat map or plan of the property.
C. Give the buyer a seven day right of rescission.
D. All of the above.

Answer: A. All of the answers are, in fact, obligations of the developer. However, the original owner or subsequent buyers of an individual unit only need to provide new buyers with dues and assessments information.

102. Who prepares the bylaws that govern the operation of a condominium community?

A. The developer.
B. The condominium's board of managers.
C. The condominium board's executive committee.
D. The registrar in the county where the condominium is located.

Answer: A. The developer creates the initial set of bylaws, which also generally provides for the creation of an owners' association and/or a board of managers elected by individual owners.

103. In terms of house construction, what does the home's foundation rest on?

A. Studs.
B. Sills.
C. Footings.
D. Joists.

Answer: C. From the ground up: a home's foundation rests on footing which are sunk into the ground. The sill is the lowest wooden member of a home's construction that rests on the footings. Studs are the main parts of a home's wooden framing sections, while joists are the smaller framing members that distribute the weight of floors.

104. What is the term for columns that add extra support to the flooring between foundation walls.

A. Interior footings.
B. Piers.
C. Support walls.
D. Support joists.

Answer: B. In many homes, there is too much distance between opposite sides of a foundation to adequately support the floors and structure. In such cases, piers are added at critical points to provide the additional support.

105. Which of these statements about a home's insulation materials is true? 1) A higher "R-value" means the material is more resistant to the transfer of heat. 2) The higher the R-value, the less the material resists heat transfer. 3) The most efficient R-value should be in the roof?

A. #1 only.
B. #2 only.
C. Both #1 and #2.
D. Both #1 and #3.

Answer: D. The higher the R-value the more energy-efficient a home will be. Further, even though factors such as tightness of doors and windows come into play, homes usually loose most of their heating and cooling efficiency through the roof so that's where to look for the highest R-values.

106. What determines the pitch of a roof?

A. The ridge beam.
B. Ceiling joists.
C. Rafters.
D. Piers.

Answer: C. The ridge beam is main roofing member to which rafters are attached. However, it is the angle of the rafters relative to the ridge beam that determines pitch.

107. What is the name for the wooden or composite material that covers the exterior wall and roof framing of a home?

A. Siding.
B. Sheathing.
C. Vapor barrier.
D. Façade.

Answer: B. The fabric-like vapor barrier goes between the framing members and sheathing. Siding, which can be of wood, brick, stone, vinyl or other material, is the final material that is applied over the sheathing to a home's exterior to protect it from the elements and add beauty. The façade of a home refers to its style and appearance, such as English, contemporary, cottage and so forth.

108. Which of these home styles is the most economical to build?

A. A two-story home.
B. A one-and-a-half story home.
C. A ranch home.
D. A ranch home with basement.

Answer: A. A two-story home is the most economical to build on a cost-per-square foot basis. That's because two full floors of living space are being accommodated on a smaller "footprint," which means lower foundation and roofing costs.

109. What document does a local building inspector issue stating that a home is complete?

A. A certificate of completion.
B. A Certificate of approval.
C. A certificate habitability.
D. A certificate of occupancy.

Answer: D. This document certifies that the structure has been inspected; meets local code requirements; has all specified systems such as water, electric, heating, cooling, etc. installed and functioning; and is ready to be occupied for daily living.

110. What is the term for the ordinance that specifies minimum standards of construction and materials?

A. A building code.
B. A construction code.
C. Variances.
D. Covenants.

Answer: A. The purpose of building codes, which can vary from one jurisdiction to another, is to ensure basic standards of health and safety. "Variances" are exceptions to a building code while "covenants" are additions to code, such as required architectural styles that a subdivision or development may adopt to achieve community consistency.

111. What is the name for a heavy material placed on top of the sheathing to insulate and waterproof the roof?

A. Roofing boards.
B. Roofing felt.
C. Shingles.
D. Insulation.

Answer: B. Typically made from synthetic materials, "roofing felt," is a heavy, cloth-like material that goes over the roof boards or sheathing and under the shingles.

112. What is "slab?"

A. Dirt graded in preparation for foundation work.
B. Bricks delivered on palates prior to installation.
C. Concrete material.
D. Wooden decking material.

Answer: C. Slab is the expression given to concrete formed into flooring for basements, garages, or rooms or as an economical foundation structure.

113. What is the name for an insurance policy that covers more risks than the basic form, including such hazards such as weight of ice, snow or sleet, falling objects, damage from accidental discharges of water or artificially-generated electricity? 1) Broad form insurance. 2) Extended all-risk insurance.

A. Either #1 or #2.
B. Neither #1 or #2.
C. #1 only.
D. #2 only.

Answer: C. The basic form of home-owners insurance is seldom used, while the much more inclusive broad form is the standard. Extended all-risk provides coverage for both real and personal property and is generally intended for owners of very expensive properties.

114. What is the most commonly-used, all-risk policy used today?

A. HO-5

B. HO-4
C. HO-3
D. HO-2

Answer: C. HO-3 offers greater coverage than HO-2 and is generally considered to provide the most favorable cost-benefit value for most people. HO-4 is renter's insurance while HO-5 is the most extensive homeowner's policy.

115. What kind of policy provides protection against damage to a homeowner's property and improvements? 1) Property insurance. 2) Casualty insurance.

A. Neither #1 or #2.
B. Either #1 or #2.
C. #1 only.
D. #2 only.

Answer: B. The terms are used interchangeably and refer to policies that protect homeowners against losses to property and improvements outside a home's structure, such as swimming pools.

116. What is the name of the clause in most insurance policies that requires a homeowner to maintain fire insurance equal to or greater than 80% of his property's

replacement cost? 1) Coinsurance clause. 2) Subrogation clause.

A. #1 only.
B. #2 only.
C. Both #1 and #2.
D. Neither #1 or #2.

Answer: A. The 80% requirement reflects the fact that the property on which a house sits will not have to be rebuilt even if the entire structure burns down. The subrogation clause assigns homeowners the right to sue a person who may have caused damage to a policy holder's home that the insurance company had to pay for.

117. What is the term for provisions excluding certain hazards from coverage under a particular insurance policy?

A. Exclusions.
B. Riders.
C. Endorsements.
D. Both #2 and #3.

Answer: A. Exclusions are perils the insurance company will not cover, such loss as a result of war. Endorsements, sometimes called riders are additions to the policy to insure or increase the standard coverage on items of particular value such as furs, jewelry, art and collections.

118. Which of these is covered by most standard homeowner policies? 1) Liability. 2) Fire. 3) Theft.

A. Only #1.
B. Only #1 and #2.
C. All of the above.
D. Only #2 and #3

Answer: C. Standard policies generally cover all three. Broader coverage policies typically add damage from storm and other hazards as well as higher limits on the amounts of coverage.

119. A $100,000 property sustains $60,000 in fire damage, but is only covered for $40,000. Under the terms of the insurance policy's 80% coinsurance requirement how much will the insured receive?

A. $60,000
B. $48,000
C. $40,000
D. $30,000.00

Answer: D. To make this calculation, begin by determining the maximum benefit the homeowner could receive under the 80% requirement, which is $80,000. Next divide the $40,000 of actual coverage by the 80% number and calculate it as a percentage. The result is 50%... and 50% of the $60,000 loss is $30,000. Had the homeowner maintained the 80% coverage, he or she would have been covered for the entire $60,000 loss.

120. Ross and Amanda Troutman own a $199,999 home that's insured with a $120,000 policy that includes an 80% coinsurance requirement. What amount will they receive from the insurance company if they sustain a loss of $175,000?

A. $165,000
B. $120,000
C. $175,000
D. $131,250.66

Answer: D. To calculate the amount due the homeowners: Step 1 - 199,999.00 X 80% = $159,999.20 Step 2 - 120,000.00 divided by $159,999.20 = 75.00038 Step 3 – Leaving 75.00038 in my calculator and multiplying by $175,000.00 the amount of the loss = exactly $131,250.66

121. Rachel Prentiss owns a beach-front property she rents out. What are her responsibilities under the North Carolina Vacation Rental Act?

A. Provide a fit and habitable premises.
B. Place all deposits and other monies received in advance in a trust or escrow account.
C. Have written rental agreements.
D. All of the above.

Answer: D. Passed in January 2000, the Vacation Rental Act has many additional provisions to help ensure positive rental experiences for vacationers and protect North Carolina's reputation as a desirable tourist destination.

122. Which of the following is NOT an example of ordinary wear and tear?

A. Paint that's peeling.
B. Plumbing fixtures leak.
C. Broken plumbing fixtures.
D. Carpet that needs cleaning.

Answer: C. Assuming that plumbing fixtures were undamaged when the tenant moved in (or promised repairs were made), a broken fixture is considered damage which can be paid for from a tenant's security deposit.

123. What is the definition of a time-share?

A. Five or more time periods of use.
B. Five or more separate periods of use over five or more years.
C. Beachfront property rented out to different tenants over five or more years.
D. Vacation property intended for rental for five years or less.

Answer: B. Time-shares can be beach-front, resort, mountain or other leisure destination and their sale and development are subject to strict statutes.

124. Which of the following is required to develop a time-share in North Carolina?

A. A certificate of registration and a project broker.
B. A certificate of registration from the state.
C. A project broker.
D. A real estate license.

Answer: A. Although a developer does not need to be licensed by the Real Estate Commission, he or she does need a broker to handle sales as well as appropriate registrations.

125. Which is true regarding time-share developers and registration certificates?

A. It is the project broker's responsibility to obtain registrations.
B. Registrations must be obtained before 10% of the units are committed.
C. Registrations must be obtained by developers before any units are offered for sale or they are guilty of a felony.
D. #1 and #2 are both true.

Answer: C. Because of past time-share abuses here and in many other states, North Carolina has put strict statutes into place with criminal penalties for certain violations.

126. Who is responsible for recording the instruments conveying ownership in timeshare units?

A. The developer.
B. The registrar.
C. The project broker.
D. Either the developer or the project broker.

Answer: B. Additionally, the registrar does not need to hold a real estate license if he or she does not engage in the sales process.

127. Every purchaser of a time-share unit is entitled to which of the following?

A. A guarantee that they will be able to trade weeks with other owners.
B. A free weekend to evaluate the property.
C. A three-day right of rescission to make certain they want to complete the transaction.
D. None of the above.

Answer: D. The right of recession period is five days, not three. They must be given accurate information on any exchange program, but not a guarantee per se. In addition, they must receive a complete public offering statement.

128. How long must a purchaser's monies be kept in a time-share escrow account?

A. At least five days.
B. At least seven days.
C. At least ten days.
D. At least thirty days.

Answer: C. Although purchasers have a five-day right of rescission, the state requires their funds be kept in escrow for ten days to ensure the money will be available if the purchaser elects to send their rescission by regular mail.

129. Time-share project brokers who violate provisions of G.S. 93A are subject to disciplinary action by which of the following?

A. The SEC.
B. The Justice Department.
C. The attorney general.
D. The Real Estate Commission.

Answer: D. Time-share regulations and the statutes of G.S. 93A are under the jurisdiction of the North Carolina Real Estate Commission. It goes without saying, of course, that project brokers can also break the rules of other statutes and regulatory bodies and be subject to additional penalties beyond those the Commission may impose.

130. Which of the following is NOT an obligation of developers under the North Carolina Condominium Act of 1986?

A. Give prospective buyers the right of rescission.
B. Arrange financing for prospective buyers.
C. Give buyers a set of bylaws.
D. File a plan of the property or plat map.

Answer: B. Developers do not have to provide or find financing for buyers. All the other choices, among many others, are required of developers.

131. Which of the following IS an obligation of the seller of a condominium who is not the developer and owns a unit built after 1986?

A. Provide dues and assessments information to the buyer.
B. Provide the buyer with the original or updated plat map or plan of the property.
C. Give the buyer a seven day right of rescission.
D. All of the above.

Answer: A. All of the answers are, in fact, obligations of the developer. However, the original owner or subsequent buyers of an individual unit only need to provide new buyers with dues and assessments information.

132. Who prepares the bylaws that govern the operation of a condominium community?

A. The developer.
B. The condominium's board of managers.
C. The condominium board's executive committee.

D. The registrar in the county where the condominium is located.

Answer: A. The developer creates the initial set of bylaws, which also generally provides for the creation of an owners' association and/or a board of managers elected by individual owners.

133. In terms of house construction, what does the home's foundation rest on?

A. Studs.
B. Sills.
C. Footings.
D. Joists.

Answer: C. From the ground up: a home's foundation rests on footing which are sunk into the ground. The sill is the lowest wooden member of a home's construction that rests on the footings. Studs are the main parts of a home's wooden framing sections, while joists are the smaller framing members that distribute the weight of floors.

134. What is the term for columns that add extra support to the flooring between foundation walls.

A. Interior footings.
B. Piers.
C. Support walls.
D. Support joists.

Answer: B. In many homes, there is too much distance between opposite sides of a foundation to adequately support the floors and structure. In such cases, piers are added at critical points to provide the additional support.

135. Which of these statements about a home's insulation materials is true? 1) A higher "R-value" means the material is more resistant to the transfer of heat. 2) The higher the R-value, the less the material resists heat transfer. 3) The most efficient R-value should be in the roof.

A. #1 only.
B. #2 only.
C. Both #1 and #2.
D. Both #1 and #3.

Answer: D. The higher the R-value the more energy-efficient a home will be. Further, even though factors such as tightness of doors and windows come into play, homes usually loose most of their heating and cooling efficiency through the roof so that's where to look for the highest R-values.

136. What determines the pitch of a roof?

A. The ridge beam.
B. Ceiling joists.
C. Rafters.
D. Piers.

Answer: C. The ridge beam is main roofing member to which rafters are attached. However, it is the angle of the rafters relative to the ridge beam that determines pitch.

137. What is the name for the wooden or composite material that covers the exterior wall and roof framing of a home?

A. Siding.
B. Sheathing.
C. Vapor barrier.
D. Façade.

Answer: B. The fabric-like vapor barrier goes between the framing members and sheathing. Siding, which can be of wood, brick, stone, vinyl or other material, is the final material that is applied over the sheathing to a home's exterior to protect it from the elements and add beauty. The façade of a home refers to its style and appearance, such as English, contemporary, cottage and so forth.

138. Which of these home styles is the most economical to build?

A. A two-story home.
B. A one-and-a-half story home.
C. A ranch home.
D. A ranch home with basement.

Answer: A. A two-story home is the most economical to build on a cost-per-square foot basis. That's because two full floors of living space are being accommodated on a smaller "footprint," which means lower foundation and roofing costs.

139. What document does a local building inspector issue stating that a home is complete?

A. A certificate of completion.
B. A Certificate of approval.
C. A certificate habitability.
D. A certificate of occupancy.

Answer: D. This document certifies that the structure has been inspected; meets local code requirements; has all specified systems such as water, electric, heating, cooling, etc. installed and functioning; and is ready to be occupied for daily living.

140. What is the term for the ordinance that specifies minimum standards of construction and materials?

A. A building code.
B. A construction code.
C. Variances.
D. Covenants.

Answer: A. The purpose of building codes, which can vary from one jurisdiction to another, is to ensure basic standards of health and safety. "Variances" are exceptions to a building code while "covenants" are additions to code, such as required architectural styles that a subdivision or development may adopt to achieve community consistency.

141. What is the name for a heavy material placed on top of the sheathing to insulate and waterproof the roof?

A. Roofing boards.
B. Roofing felt.
C. Shingles.
D. Insulation.

Answer: B. Typically made from synthetic materials, "roofing felt," is a heavy, cloth-like material that goes over the roof boards or sheathing and under the shingles.

142. What is "slab?"

A. Dirt graded in preparation for foundation work.
B. Bricks delivered on palates prior to installation.
C. Concrete material.
D. Wooden decking material.

Answer: C. Slab is the expression given to concrete formed into flooring for basements, garages, or rooms or as an economical foundation structure.

143. What is the name for an insurance policy that covers more risks than the basic form, including such hazards such as weight of ice, snow or sleet, falling objects, damage from accidental discharges of water or artificially-generated electricity? 1) Broad form insurance. 2) Extended all-risk insurance.

A. Either #1 or #2.
B. Neither #1 or #2.
C. #1 only.
D. #2 only.

Answer: C. The basic form of home-owners insurance is seldom used, while the much more inclusive broad form is the standard. Extended all-risk provides coverage for both real and personal property and is generally intended for owners of very expensive properties.

144. What is the most commonly-used, all-risk policy used today?

A. HO-5
B. HO-4
C. HO-3
D. HO-2

Answer: C. HO-3 offers greater coverage than HO-2 and is generally considered to provide the most favorable cost-benefit value for most people. HO-4 is renter's insurance while HO-5 is the most extensive homeowner's policy.

145. What kind of policy provides protection against damage to a homeowner's property and improvements? 1) Property insurance. 2) Casualty insurance.

A. Neither #1 or #2.
B. Either #1 or #2.

C. #1 only.
D. #2 only.

Answer: B. The terms are used interchangeably and refer to policies that protect homeowners against losses to property and improvements outside a home's structure, such as swimming pools.

146. What is the name of the clause in most insurance policies that requires a homeowner to maintain fire insurance equal to or greater than 80% of his property's replacement cost? 1) Coinsurance clause. 2) Subrogation clause.

A. #1 only.
B. #2 only.
C. Both #1 and #2.
D. Neither #1 or #2.

Answer: A. The 80% requirement reflects the fact that the property on which a house sits will not have to be rebuilt even if the entire structure burns down. The subrogation clause assigns homeowners the right to sue a person who may have caused damage to a policy holder's home that the insurance company had to pay for.

147. What is the term for provisions excluding certain hazards from coverage under a particular insurance policy?

A. Exclusions.
B. Riders.
C. Endorsements.
D. Both #2 and #3.

Answer: A. Exclusions are perils the insurance company will not cover, such loss as a result of war. Endorsements, sometimes called riders are additions to the policy to insure or increase the standard coverage on items of particular value such as furs, jewelry, art and collections.

148. Which of these is covered by most standard homeowner policies? 1) Liability. 2) Fire. 3) Theft.

A. Only #1.
B. Only #1 and #2.
C. All of the above.
D. Only #2 and #3

Answer: C. Standard policies generally cover all three. Broader coverage policies typically add damage from storm and other hazards as well as higher limits on the amounts of coverage.

149. A $100,000 property sustains $60,000 in fire damage, but is only covered for $40,000. Under the terms of the insurance policy's 80% coinsurance requirement how much will the insured receive?

A. $60,000
B. $48,000
C. $40,000
D. $30,000.00

Answer: D. To make this calculation, begin by determining the maximum benefit the homeowner could receive under the 80% requirement, which is $80,000. Next divide the $40,000 of actual coverage by the 80% number and calculate it as a percentage. The result is 50%... and 50% of the $60,000 loss is $30,000. Had the homeowner maintained the 80% coverage, he or she would have been covered for the entire $60,000 loss.

150. Ross and Amanda Troutman own a $199,999 home that's insured with a $120,000 policy that includes an 80% coinsurance requirement. What amount will they receive from the insurance company if they sustain a loss of $175,000?

A. $165,000
B. $120,000
C. $175,000

D. $131,250.66

Answer: D. To calculate the amount due the homeowners: Step 1 - 199,999.00 X 80% = $159,999.20 Step 2 - 120,000.00 divided by $159,999.20 = 0.7500038 Step 3 – Leaving 0.7500038 in my calculator and multiplying by $175,000.00 the amount of the loss = exactly $131,250.66

REAL ESTATE MATH EXAM

1. The fastest way to calculate one month's interest on a real estate loan with an interest rate of 7.2% interest per annum is to multiply the principal balance by:

A.   0.006
B.   0.6
C.   7.2% and divide by 12
D.   12 and divide by 7.2%

Answer: A. By dividing the 7.2% rate by 12 first, you can find one month's interest by multiplying the loan amount by .006; 7.2% divided by 12 = .006, rate for one month.

2. A duplex with a fair market value of $20,000 and an outstanding loan balance of $12,000 was exchanged for a four-plex with a market value of $35,000 and an outstanding $18,000 loan balance. The owner of the duplex would pay in cash or secondary financing

A. $6,100
B. $8,100
C. $9,100
D. $15,100

Answer: C. Market Value - Loan = Equity Duplex $20,000 - $12,000 = $8,000 Four-plex $35,000 - $18,000 = $17,000 Difference in equities amounts to $9,000.

3. Mr. Brown, licensed broker, took an offer from Mr. Green on land for $6,000 with the following terms: $2,000 down and purchase money trust deed and note for the balance, payable $70 per month including interest at 7.2%. If the offer was accepted by the seller, what is the balance of the loan after the first 3 months payment?

A. $3,186
B. $3,467
C. $3,861
D. $3,790

Answer: C. $6,000 price - $2,000 down = $4,000 first trust deed. $4,000 x .006 = $24.00 interest first month. $70 - $24 = $46.00 applied to principal. $4,000 - $46 = $3,954 balance after first month. $3,954 x .006 = $23.72 interest second month. $70 - $23.72 = $46.28 applied to principal. $3954 - $46.28 = $3907.72 balance after second month $3,907.72 x .006 = $23.45. $70 - $23.45 = $46.55 applied to principal. $3,907.72 - $46.55 = $3,861.17.

4. After subtracting $140.00 escrow fees and 6% commission on gross sales price, a seller receives $13,584.00. What is the selling price?

A. $12,770
B. $14,440
C. $14,540
D. $14,600

Answer: D. Selling price (100%) = $13,584 + $140 + 6% 94% = $13,584 + $140 = $13,724 $13,724 divided by 94% = $14,600.

5. Keith Johnson purchased a property at 20% less than the listed price and later sold the property for the original listed price. What was the percentage of profit?

A.   10%
B.   20%
C.   25%
D.   40%

Answer: C. Assume that the property was listed at $10,000. Listed price less 20% = $8,000 purchase price. If it was sold at the listed price of $10,000, the owner made $2,000 profit. $2,000 profit divided by $8,000 cost = 25%.

6. Lots "A", "B" and "C" sold for a total price of $39,000. If lot "B" was priced at $6,400 more than lot "A", and lot "C" was priced at $7,100 more than lot "B", the price of lot "A" was:

A. $13,000.00
B. $6,366.67
C. $5,433.33
D. $4,633.00

Answer: B. $39,000 = A + B + C = A + $6,400 + A + $7,100 + $6,400 + A; 39,000 = 19,900 + (3 x A); 39,000 - 19,900 = 3 x A; 19,100 = 3 x A; 19,100 divided by 3 = A; $ 6,366.67 = A

7. Assume a real estate salesman sold a residence for $31,000. If the broker's commission was 6% and the salesman was to receive 45% of the total commission for selling the property, the salesman would receive:

A. $837.70
B. $959.95
C. $1,860.00
D.   None of the above

Answer: D. $31,000 x 6% = $1,860 Total commission $1,860 x 45% = $837.00 Choice "A" is close, but not exactly $837.00

8. Smith and Allen wish to exchange real property. Smith owns a property valued at $150,000 against which there is a $35,000 trust deed. Allen owns property worth $105,000 on which there is an existing first trust deed of $25,000 and a second trust deed of $20,000. Allen has $15,000 in cash which he is willing to pay towards the exchange. If Smith is willing to accept a second trust deed and note from Allen in order to effect the exchange, the amount of the note would be:

A. $20,000
B. $40,000
C. $50,000
D. $70,000

Answer: B. Market Value - Loan = Equity Smith $150,000 - $35,000 = $115,000 Allen $105,000 - $25,000 = $60,000 Differences in Equity $115,000 - $60,000 = $55,000; $55,000 - $15,000 Cash = $40,000 Second

9. An apartment house property costs $240,000 and this price has been verified to be an accurate estimate of the property value. In comparable circumstances it is also verified that the owner may use a 10% capitalization rate to the purchase price in determining his net income. Should there be a 10% increase in rental income with no increase in the owner's expense and should the capitalization rate of the property be increased to 12%, what would be the estimated value of the property be?

A. $220,000
B. $240,000
C. $264,000
D.   None of the above

Answer: A. Value x Cap Rate = Income $240,000 x 10% = $24,000 Income; 10% income increase = $2,400; New income = $26,400; new Cap Rate = 12%; Value = $26,400 divided by 12% = $220,000

10. Able purchased a $15,000 home. His down payment amounted to 6 2/3% of the purchase price; the balance was carried as a first trust deed bearing interest at 8.4% per annum. The principal is to be repaid at $50.00 per month. A three-year insurance policy costs $72.00; the property taxes are $360.00 per year. Able is required to make a proportionate monthly payment to a loan trust fund for

these items. The total amount of the first monthly payment most nearly would be:

A. $267
B. $182
C. $186
D. $188

Answer: B. 6 2/3% = Fraction 1/15; $15,000 x 6 2/3% (or 0.07) = $1,000; $15,000-$1,000=$14,000 Loan; $14,000 x 0.084 = $1,176 Interest per year; $1,176 divided by 12 = $98 Interest per month Principal = 50.00 Principal 3-Year $72.00 divided by 36 months = 2.00 Insurance; $360 Taxes divided by 12 = $30.00 Taxes; 98 + 50 + 2 + 30 = $180.00 most nearly.

11. A husband and wife own a vacation home in the mountains. The annual taxes on the property are $400.00. Since the total taxes cannot exceed 1% of the full cash value of the property, the "full cash value" of the property would be:

A. $10,000
B. $20,000
C. $40,000
D. $80,000

Answer: C. $400 divided by 1% = $40,000

12. A house sold for $16,350, which amount was 9% more than the cost of the house. The cost of the house was:

A. $14,878.50
B. $15,000.00
C. $16,000.00
D. $17,821.50

Answer: B. Cost (100%) + Profit (9%) = $16,350 109% = $16,350 $16,350 divided by 109% = $15,000

13. The Southern Pacific Railroad Company sold ABS Developers three sections of land that had been divided into 20 acre parcels. 16 sold at $4,000 each and the remainder sold at $5,000 each. Which of the following was most nearly the total amount realized by the seller?

A. $350,000
B. $358,000
C. $475,000
D. $500,000

Answer: C. Three sections = 3 x 640 acres = 1920 acres; 1920 divided by 20 acres per parcel = 96 parcels; 16 parcels x $4,000

each = $ 64,000; 80 parcels x $5,000 each = $400,000; 96
parcels = $464,000; Closest answer is $475,000

**14. An acre is to be divided into four equal lots. If the lots
are parallel to each other, rectangular, and 200 feet deep,
the width of each lot would most nearly be:**

A.   15 feet
B.   55 feet
C.   200 feet
D.   218 feet

Answer: B. One acre = 43,560 square feet; 43,560 divided by
200 = 217.80; 217.80 divided by 4 = 54.45 feet; 55 is nearest

**15. A prospect is considering the purchase of an income
property which has an operating statement showing
$94,500.00 deducted from gross income to arrive at the net
income. The deductions amount to 60% of the gross income.
If the prospect wants a 12% return on the purchase price of
any investments he makes, what should he pay for the
property?**

A. $81,000
B. $196,000

C. $504,000

D. $720,000

Answer: C. Expenses = $94,500 = 60% of Gross Income or $94,500 = 0.6 x Gross Income $94,500 divided by 0.6 = Gross Income = $157,500 Gross Income - Expenses = Net Income $157,500 Gross income - $94,500 Expenses = $63,000 Net Income Value = Net Income divided by Rate of Return; Value = $63,000 divided by 12% = $36,000 divided by 0.12 = $525,000

16. Richard Rock sold his residence which was unencumbered. Total deductions in escrow amounted to $215.30 in addition to a broker's commission of 6% of the selling price. The selling price was the only credit item. Richard Rock received a check for escrow amounting to $15,290. The selling price was most nearly:

A. $16,200

B. $16,266

C. $16,430

D. $16,495

Answer: D. Selling price (100%) = $15,290 + $215.30 + 6%; $15,290 + $215.30 = $15,505.30 or 94%; $15,505.30 divided by 94% = $16,495

17. Mr. and Mrs. Smith acquired a home in 1977 for

$48,000. In 1987 they sold it for $60,500 and moved into an apartment unit. During the ten year period of ownership, permanent improvements totaling $12,750 were made to their house. If Mr. Smith's income consists entirely of wages, how would the sale affect his 1987 federal income return?

A.   No affect
B. $125.00 loss
C. $250.00 loss
D. $12,500 gain

Answer: A. Cost $48,000 + Additions $12,750 = $60,750; Book value = $60,500; Selling price = $ 250 loss Losses are not deductible on the sale of a residence.

18. Eddie Ronquillo sold his house and took back a note for $4,200 secure a second deed of trust. He promptly sold the note for $2,730. This represents a discount of:

A.   28%
B.   35%
C.   55%
D.   65%

Answer: B. Face amount: $4,200; Net amount: $2,730; $4,200 - $2,730 = $1,470 % discount = $1,470 divided by $4,200 = 35%

19. An owner depreciated the improvements based on a cost basis of $160,000 using the straight line method. Improvements are depreciated 37.5% to date and the remaining economic life is estimated to be 15 years. Which of the following is correct? The:

A.   Rate of depreciation exceeds 4% per annum
B.   Time of depreciation to date is over ten years
C.   Value of the building is $120,000
D.   Rate of depreciation cannot be determined from the data given

Answer: A. 100% - 37.5% = 62.5% remaining to depreciate; 62.5% divided by 15 years = 4.17% per year

20. What is the monthly return on an income property with a 6 1/2% return on its value of $46,500?

A. $251.88
B. $302.50
C. $151.25
D. $3,630.00

Answer: A. $46,500 x .065 = $3,022.50 Income; $3,022.50

divided by 12 = $251.88 per month.

21. Andrew Blacker was the owner of a straight note with an annual interest rate of 8.4%. In 5 years, he had received $5,460 in interest. What was the principal amount of the note?

A. $1,092
B. $13,000
C. $6,500
D. $3,250

Answer: B. $5,460 divided by 5 years = $1,092 annual interest; $1,092 divided by .084 = $13,000 principal amount

22. The Phillips sold their home for $36,850, which represents a 17% profit over the original price. What was the original price?

A. $31,495
B. $35,000
C. $53,540
D. $19,850

Answer: A. Cost Rule: Selling Price divided by (100% + %) 100 + 17 = 1.17 $36,850 divided by 1.17 = $31,495

23. If a building's costs increased 20 percent, the value of the investor's dollar has decreased by:

A.   16 and 2/3%
B.   20%
C.   25%
D.   33 and 1/3%

Answer: A. The material I bought yesterday for $100 now costs 20% more or $120. If I only have $100, I can only buy 100/120 or 5/6ths of what I could yesterday. My dollar has decreased 1/6 or 16 2/3%.

24. One month's interest on a 5 year straight note amounted to $225.00. At a 7 1/2% per year interest rate, what was the face amount of the note?

A. $2,700
B. $1,688
C. $36,000
D. $44,000

Answer: C. 12 x $225 = $2,700; $2,700 divided by .075 = $36,000

25. Escrow closed May 1 with interest on a $4,415 second trust deed paid to June 1. The interest rate is 7 2/10%. What is the debt to the buyer, if the buyer assumes the loan?

A. $22.09
B. $26.49
C. $4,415.00
D.   None of the above

Answer: B. Since the sellers paid one month's interest in advance, this must be returned to them by the buyer. This will be a debit on the buyer's statement. $4,415 x .006 (7.2% divided by 12) = $26.49

26. A man owns an apartment building with 20,000 square feet of living space and wants to carpet 60% of the area. If the carpet costs $6.00 a square yard, what is the total cost of the carpeting?

A. $3,996
B. $4,000
C. $7,998
D. $24,000

Answer: C. 20,000 x .60 = 12,000 square feet; 12,000 divided by 9 (9 square feet = 1 square yard) = 1,333 square yards; 1,333 x $6.00 = $7,998

27. One month's interest on a straight note amounted to $45. At 4 1/2% per year, what was the face amount of the note?

A. $2,025
B. $1,200
C. $12,000
D. $24,000

Answer: C. $45 x 12 = $540 interest/year; $540 divided by .045 = $12,000

28. If the interest is paid at a rate of $60 per month and the rate of interest is 8% per year, what is the principal amount of the loan?

A. $5,760
B. $8,560
C. $9,000
D. $90,000

Answer: C. 12 months x $60 = $720 interest/year; $720 divided by .08 = $9,000

29. Mr. Morton paid $945 interest on a straight note loan of $7,000, at a rate of 9%. What was the term of the loan?

A.   18 months
B.   36 months
C.   48 months
D.   60 months

Answer: A. $7,000 x .09 = $630 interest for 1 year; $630 divided by 12 = $52.50 interest/month; $945 (interest) / $52.50 = 18 months

30. A man paid $140 in interest for a 90 day period on a $7,000 loan. What was the interest rate on the loan?

A.   6%
B.   8%
C.   10%
D.   11%

Answer: B. $140 x 4 (12 months divided by 3 months) = $560; $560 divided by $7,000 = 8%

31. A rectangular parcel containing 540 square yards which has a frontage of 45' would be how many feet deep?

A.   54' deep
B.   108' deep
C.   270' deep
D.   540' deep

Answer: B. 1 sq. yard = 9 sq. ft. 540 x 9 = 4,860 sq. ft. Area = L x W W = 45, so 4,860 divided by 45 = 108 ft.

32. How many acres are contained in a parcel of land 1,320' by 2,640'?

A.   40 acres
B.   60 acres
C.   80 acres
D.   120 acres

Answer: C. 1,320' x 2,640' = 3,484,800'; 3.484,800' divided by 43,560' = 80 acres

33. If $150 interest is paid in 8 months on a straight note loan of $2,500, what is the annual rate of interest?

A.   9%
B.   10%
C.   11.50%
D.   12%

Answer: A.8 months = 2/3 year = $150 interest; $150 divided by 0.67 = $227.27 interest for 8 months; $2257.27 divided by $2,500 = .09 = 9%

34. A parcel of land 1/4 mile by 1/4 mile is how many acres?

A.   Ten acres
B.   Twenty acres
C.   Forty acres
D.   Eighty acres

Answer: C. 5280 divided by 4 = 1320; 1320 x 1320 = 1,742,400; 1,742,400 divided by 43,560 = 40 acres

35. A man bought a home for $31,680 and now wishes to sell. He is informed that the cost of selling will amount to 12% of the selling price. He wishes to sell at a price so as not to have a loss. How much would the home have had to appreciate in order to offset the selling costs?

A. $1,080
B. $2,160
C. $4,320
D. $5,400

Answer: C. Selling Price Rule: 100% - (Net divided by %) = Gross Selling Price; 100% - 12% = 88%; $31,680 divided by .88 = $36,000; $36,000 (gross selling price) - $31,680 (purchase price) = $4,320 (appreciation)

36. A building that has interior dimensions of 26' x 30' and has 6" walls would cover how much square footage of land?

A.   58
B.   428
C.   837
D.   3,680

Answer: C. L = 26' + 6" + 6" = 27'; W = 30' + 6" + 6" = 31'; 27' x 31' = 837 square feet

37. A rectangular parcel of land measures 1,780' x 1,780' and contains how many acres?

A.   73
B.   316
C.   632
D.   1,780

Answer: A. 1,780 x 1,780 = 3,168,400 square feet; 3,168,400 divided by 43,560 = 73 acres

38. A borrower paid $120 interest on a 90-day straight note. The principal was $6,000. What was the interest rate?

A. 6%
B. 7%
C. 8%
D. 9%

Answer: C. $120 x 4 = $480; $480 divided by $6,000 = .08 = 8%

39. A man borrowed $750 on a straight note at an interest rate of 7.2%. If his total interest payment was $67.50, the length of the loan was?

A. Twelve months
B. Fifteen months
C. Twenty four months
D. Thirty months

Answer: B. $750 x 7.2% = $54; $54 divided by 12 months = $4.50 interest/month; $67.50 divided by $4.50 = 15 months

40. A house sold for $16,350 which was 9% more than its original cost. What was the original cost?

A. $15,000

B. $20,000
C. $25,000
D. $30,000

Answer: A. 100% + 9% = $16,350; $16,350 divided by 1.09 = $15,000

41. A homeowner sold his house for $23,000. This selling price represented a 15% profit over what he had originally paid for the house. What was the original price of the home?

A. $15,000
B. $20,000
C. $25,000
D. $30,000

Answer: B. 100% + 15% = $23,000; $23,000 divided by 1.15 = $20,000

42. Assume that a second trust deed of $1,000 was to be paid in annual installments of $300 plus 6% interest, with a balloon payment of the balance at the end of the third year. The remaining balance of the principal after the second annual installment was paid would be:

A. $400.00

B. $424.00
C. $505.60
D. $520.00

Answer: A. Since the payments on the principal are $300 per year and the borrower has made two payments plus whatever interest was due, the balance would be $400. $1,000 - $600 = $400

43. Mr. John listed his home with Broker Bob for $35,000. The broker was to receive a commission rate of 6%. The broker brought an offer at 10% less than the listed price. The owner agreed to accept the offer if the broker reduced his commission by 20%. If they all agree to these terms, what amount of commission would the broker receive?

A. $812
B. $1,012
C. $1,312
D. $1,512

Answer: D. $35,000 x .10 = $3,500; $35,000 - $3,500 = $31,500; $31,500 x .06 = 1,890; $1,890 x .20 = $378; $1,890 - $378 = $1,512

44. A man had an income property which suffered a $300 monthly loss of net income when a freeway was built nearby.

At a capitalization rate of 12%, how much did his property lose in value?

A. $20,000
B. $30,000
C. $40,000
D. $50,000

Answer: B. $300 x 12 = $3,600; $3,600 divided by .12 = $30,000

45. Kent was the owner of a straight note with an annual interest rate of 8.4%. In five years he had received $5,460 in interest. The principal amount of the note was most nearly?

A. $12,000
B. $13,000
C. $14,000
D. $15,000

Answer: B. $5,460 divided by 5 = $1,092; $1,092 divided by 8.4% = $13,000

46. An investor owns a 20-unit apartment house. When compared to comparable apartment properties he loses $200 net income a month because his property is located next to a

busy freeway. Appraisers are using a 12% capitalization rate for this neighborhood of income properties. The subject property has suffered a loss in value in the amount of:

A. $20,000
B. $25,000
C. $30,000
D. $35,000

Answer: A. $200 x 12 = $2,400; $2,400 divided by 12% = $20,000

47. In order to earn $208 per month from an investment that yields a 6% return you would have to invest approximately:

A.   12480
B. $20,800
C. $24,960
D. $41,600

Answer: D. $208 x 12 = $2,496; $2,496 divided by 6% = $41,600

48. A man bought two 60 foot lots for $18,000 each and divided them into three lots which he sold for $15,000 each. What was his percentage of profit?

A.   15.00%
B.   25.00%
C.   28.00%
D.   30.00%

Answer: B. $18,000 x 2 = $36,000; $15,000 x 3 = $45,000; $45,000 - $36,000 = $9,000; $9,000 divided by $36,000 = .25 = 25%

49. If a man paid $50,000 for a business which gave him a 6% return on his money, how much did he make during the first year that he owned it?

A. $1,500
B. $3,000
C. $4,500
D. $6,000

Answer: B. $50,000 x 6% = $3,000

50. An investor was going to have a building constructed which was to cost $150,000 and could, when completed, be leased for $2,500 per month. The annual operating expenses for the property would be $6,000. The amount he could invest in the land to realize a 12% return would be:

A. $50,000

B. $75,000
C. $100,000
D. $150,000

Answer: A. $2,500 x 12 = $30,000; $30,000 - $6,000 =
$24,000; $24,000 divided by .12 = $200,000; $200,000 -
$150,000 = $50,000

**51. An investor purchased property for a total price of
$72,000, paying $20,000 down and financing the balance of
$52,000 using a straight note. If the investor eventually sold
the property after it had doubled in value and had made no
principal payments on the loan, each dollar invested would
show a return of:**

A. $2.00
B. $4.60
C. $5.60
D. $8.70

Answer: B. New selling price is $72,000 x 2 = $144,000;
$144,000 less $52,000 loan = $92,000 return; $92,000 divided
by $20,000 = $4.60

52. Which of the following contains the largest area?

A. 4 square miles
B. 5,280' X 10,560'
C. 2 sections
D. 1/10 of a township

Answer: A. A parcel that is 4 square miles is the largest. 1/10 of a town- ship is 3.6 square miles. 5,280' X 10,560' is a parcel that is 1 mile X 2 miles or 2 square miles. 2 sections contain 2 square miles.

53. Harris obtained a loan in the amount of $20,000 and paid the mortgage lender four discount points and an origination fee of 2%. If the payments on the loan were $163.00 per month, including 8% interest and the average balance over a five year period was $18,500, the gross amount earned by the lender is the 5 years was most nearly:

A. $5,100
B. $6,000
C. $7,400
D. $8,600

Answer: D. The lender earned the discount points, origination fee and interest. $20,000 x 4% = $800 in points; $20,000 X 2% = $400 in origination fee; $18,500 X 8% = $1480 annual interest x 5 years = $7400 Total of these three amounts is $8600

54. An individual who receives $225 per month on a money market savings account that pays 7 1/2% per year, has invested which of the following amounts?

A. $12,500
B. $27,000
C. $36,000
D. $48,000

Answer: C. $225 x 12 = $2700 per year; $2700 divided by 7.5% = $36,000

55. A seller took back a second trust deed and note in the amount of $11,400 payable $240 per month, including interest at 7% per annum. If interest on the note begins July 15 and the first payment is made on August 15, the amount of the first payment that is applied to the principal is:

A. $66.50
B. $79.80
C. $173.50
D. $240.00

Answer: C. $11,400 x 7% = $798 per year; $798 divided by 12 = $66.50 per month; $140 - $66.50 = $173.50

56. Humphreys sold his residence which was unencumbered. Total de- ductions in escrow amounted to $215.30 in addition to a broker's commission of 6% of the selling price. The selling price was the only credit item. Humphreys received a check from escrow amounting to $15,290. The selling price was most nearly:

A. $16,200
B. $16,266
C. $16,430
D. $16,495

Answer: D. Selling price (100%) = $15,290 + $215.30 + 6%; $15,290 + $215.30 = $15,505.30 or 94%; $15,505.30 divided by 94% = $16,495

57. Ms. Rodgers sold her house and took back a note for $4200 secured by a second deed of trust. She promptly sold the note for $2730. This represents a discount of:

A.   28%
B.   35%
C.   51%

D.   73%

Answer: B. Face amount = $4200; Net amount = $2730; $4200 - $2730 = $1470; Discount = $1470 divided by $4200 = 35%

58. After subtracting $140 escrow fees and 6% commission on gross sales price, a seller receives $13,584. What is the selling price?

A. $12,770
B. $14,440
C. $14,540
D. $14,600

Answer: D. Selling price (100%) = $13,584 + $140 + 6%; $13,584 + $140 = 94% or $13,724; $13,724 divided by 94% = $14,600

59. A man purchased a property at 20% less than the listed price and later sold the property for the original listed price. What was the percentage of profit?

A.   10%
B.   20%
C.   25%

D.   40%

Answer: C. Assume the property was listed at $10,000. Listed price less 20% is $8000 purchase price. If it was sold at the listed price of $10,000, the owner made $2000 profit. $2000 profit divided by $8000 cost = 25%

60. Escrow closed May 1st with interest on a $4415 second trust deed paid to June 1st. If the interest rate is 7.2%, the debit to the buyer, if the buyer assumed the loan, would be:

A. $22.09
B. $26.49
C. $4,415.00
D.   None of the above

Answer: B. Since the sellers paid one month's interest in advance, this must be returned to them by the buyer. This will be a debit on the buyer's statement. $4415 X .006 (7.2% divided by 12) = $26.49

61. A board foot of lumber could be obtained from a piece of lumber that is:

A.   6" X 6" X 1"
B.   6" X 12" X 1"

C.   12" X 1" X 1"
D.   6" X 12" X 12"

Answer: D. A board foot of lumber contains 144 cubic inches of lumber. Choice "D" is the only one that exceeds 144 cubic inches.

62. Assume that a second trust deed of $1000 was to be paid in annual installments of $300 plus 6% interest, with a balloon payment of the balance at the end of the third year. The remaining balance of the principal after the annual installment had been paid was:

A. $400
B. $424
C. $506
D. $520

Answer: A. Since the payments on the principal are $300 per year and the borrower has made two payments plus whatever interest was due, the balance is $400. $1000 - $600 = $400

63. Assume a real estate salesman sold a residence for $31,000. If the broker's commission was 6% and the salesman was to receive 45% of the total commission for

selling the property, the salesman would receive:

A. $837.70
B. $959.95
C. $1,860.00
D.   None of the above

Answer: D. $31,000 X 6% =$1860 total commission; 45% of
$1860 = $837.00 Choice "A" is close, but not exactly $837.00

**64. If Broker Christianson brought in an offer of 10% less
than the listing price of $15,300 and the seller would agree to
the price if the broker would accept a 20% reduction of his
commission, the broker's commission would amount to:**

A. $660.96
B. $689.85
C. $735.84
D. $827.82

Answer: A. $15,300 - $1530 (10%) = $13,770; $13,770 x 6% =
$826.20; 80% of $826.20 (less 20%) = $660.96

**65. A man enters into a lease agreement on a grocery store
with the following terms: $350 minimum monthly rent or
5% grocery sales, 7% of meat sales, 6% of deli sales, and**

8% of produce sales, whichever is greater. The grocery sales were $27,000 annually, meat sales $500 per month, deli sales $300 per month and produce sales $3,000 annually. What was the annual rent on the store?

A. $3,180
B. $4,200
C. $4,386
D. $5,120

Answer: B. Grocery Sales: $27,000 x 5% = $1350; Meat Sales: ($500 x 12) x 7% = $420; Deli Sales: ($300 x 12) x 6% = $216; Produce Sales: $3,000 x 8% = $240; Total of above = $2226 (or) the minimum rent would be $350 x 12 = $4,200, since $4,200 is greater, then the annual rent would be $4,200.

66. A building was insured for $19,500 at a rate of .18 per hundred. If the three year policy was 2 1/2 times the one year rate, what amount per month should be added to the monthly payments to properly cover the insurance cost?

A. $7.31
B. $2.92
C. $2.44
D. $1.46

Answer: C. $0.18 x 2.5 = $0.45 per $100; ($19,500 x $0.45) divided by 100 = $87.75; $87.75 divided by 36 = $2.44

67. What is the annual interest rate on a $16,000 loan when the interest payments are $160.00 per quarter on the full amount? At least:

A.   3%, but less than 4%
B.   4%, but less than 5%
C.   5%, but less than 6%
D.   6%, but less than 7%

Answer: B. $160.00 x 4 = $640.00; $640.00 divided by $16,000 = 4%

68. A homeowner sold his house for $23,000. If the selling price represented a 15% profit over what he had originally paid for the house, the original price of the home was:

A. $19,550
B. $20,000
C. $27,000
D.   None of the above

Answer: B. Selling price = cost (100%) + profit (15%) = 115% = $23,000; $23,000 divided by 1.15 = $20,000

69. An owner of a section of land dedicates an easement for a road along the south side of his section. The easement contained 3 acres. The width of the road was approximately:

A.   Twenty feet
B.   Thirty feet
C.   Forty feet
D.   Fifty feet

Answer: A. The length of the road is one mile, or 5280 feet. The total area is three acres, or 130,680 square feet (43,560 x 3 = 130,680 square feet) 130,680 divided by 5280 feet = 24.75 feet

70. There are five units in a condo. Smith paid $12,600, Jones paid $13,500, Kahn paid $13,750, Poe paid $14,400 and Clark paid $15,250. If there was an $1800 annual maintenance fee and each owner was to pay his proportionate share based upon the ratio of his unit purchase price to the total purchase price of all units, the monthly share of Smith's unit would be:

A. $8.00
B. $27.00
C. $32.40

D. $36.00

Answer: B. Total purchase price was $69,500 $12,600 divided by $69,500 = 18%; $1800 divided by 12 months = $150 per month; $150 x 18% = $27.00

71. A property in probate was offered for sale and an offer of $12,000 was received. If anyone else wishes to bid on the property at the time of the confirmation, the initial minimum overbid must be:

A. $12,000
B. $13,000
C. $13,100
D. $13,500

Answer: C. The first additional bid (overbid) must be at least the original bid plus 10% of the first $10,000 of the original bid and 5% of any excess. Original bid = $12,000 $10,000 x 10% = $1,000 $2,000 excess at 5% = $100 Total of above = $13,100

72. The total number of lineal feet on one side of a Section is:

A.   1,000
B.   2,640
C.   5,280

D.   43,560

Answer: C. One side of a section is one mile long, or 5280 feet

73. Arnold held a straight note which carried an annual interest rate of 8.4%. If in five years he had received $5,460 in interest, the principal amount of the note was:

A. $10,000
B. $11,500
C. $13,000
D. $15,000

Answer: C. $5460 divided by 5 = $1092 interest per year; $1092 divided by 8.4% = $13,000.

74. Escrow companies normally base their prorations on an escrow year of:

A.   350 days
B.   355 days
C.   360 days
D.   365 days

Answer: C. 12 months at 30 days each = 360 days per year.

75. Eddie Ronquillo sold his home for $17,200. If this represents 9% more than what he paid for it, the cost of the home was most nearly:

A. $15,424
B. $15,500
C. $15,800
D. $16,000

Answer: C. $17,200 divided by 1.09 = $15,779.82 Closest answer is $15,800.

76. An individual borrowed $750 on a straight note at an interest rate of 7.2%. If the total interest payment on the loan was $81.00, the term of the loan was:

A.   15 months
B.   18 months
C.   21 months
D.   24 months

Answer: B. Calculate the amount of interest expense for one month and then find how many months worth of interest was paid. $750 x 7.2% = $54.00 per year; $54.00 divided by 12 = $4.50 per month; $81.00 divided by $4.50 = 18 months.

77. The Richard Rock sold his home and had to carry back a second trust deed and note of $5310. If he sold the note for $3823.20 before any payments had been made on the note, the rate of discount amounted to:

A. 25%
B. 28%
C. 54%
D. 72%

Answer: B. $5310 (original amount of note) $3823.20 (net received from sale) 5310 - 3823.20 = $1486.80 (amount of discount) $1486.20 divided by $5310 = 28% discount.

78. A real estate syndicate paid $193,600 for a lot on which they planned to build a high rise apartment. If the lot was 200 feet deep and they paid $4.40 per square foot, the cost per front foot was:

A. $220
B. $440
C. $880
D. $960

Answer: C. $193,600 divided by $4.40 = 44,000 square feet of lot; 44,000 divided by 200 feet = 220 feet frontage; $193,600 divided by 220 feet = $880 per front foot.

79. A rectangular parcel of land that measures 220' X 330' contains most nearly:

A.   1 1/4 acres
B.   1 3/5 acres
C.   1 2/3 acres
D.   2 acres

Answer: C. 220' x 33' = 72,600 square feet; 72,600 divided by 43,560 square feet per acre = 1.67 acres; 1.67 = 1 2/3 acres.

80. A borrower signed a straight note for a term of eight months in the amount of $2500. If she paid $150 in interest on the loan, the interest rate was:

A.   8%
B.   9%
C.   9%
D.   10%

Answer: C. $150 divided by 8 months = $18.75 per month; $18.75 x 12 = $225 per year; $225 divided by $2500 = 9%.

81. An income property was appraised for $100,000 based on a 6% capitalization rate. If an investor used an 8% cap rate, the value of the property would be:

A. $60,000
B. $75,000
C. $80,000
D. $90,000

Answer: B. $100,000 x 6% = $6000 net income; $6000 divided by 8% = $75,000 value

82. If a note in the amount of $22,250 specifies monthly payments over a period of 30 years at 6.6% interest per annum, what is the first month's interest payment?

A. $111.25
B. $122.38
C. $130.71
D. $140.50

Answer: B. $22,250 x 6.6% = $1468.50 $1468.50 divided by 12 = $122.38

83. If Haeli McDonald paid a commission of 6% of the selling price of a property valued at $54,375, the selling broker would receive:

A. $4,275.00
B. $3,375.00
C. $3,262.50
D. $3,191.50

Answer: C. $54,375 x 6% = $3262.50

84. A bank agreed to lend the owner of a piece of property a sum equal to 66 2/3% of its appraised valuation. The interest rate charged on the amount borrowed is 5% per annum. The first year's interest amounted to $200.00. What was the valuation placed upon the property by the bank?

A. $3,000.00
B. $4,000.00
C. $5,333.33
D. $6,000.00

Answer: D. $200.00 divided by 5% = $4000 loan $4000 divided by 66.66% = $6000

85. A married couple purchased a property for a total price of $18,000, paying $5000 down and having the seller take back a first trust deed in the amount of $13,000. The terms of the $13,000 trust deed called for no payments in the first year. If at the end of the first year, they were to sell the property at twice its original cost, their original dollar is now worth:

A. $2.00
B. $4.60
C. $7.20
D. $8.00

Answer: B. The owners had an equity or investment of $5000. If the property doubles in value to $36,000 and you deduct the $13,000 loan, their equity increased to $23,000. $5000 divided into $23,000 equals $4.60.

86. If a borrower pays $1650 interest per quarter on a straight note of $60,000, the interest rate would be:

A.   8.50%
B.   9.00%
C.   10.50%
D.   11.00%

Answer: D. $1650 = interest for 3 months; $1650 x 4 = $6600 interest for one year; $6600 divided by $60,000 = .11 or 11%.

87. Maria Watson sold a residence that was free and clear of all liens and received a check for $30,580. If closing costs of $430.60 had been deducted as well as the broker's 6& commission, the actual selling price would have been most nearly:

A. $31,590
B. $31,825
C. $32,885
D. $32,990

Answer: D. $30,580.00 (net) + 430.00 (closing costs) + 6% commission = selling price ; $31,010.60 divided by 94% = $32,990.00.

88. The number of townships in a tract of land that is 28 miles square is most nearly:

A. Eleven
B. Seventeen
C. Twenty two
D. Fifteen

Answer: C. A township is 6 miles square and contains 36 square miles 28 miles x 28 miles = 784 square miles; 784

divided by 36 = 21.77 townships.

89. Clever executed a promissory note in the amount of $7000. If the note called for the payment of interest only and Clever paid off the entire sum in 90 days together with interest of $210, the interest rate on the note was most nearly:

A.   9%
B.   10%
C.   11%
D.   12%

Answer: D. 90 = approximately 1/4 of a year $210 interest for 90 days x 4 = $840 interest for one year $840 divided by $7000 = 12%.

90. Broker Thomas is listing a property owned by Gibson. Gibson has advised Thomas that he wished to realize $37,000 cash from the sale after paying Thomas a 4% commission and paying $600 in closing costs. To accomplish this and assuming that the property is free and clear, the selling price must be at least:

A. $37,856
B. $38,480
C. $39,110

D. $39,167

Answer: D. $37,000 + $600 + 4% = selling price; $37,600 divided by 96% = $39,167

91. The interest rate on a straight note in the amount of $27,000 that calls for interest payments of $573.75 each quarter would most nearly be:

A.   6.6%
B.   7.2%
C.   8.6%
D.   9.2%

Answer: C. $573.75 x 4 = $2295 interest for one year $2295 divided by $27,000 = 0.85 or 8.5% 8.6% is closest.

92. A commercial office building yields an annual net income of $174,000. If an appraiser applied a capitalization rate of 8% to the property, the market value of the property would most nearly be:

A. $1,392,000
B. $1,666,000
C. $1,932,000
D. $2,175,000

Answer: D. $174,000 income divided by 8% = $2,175,000.

93. An individual who receives $225.00 per month on a money market savings account that pays 7.5% per year, has invested which of the following amounts?

A. $125,000
B. $27,000
C. $36,000
D. $48,000

Answer: C. $225 x 12 = $2700 per year $2700 divided by 7.5% = $36,000   .

94. A holder of a second trust deed and straight note with a face amount of $3740 sold it for $2431. This amounted to a discount of:

A.   26%
B.   35%
C.   45%
D.   55%

Answer: B. $3740 - $2431 = $1309 discount $1309 divided by $3740 = 35%

95. A seller took back a second trust deed and note in the amount of $11,400, payable $240 per month, including interest at 7% per annum. If interest on the note begins July 15 and the first payment is made on August 15, the amount of the first payment that is applied to the principal is:

A. $66.50
B. $79.80
C. $173.50
D. $240.00

Answer: C. $11,400 x 7% = $798 per year $798 divided by 12 = $66.50 per month $240 - $66.50 = $173.50.

96. A homeowner made a regular monthly payment of $550 on her home loan. Out of the total payment, the lender deducted the interest that was due for the month and applied the remaining balance of $43.85 to the principal. If the outstanding balance of the loan was $56,500, the interest rate on the load was most nearly:

A.   8.50%
B.   9.25%
C.   10.75%
D.   12.50%

Answer: C. $550 - $43.85 = $506.15 interest for 1st month

$506.15 x 12 = $6073.80 per year $6073.80 divided by $56,500 = 11%.

97. A square parcel of land that is 1780' X 1780' contains most nearly:

A.   27 acres
B.   54 acres
C.   65 acres
D.   73 acres

Answer: D. 1780' X 1780' = 3,168,400 square feet 3,168,400 divided by 43,560 = 72.736 acres.

98. An investor purchased two lots and paid $18,000 for each one. Since each lot had a 60' frontage he was able to subdivide the combined parcels in 3 lots with equal front footage. If the 3 lots sold for $15,000 each, his rate of profit on his investment was:

A.   20%
B.   25%
C.   33%
D.   40%

Answer: B. 3 lots x $15,000 each = $45,000 selling price $45,000 less cost of $36,000 (2 x $18,000) = $9000 profit;

$9000 divided by $36,000 = 25%.

99. A one acre parcel of land that is square is divided into four lots of equal size. If the lots are rectangular, parallel to each other and are 240' deep, the width of each lot is most nearly:

A.   45.4'
B.   90.8'
C.   181'
D.   240'

Answer: A. 43,560 square feet divided by 240' = 181.5' wide 181.5 divided by 4 = 43.375' 45.4' is closest.

100. Natalie Johnson owns a $100,000 property based on a 6% capitalization rate. If due to changes in economic conditions investors now require a higher capitalization rate or 8%, what would the value of the property be using the same dollar income?

A. $90,000
B. $75,000
C. $80,000
D. $60,000

Answer: B. $100,000 if capitalized at 6% would give a net income projection of $6,000. $6,000 net income capitalized at 8% would give $75,000 in value. $6,000 divided by 0.08 (8%) = $75,000.

In this section there will be no answers to the questions. You will be able to test yourself here by answering the questions on a separate sheet of paper. Number your papers 1 through 232 (Vocabulary) 1 through 200 (State Exam) 1 through 100 (Math Exam) and write down the letter of the answer you think is correct. Score yourself at the end by using the correct answers in the Study Section to see how you did. If you did not score at least 90%, go back to the Study Section and read through the exam again and continue to study and memorize the answers until you are scoring 90% or better. This will insure you pass your actual exam on the 1st try.

1. Which of the following describes the term "appreciation"?

A.   Kind words expressed to someone about something they did

B.   An increase in the value of property

C.   An item of value owned by an individual

D.   None of the above

2. When ownership of a mortgage is transferred from one company or individual to another, it is called

A.   an assumption

B.   an assignment

C.   an assessment

D.   all of the above

3. A mortgage loan which requires the remaining balance be paid at a specific point in time is called a/an

A.   balloon mortgage

B.   early due mortgage

C.   mortgage of convenience

D.   promissory note

4. The following reason accounts for why bridge loans are not used much anymore:

A.   More second mortgage lenders now will lend at a high loan to value

B.   Sellers would rather accept offers from Buyers who have already sold their property

C.   Neither A or B

D.   Both A and B

5. A title which is free of liens or legal questions as to ownership of the property is called a _____ title.

A.   good

B.   cloudy

C.   clear

D.   free

6. What is the collateral in a home loan?

A.   The property itself

B.   A person's good name

C.   The amount of savings a person has

D.   The current automobile the person owns

7. The adjustment date on an adjustable-rate mortgage is

A.   the date the interest rate changes
B.   the date the stock market goes up
C.   30 days from the date the mortgage was taken out
D.   all of the above

8. What is the deposit made by a potential buyer to show he is serious about buying a house called?

A.   Serious money deposit
B.   Earnest money deposit
C.   "Nothing ventured, nothing gained" deposit
D.   Down payment

9. A right-of-way which gives persons other than the owner access to or over a property is known as an

A.   easement
B.   ingress
C.   egress
D.   none of the above

10. Which best describes a "subdivision"?

A.   Houses in the same neighborhood similar in style and size

B.   A housing development created by dividing a tract of land into individual lots

C.   A development which is "substandard"

D.   None of the above

11. When someone contributes to the construction or rehabilitation of a property with labor or services rather than cash, that contribution is called

A.   a personal contribution

B.   sweat equity

C.   a big help to the contractors

D.   toil and labor

12. A two-step mortgage is defined as

A.   an adjustable rate mortgage with one interest rate for the first five or seven years and a different rate for the remainder of the term.

B.   a mortgage which is both adjustable and fixed

C.   a mortgage which is named after a dance step

D.   all of the above

13. A legal document evidencing a person's right to or

ownership of a property is called a

A.   quitclaim deed
B.   title
C.   yearly lease
D.   accurate appraisal

14. If you were buying a house that included furnishings, you would receive a written document transferring title to the personal property. This document is called a/an

A.   title
B.   deed
C.   bill of sale
D.   evidence of payment

15. An oral or written agreement that is binding in a court of law is called a

A.   gentlemen's agreement
B.   contract
C.   business deal
D.   promissory note

16. The part of the purchase price of a property that the buyer pays in cash and does not finance with the mortgage is called the

A. deposit
B. second mortgage
C. down payment
D. deed of trust

17. A female named in a will to administer an estate is called an

A. executor
B. executrix
C. individual representative
D. able inheritor

18. The greatest possible interest a person can have in real estate is called

A. fee complex
B. fee simple
C. no additional fees
D. ownership

19. Required for properties located in federally designated flood areas, this type of insurance compensates for physical property damage resulting from flooding. It is called

A. water damage insurance
B. hurricane insurance
C. there's no such thing

D.   flood insurance

20. The following is true of a government loan:

A.   It is guaranteed by the Department of Veterans Affairs (VA)
B.   It is guaranteed by the Rural Housing Service (RHS)
C.   It is insured by the Federal Housing Administration (FHA)
D.   All of the above

21. The person conveying an interest in real property is called

A.   the buyer
B.   the grantee
C.   the grantor
D.   the mortgagor

22. Insurance that covers in the event of physical damage to a property from fire, wind, vandalism, or other hazards is called

A.   act of God insurance
B.   hazardous insurance
C.   hazard insurance
D.   there is no such insurance

23. A liquid asset is

A.   an asset which is not in solid form
B.   an asset which cannot be frozen
C.   a cash asset or an asset easily turned into cash
D.   an asset that is hard to get to

24. Another term for the lender in a mortgage agreement is the

A.   banker
B.   mortgagee
C.   mortgagor
D.   private mortgage company

25. If you are buying a house and asking the Seller to provide all or part of the financing, you are asking for _____financing.

A.   special
B.   owner
C.   personal
D.   non-bank

26. A point is

A.   the part of the pen you sign a contract with
B.   a score in a basketball game
C.   the reason for telling the story
D.   1% of the amount of the mortgage

27. What does a power of attorney grant someone?

A.   The ability to attend law school
B.   Complete or limited authority on behalf of someone else
C.   Complete control over which medical facility someone uses
D.   The right to inherit an estate

28. The principal is

A.   the amount borrowed or remaining unpaid
B.   part of the monthly payment that reduces the remaining balance of a mortgage
C.   an ethic or value
D.   both A and B

29. A promissory note is

A.   a written promise to repay a specified amount over a specified period of time
B.   an oral promise to repay a specified amount over a specified period of time

C.   a note passed back and forth in class

D.   a note you deliver to another telling them of your intentions

30. Which of the following best describes a real estate agent?

A.   A licensed person who negotiates and transacts the sale of real estate

B.   The owner of a real estate firm

C.   A person who negotiates and transacts the sale of real estate but is not licensed

D.   A person who sells both property and insurance

31. When does an assumption take place?

A.   When someone believes something and it turns out to be true

B.   When the buyer assumes the seller's mortgage

C.   When the seller assumes the buyer's mortgage

D.   All of the above

32. A legal document conveying title to a property is called a/an

A.   sales contract

B.   option to purchase

C.   deed
D.   contract for deed

33. If you have a loan and transfer the title to another individual without informing the lender, it is likely that the lender will demand payment of the outstanding loan balance. He is able to do this because of a clause in your mortgage called the

A.   due on demand clause
B.   acceleration clause
C.   amortization schedule
D.   both A and B

34. The most common type of bankruptcy is called

A.   Chapter 11 bankruptcy
B.   Chapter 11 no asset bankruptcy
C.   Chapter 7 no asset bankruptcy
D.   Chapter 7 bankruptcy

35. Which of the following best describes a "broker"?

A.   Someone who owns a real estate firm
B.   Some real estate agents working for brokers
C.   Someone who acts as an agent and brings two parties together for a transaction and earns a fee for this
D.   All of the above

36. A normal contingency in a real estate contract would be that the

A.   purchaser is able to obtain a satisfactory home inspection from a qualified inspector.

B.   seller is allowed to come back and spend 2 weeks in the house each year

C.   purchaser is able to have occupancy as soon as the sales contract is signed

D.   seller is allowed to dig up some of the landscaping and take it with him

37. If you go to a bank or mortgage company to apply for a home, what type of mortgage would you be applying for?

A.   Government

B.   Conventional

C.   American

D.   Adjustable rate

38. A report of someone's credit history which is prepared by a credit bureau and used by a lender in the loan qualification process is called a

A.   personal affidavit

B.   credit card history

C.   savings account history

D.   credit report

39. If you have not made your mortgage payment within 30 days of the due date, the mortgage is considered to be in

A.   arrears

B.   default

C.   trouble

D.   bankruptcy

40. A term used by appraisers to estimate the physical condition of a building. It may be different from the building's actual age.

A.   Estimated age

B.   Longevity

C.   Preferred age

D.   Effective age

41. The difference between the fair market value of a property and the amount still owed on the mortgage and other liens is the owner's financial interest in the property and is called his

A.   equity

B.   balance due

C.   indebtedness

D.   none of the above

42. You put in a new driveway to your property, but in the process the paving goes across your property line onto your neighbor's property a few inches. This is called an

A.   illegal driveway
B.   extra benefit for your neighbor
C.   encroachment
D.   easement

43. A government loan that is not a VA loan would be a/an

A.   FHA mortgage
B.   FDA mortgage
C.   This type loan does not exist
D.   ARM mortgage

44. If you convey an interest in real property to a relative, that person is known as the

A.   receiver
B.   mortgagor
C.   grantee
D.   lucky relative

45. You decide you want to buy a boat and you want to borrow against the equity in your home. You would get a mortgage loan up to a specified amount which is in second position to your first mortgage. This arrangement is called a

A.   perfectly acceptable way to buy a boat
B.   leverage against your house
C.   home equity line of credit
D.   line of credit for personal purposes

46. You are your sister are joint tenants in a home your mother left you. Your sister has three children in her will and you have one. If she dies first, who does the property go to?

A.   It is divided equally between her three children
B.   It goes entirely to you
C.   It is divided equally between her three children and your one
D.   It goes into her estate

47. What is the best description of a lien?

A.   Something that doesn't stand up straight in a house
B.   Something that's illegal
C.   A legal claim against property that must be paid off when it's sold
D.   None of the above

48. What is a lock-in?

A.   A gated community which locks the gate at midnight
B.   An agreement from a lender guaranteeing a specific interest rate for a specific time at a certain cost
C.   What parents do with wayward children
D.   A type of key available at most hardware stores

49. The right of a government to take private property for public use upon payment of its fair market value. It is the basis for condemnation proceedings.

A.   Eminent domain
B.   Governmental domain
C.   Encroachment
D.   Both A and B

50. A mortgage with a lien position subordinate to the first mortgage on a piece of property is called a

A.   second mortgage
B.   first subordinate mortgage
C.   mortgage which isn't legal
D.   lien position mortgage.

51. An adjustable-rate mortgage, also known as an ARM is

A.   one in which the interest rate is fixed over time
B.   one in which the interest rate changes periodically, depending on index changes
C.   one in which the interest rate changes periodically, depending on the stock market
D.   a type of mortgage that the mortgagor can adjust himself

52. A schedule that shows how much of each payment will be applied to principal and how much toward interest over the life of the loan is called a/n

A.   amortization schedule
B.   annual percentage rate
C.   assumption
D.   both A and C

53. The term applied to a mortgage in which you make the payments every two weeks, thereby making thirteen payments a year rather than twelve. This mortgage is paid off faster than a normal mortgage.

A.   Twice-monthly mortgage
B.   Accelerated mortgage
C.   Bi-weekly mortgage
D.   None of the above

54. The limitation of how much an adjustable rate mortgage may adjust over a six-month period, annual period, and over the life of the loan is called a

A.   buy-down
B.   high point
C.   top stop
D.   cap

55. When is a real estate transaction considered to be "closed"?

A.   When the buyer has signed all the sales contracts
B.   When the closing documents have been recorded at the local recorder's office
C.   When all the documents are signed and money changes hands
D.   Both B and C.

56. A record of an individual's repayment of debt, reviewed by mortgage lenders in determining credit risk is called a

A.   credit affidavit
B.   credit history
C.   there is no such record
D.   credit worthiness

57. If you sell your property to a neighbor and the lender demands repayment in full, this means you have a _____ in your mortgage.

A.   seller pays all provision
B.   buyer pays all provision
C.   due-on-sale provision
D.   none of the above

58. The sum total of all the real and personal property owned by an individual at time of death is called their

A.   estate
B.   probate
C.   will
D.   all of the above.

59. If you list your property with a real estate agent and sign a written agreement that they are the only ones entitled to a listing for a specific time you have given them an

A.   exclusive listing
B.   exclusive right to advertise
C.   exclusive right to show
D.   inclusive listing

60. Fair market value could be defined as

A.   how much a property is worth, determined by a realtor's market analysis
B.   the most a buyer, willing, but not compelled to buy, would pay
C.   the least a seller, willing, but not compelled to sell, would take
D.   both B and C

61. If a lender agrees to make a loan to a specific borrower on a specific property, he has made a

A.   decision to make the loan
B.   statement that both the buyer and the property pass inspection
C.   firm commitment
D.   both B and C

62. If you buy a house and build cabinets into the wall, then sell that house, the cabinets stay because they have become a

A.   type of attachment
B.   fixture
C.   part of the house
D.   none of the above

63. A home inspection is

A.   a thorough inspection by a professional which evaluates the structural and mechanical condition of a property

B.   not required by law

C.   often a contingency in a contract that it turns out satisfactorily

D.   both A and C.

64. An insurance policy which combines personal liability insurance and hazard insurance coverage for a dwelling and its contents is called

A.   homeowner's insurance

B.   buyer's insurance

C.   errors and omissions insurance

D.   all of the above

65. Which of the following is true of a lease-option?

A.   It is an alternative financing option

B.   Each month's rent may also consist of an additional amount applied toward the

purchase

C.   The price is already set in the beginning

D.   All of the above

66. In simple terms, a sum of borrowed money (principal) usually repaid with interest is called a

A.   mortgage
B.   loan
C.   conventional loan
D.   alternative mortgage

67. A property description which is recognized by law and is sufficient to locate and identify the property without oral testimony is known as the property's

A.   address
B.   911 address
C.   legal description
D.   identifying information

68. The date on which the principal balance of a loan, bond, or other financial instrument becomes due and payable is called

A.   its due date
B.   maturity
C.   end of the paper trail
D.   delivery

69. The person borrowing money in a mortgage agreement is called the

A.   mortgagor
B.   mortgagee
C.   borrower
D.   lessee

70. Which of the following is true about an origination fee?

A.   It applies to both government and conventional loans
B.   It is usually 1% on a government loan
C.   It is usually 2% on a conventional loan
D.   Both A and B

71. Which of the following falls under the term "personal property"?

A.   A garage attached to a house
B.   A sofa
C.   The front porch of a home
D.   The windows in a home

72. In some cases if a borrower pays off a loan before it is due he may encounter a penalty called a

A.   penalty for early withdrawal

B.   loan to value penalty

C.   prepayment penalty

D.   there is never a penalty for paying a loan off early

73. Which of the following statements is true regarding the term "pre-approval"?

A.   It applies only to the property

B.   It is done before the loan application is complete

C.   It s a loosely used term

D.   None of the above

74. PITI reserves applies to

A.   a cash amount the borrower must have on hand after down payment and closing Costs.

B.   an amount which is financed with the mortgage

C.   both A and B

D.   none of the above

75. Why would a public auction take place?

A.   It's a good way to buy property

B.   To inform the public about property for sale

C.   To help auctioneers get employment

D.   To sell property to repay a mortgage in default

76. The term "realtor" applies to

A.　　any real estate agent who has passed the state exam

B.　　any real estate agent whose license is active

C.　　any real estate agent who is a member of a local real estate board affiliated with

　　　the National Association of Realtors.

D.　　any real estate agent who belongs to his local board

77. "Remaining term" refers to

A.　　the remaining school term for a real estate class

B.　　the original amortization term minus the number of payments that have been applied

C.　　the months left in a pregnancy

D.　　all of the above

78. Which of the following is not true of a "revolving debt"?

A.　　It is a type of credit arrangement, like a credit card

B.　　It revolves around no interest for the first six months

C.　　A customer borrows against a pre-approved line of credit

D.　　The customer is billed for the amount borrowed plus any interest due

79. Which of the following does a survey not show?

A.   Precise legal boundaries of a property
B.   Location of improvements, easements, rights of way
C.   Encroachments
D.   Location of furnishings within the dwelling

80. What is meant by "seller carry-back"?

A.   The seller physically carries his furnishings out of the house on the day of closing
B.   The seller agrees to be on the mortgage with the buyer
C.   the seller provides financing, often in combination with an assumable mortgage
D.   The seller carries the principal, but not the interest on a loan

81. A title company is one which

A.   is usually not needed in a real estate transaction
B.   is not called upon until one year after the sale is closed
C.   specializes in examining and insuring titles to real estate
D.   specializes in preparing deeds and deeds of trust

82. A state or local tax which is payable when title passes from one owner to another is called a

A.   title tax
B.   transfer tax
C.   revenue stamps
D.   real estate tariff

83. What is Truth-in-Lending?

A.   A state law requiring lenders to fully disclose in writing all terms and conditions

of a mortgage
B.   A federal law requiring lenders to fully disclose in writing all terms and

conditions of a mortgage
C.   A local law requiring lenders to fully disclose in writing all terms and conditions of a mortgage
D.   None of the above

84. A VA mortgage

A.   is a conventional mortgage for the state of Virginia
B.   is guaranteed by the Department of Veterans Affairs
C.   originates in Texas but ends up in Virginia
D.   in available to anyone applying for a mortgage

85. Which of the following is not true of "amortization"?

A.   Over time the interest portion increases as the loan balance decreases

B.   Over time the interest portion decreases as the loan balance decreases

C.   Over time the amount applied to principal increases so the loan is paid off in the

specified time

D.   None of the above

86. The valuation placed on property by a public tax assessor for taxation purposes is called

A.   real value
B.   fair market value
C.   assessed value
D.   predicted value

87. If a veteran is eligible for a VA loan, he or she would receive a document from the VA called

A.   Certificate of Authenticity
B.   Certificate of Approval
C.   Certificate of Met Requirements
D.   Certificate of Eligibility

88. Which of the following usually earns the largest commissions in a real estate transaction?

A.   Attorneys
B.   Realtors
C.   Loan officers
D.   Home warranty companies

89. An unwritten body of law based on general custom in England and used to an extent in some states is called

A.   common law
B.   uncommon law
C.   casual law
D.   it isn't law if it's not written down

90. If a real estate agent is trying to determine the market value of a property, one thing they would use is recent sales of similar properties or

A.   neighbors' estimates of the value of the property
B.   records from several years back in the same neighborhood
C.   comparable sales
D.   sales they estimate to happen in the future

91. A person to whom money is owed is known as a

A.   debtor
B.   creditor
C.   mortgagee
D.   lender

92. Discount points refer to

A.   a system of figuring out how much the property will be discounted
B.   points paid in addition to the one percent loan origination fee
C.   usually only FHA and VA loans
D.   both B and C

93. Which of the following can the Equal Credit Opportunity Act (ECOA) not discriminate against?

A.   Race, color or religion
B.   National origin
C.   Age, sex, or marital status
D.   All of the above

94. An exclusive listing is one which gives a licensed real estate agent the exclusive right to sell a property

A.   until it sells
B.   until the owner takes it off the market
C.   for a specified period of time
D.   none of the above

95. Which of the following is true about Fannie Mae's Community Home Buyer's Program?

A.   It is an income-based community lending model
B.   It has flexible underwriting guidelines to increase low to moderate income

      family's buying power
C.   Borrows who participate must attend pre-purchase home-buyer education sessions
D.   All of the above

96. The mortgage that is in first place among any loans recorded against a property and usually refers to the date in which loans are recorded, but not always, is called a

A.   primary mortgage
B.   first in line mortgage
C.   first mortgage
D.   both A and B

97. The legal process by which a borrower in default under a

mortgage is deprived of his or her interest in the mortgaged property is called a

A. takeover by the mortgage company
B. public auction
C. foreclosure
D. proceeds sale

98. Loans against 401K plans are

A. not allowed for down payments on property
B. an acceptable source of down payment for most types of loans
C. too great a risk for most people to take
D. only allowed if you're accumulated $50,000 in the plan

99. A late charge is

A. the penalty a borrower pays when a payment is late a stated number of days
B. usually put into play when the payment is fifteen days late on a first mortgage
C. usually not applicable to most people
D. both A and B

100. A person's financial obligations are known as his

A. payments

B.   assets
C.   liabilities
D.   credit risks

101. Which of the following is not true of annual percentage rate (APR)?

A.   It is the note rate on your loan
B.   It is not the note rate on your loan
C.   It is a value created according to a government formula intended to reflect the true

cost of borrowing and expressed as a percentage
D.   It is always higher than the actual note rate on your loan

102. An individual qualified by education, training, and experience to estimate the value of real property and personal property and who usually works independently is called an

A.   estimator of value
B.   appraiser
C.   on-site inspector
D.   underwriter

103. Which of the following best describes a "balloon payment"?

A. Payment delivered with a "bang"

B. First of many payments on a mortgage

C. The final lump sum payment due at the termination of a balloon mortgage

D. Payments which go higher and higher each year

104. When a borrower refinances his mortgage at a higher amount than the current loan balance with the intention of pulling out money for personal use, it is referred to as a

A. refinance extra

B. cash-out refinance

C. home equity refinance

D. adjustable lump sum refinance

105. A certificate of deposit is

A. the same as a down payment

B. a liquid asset

C. a deposit held in a bank paying a certain amount of interest to the depositor over a

certain time

D. a deposit held in a bank which pays double the amount of normal interest over

time

106. Common area assessments are

A.   sometimes called Homeowners Association Fees
B.   paid by individual owners of condominiums or planned unit developments
C.   used to maintain the property and common areas
D.   all of the above

107. A short-term interim loan for financing the cost of construction is called a

A.   flexible loan
B.   convertible loan
C.   construction loan
D.   not a loan, but a promissory note

108. In simple terms, debt is

A.   credit extended to someone
B.   an amount owed to another
C.   an amount owed to another with interest
D.   repayable

109. Which of the following is not true of the term "depreciation"?

A.   It is a decline in the value of property
B.   It is an accounting term showing the declining monetary value of an asset
C.   It is a true expense where money is actually paid
D.   Lenders add back depreciation expense for self-employed borrowers and count it

      as income

110. Which of the following would not be paid by escrow disbursements?

A.   Real estate taxes
B.   Hazard insurance
C.   Mortgage insurance
D.   Personal property taxes

111. The lawful expulsion of an occupant from real property is called

A.   conviction
B.   divorce from bed and board
C.   eviction
D.   there is no way to lawfully remove an occupant from real property

112. If you have a loan in which the interest rate does not

change during the term of the loan you have a
_____ mortgage.

A.   fixed-rate
B.   conventional fixed-rate
C.   owner financing
D.   all of the above

113. The following is true of a Home Equity Conversion Mortgage (HECM).

A.   It is also known as reverse annuity mortgage
B.   You don't make payments to the lender, the lender makes payments to you
C.   It enables older homeowners to convert their equity into cash
D.   All of the above

114. A written agreement between property owner and tenant stipulating the conditions under which the tenant may possess the property for a specified period of time and the payment due is called a/an

A.   contract
B.   option
C.   lease
D.   lease-option

115. A lender is

A.   the firm making the loan
B.   the individual representing the firm making the loan
C.   the individual offering owner financing
D.   both A and B

116. A margin is

A.   a measurement of error
B.   an artificial line not to write in on a loan document
C.   both A and B
D.   the difference between the interest rate and the index on an adjustable rate mortgage

117. Which of the following is the best definition of a mortgage broker?

A.   A mortgage company which originates loans, then places with other lending institutions
B.   A mortgage company which originates loans, then keeps them in house
C.   An individual which originates loans, then sells on the secondary market
D.   Much like a real estate broker, receives a commission on

loans

118. The term "note rate" refers to

A.   the speed at which a musician plays scales
B.   the interest rate stated on a mortgage note
C.   the interest rate stated on a personal loan
D.   the rate at which a note is amortized

119. If you have not made your mortgage payment, you are likely to receive which of the following?

A.   Notice of non-payment
B.   A written eviction notice
C.   Notice of default
D.   A letter from an attorney

120. A payment that is not sufficient to cover the scheduled monthly payment on a mortgage loan is called a

A.   late payment
B.   partial payment
C.   "too little, too late" payment
D.   a drop in the bucket

121. PITI stands for

A.   principal, interest, taxes and insurance

B.   principle, interest, taxes and insurance
C.   prepayment, interest, tariff and insurance
D.   none of the above

122. Which of the following describes "prepayment"?

A.   An amount paid to reduce the interest on a loan before the due date
B.   An amount paid to reduce the principal on a loan before the due date
C.   Can result from a sale, owner's decision to pay off the loan, or foreclosure
D.   Both B and C

123. What is private mortgage insurance?

A.   Mortgage insurance that is arranged for by the buyer privately

B.   Mortgage insurance provided by a private mortgage insurance company
C.   Insurance required for loans with a loan-to-value percentage in excess of 80%
D.   Both B and C

124. If you were trying to buy a home you and the seller would need to sign a written contract called a/an

A.   purchase agreement
B.   down payment agreement
C.   option to purchase
D.   all of the above

125. What is a recorder?

A.   A public official who keeps records of real property transactions
B.   The county clerk
C.   The registrar of deeds
D.   All of the above.

126. The principal balance on a mortgage is

A.   the outstanding balance of principal and interest
B.   the outstanding balance of principal only
C.   the amount the mortgage has been paid down
D.   none of the above

127. Which of the following is not true about qualifying ratios?

A.   There are two types of ratios—"top" or "front" and "back" or "bottom"

B.   The "top" ratio is a calculation of the borrower's monthly housing costs (principal, taxes, insurance, mortgage insurance, homeowners' association fees) as a percentage of monthly income

C.   the "back" ratio includes all monthly costs as well as "back" taxes

D.   Both calculations are used in determining whether a borrower can qualify for a mortgage

128. The definition of "real" property is

A.   property that has nothing artificial on it, only natural materials

B.   land and appurtenances, including anything of a permanent nature such as structures, trees and minerals

C.   things located within houses such as furniture, accessories, appliances, and clothing

D.   all of the above

129. In joint tenancy, if one person dies and the other inherits the property, this is called

A.   tenants in common

B.   whatever is stated in the will

C. following the wishes of the deceased
D. right of survivorship

130. A secured loan is

A. backed by collateral
B. when the borrower promises something of value to the lender
C. when the bank is not in danger of failing
D. when the bank has been bailed out

131. A mortgage or other type of lien that has a priority lower than that of the first mortgage is called

A. a second mortgage
B. subordinate financing
C. first subordinate financing
D. all of the above

132. If you were buying a house and wanted to protect yourself against any loss arising from disputes over ownership of your property, you would purchase

A. hazard insurance
B. errors and omissions insurance
C. title insurance
D. deed insurance

133 **Which of the following is true of the Veteran's Administration (VA)?**

A. It encourages lenders to make mortgages to veterans
B. It is an agency of the federal government which guarantees residential mortgages made to eligible veterans
C. The guarantee protects the lender against loss
D. All of the above

134. The form used to apply for a mortgage loan, which contains information about a borrower's income, savings, assets, debts, and more is called a/an

A. application for funds
B. income documentary
C. both A and B
D. application

135. An assessment does which of the following?

A. Places a value on property for the purpose of real estate sales
B. Is the same as a competitive market analysis
C. Places a value on property for the purpose of taxation
D. Is usually carried out by the mayor of a town

136. Which of the following is not true about the "bond market"?

A.   It refers to the daily buy and selling of thirty-year treasury bonds

B.   Lenders do not usually follow this market closely

C.   The same factors that affect the bond market affect mortgage rates at the same time

D.   Fluctuations in this market cause mortgage rates to change daily

137. What does the term "buydown" mean?

A.   Usually refers to a fixed rate mortgage where the interest rate is "bought down" for a temporary period, usually one to three years.

B.   A lump sum is paid and held in an account used to supplement the borrower's monthly payment

C.   These funds can sometimes come from the seller to induce someone to buy their property

D.   All of the above

138. Certificate of Reasonable Value (CRV) applies to

A.   an FHA loan

B.   a conventional loan

C.   a VA loan

D.   a car loan

139. If you are buying a piece of property and have someone else who is obligated on the loan and is on the title to the property, that person is called a

A.   spouse
B.   family member or friend who shares the property and payments with you
C.   co-borrower
D.   none of the above

140. How would you define "collection"?

A.   A plate, usually at church, where money is donated
B.   It goes into effect when a borrower falls behind
C.   It applies to several or many things in the same category on a loan application
D.   It only applies to trash

141. Which of the following is true of "condominium"?

A.   It applies to ownership, not to construction or development
B.   It is a type of ownership where all of the owners own each other's interior units
C.   It is an ownership where owners own the property,

common areas, and buildings together

D.   both A and C

142. An organization which gathers, records, updates, and stores financial and public records information about the payment records of individuals being considered for credit is called a

A.   credit repository
B.   credit reporting agency
C.   mortgage company
D.   bank

143. In some states a recorded mortgage is replaced by a

A.   contract for deed
B.   promissory note
C.   deed of trust
D.   deed

144. If you have failed to pay mortgage payments when they are due, it is called

A.   delinquency
B.   foreclosure
C.   collections

D.   no big deal

145. Which of the following would not be considered an "encumbrance", limiting the fee simple title, on a piece of property?

A.   Leases
B.   Mortgages
C.   Easements or restrictions
D.   Furniture not paid for

146. An earnest money deposit is put into this until delivered to the seller when the transaction is closed.

A.   the realtor's bank account
B.   the attorney's bank account
C.   the buyer's bank account
D.   an escrow account

147. Which of the following is true of the Federal National Mortgage Association (Fannie Mae)?

A.   It is the nation's largest supplier of mortgages
B.   It is congressionally chartered, shareholder owned
C.   It is the same as Freddie Mac
D.   both A and B

148. An employer-sponsored investment plan allowing individuals to set aside tax-deferred income for retirement or emergency purposes is called a _____ plan.

A.   436(k)/401B
B.   339(k)/372B
C.   401(k)/403B
D.   both A and B

149. Which of the following is true of the Government National Mortgage Association, also known as Ginnie Mae?

A.   It is government owned
B.   It was created by Congress on September 1, 2002
C.   Provides funds to lenders for making home loans
D.   Both A and C

150. At what amount is a loan considered to be a "jumbo" loan, which exceeds Fannie Mae's and Freddie Mac's loan limits? It is also known as a non-conforming loan.

A. $417,000
B. $227,150
C. $300,000
D.   Jumbo refers to the percentage borrowed, not the amount

151. Usually part of a homeowner's insurance policy, this type insurance offers protection against claims alleging that a property owner's negligence or inappropriate action resulted in bodily injury or property damage to another party.

A. Malpractice insurance
B. Liability insurance
C. Hazard insurance
D. Collision insurance

152. A lender refers to the process of getting new loans as

A. selling his product
B. loan origination
C. his bread and butter
D. more than just a job

153. The percentage relationship between the amount of the loan and the appraised value or sales price (whichever is lower) is called

A. value to loan
B. first-time homebuyer's loan
C. loan to value
D. both B and C

154. If you are applying for a loan, the lender gives and guarantees you a specific interest rate for a specific time. This period of time is called the

A.   period of no return
B.   rate-freeze period
C.   lock-in period
D.   period at which you cannot seek other financing

155. A credit report which reports the raw data pulled from two or more of the major credit repositories is called a

A.   multi-credit report
B.   merged credit report
C.   this is not legal
D.   none of the above

156. Sometimes called a first trust deed, this is a legal document pledging a property to the lender as security for payment of a debt.

A.   promissory note
B.   deed of trust
C.   owner financing document
D.   mortgage

157. Which of the following is not true of mortgage insurance?

A.   It covers the lender against some of the losses incurred resulting from default on a home loan

B.   It is sometimes is mistakenly referred to a PMI (private mortgage insurance)

C.   It is required on all loans having a loan to value of more than 90%

D.   No "MI" loans are usually made at higher rates

158   A no-point loan has an interest rate

A.   lower than if you pay one point

B.   the same as if you pay one point

C.   higher than if you pay one point

D.   a no-point loan does not exist

159. The total amount of principal owed on a mortgage before any payments are made is called the

A.   total amount due

B.   original principal balance

C.   a lot less than you'll actually pay

D.   your down payment times ten

160. A planned unit development (PUD) is different from a

condominium because

A.   a condominium usually has more amenities
B.   there are fewer units in a condominium development
C.   in a condominium the individual owns the airspace of
the unit
D.   all of the above

161. The term that means a limit on the amount that the interest rate can increase or decrease over the life of an adjustable rate mortgage is

A.   term cap
B.   life cap
C.   ARM cap
D.   none of the above

162. If a commercial bank or other financial institution extends you credit up to a certain amount for a certain time, you are receiving a

A.   line of credit
B.   personal loan
C.   unsecured loan
D.   both B and C

163. The term "modification" means

A. a change in your mortgage without having to refinance
B. a change in house plans before building begins
C. the right of the bank to modify the interest rate without telling you
D. both B and C

164. Which of the following is true of the term "mortgage banker"?

A. They are generally assumed to originate and fund their own loans
B. It is a loosely applied term to those who are mortgage brokers or correspondents
C. They usually sell loans on the secondary market to Fannie Mae, Freddie Mac, or Ginnie Mae.
D. All of the above.

165. Which of the following describes "prime rate"?

A. It is the interest rate banks charge to their preferred customers
B. The same factors that influence the prime rate also affect interest rates of mortgage loans
C. Changes in the prime rate are usually not widely publicized in the news media
D. Both A and B

166. A no cash-out refinance is

A.   intended to put cash in the hands of the borrower
B.   calculated to cover the balance due on the current loan
and any costs associated with obtaining the new mortgage
C.   often referred to as a "rate and term refinance"
D.   both B and C

**167. A legal document requiring a borrower to repay a
mortgage loan at a stated interest rate during a specified
period of time is called a**

A.   note
B.   deed of trust
C.   mortgage
D.   both B and C

**168. The date when a new monthly payment amount takes
effect on an adjustable-rate mortgage or graduated-payment
mortgage is called the**

A.   new payment date
B.   payment change date
C.   new payment due date
D.   change payment date

169. A quitclaim deed does which of the following?

A. Transfers with warranty whatever interest or title a grantor may have at the time the conveyance is made

B. Transfers without warranty whatever interest or title a grantor may have at the time the conveyance is made

C. Does not transfer interest at all

D. Quitclaim deeds are no longer used

170. In a refinance transaction, what happens?

A. One loan is paid off with the proceeds from a new loan using the same property as security

B. An additional loan is added to the present loan

C. The loan's interest rate changes

D. The term of the loan is increased

171. The amount of principal that has not yet been repaid is called the

A. amount owed

B. balance of the loan

C. remaining balance

D. all of the above

172. If you made an arrangement to repay delinquent installments or advances, you would be setting up a

A.   good faith payment plan
B.   repayment plan
C.   another loan to pay off
D.   oral contract

173. Your neighbor has given you a right of first refusal on a piece of land he plans to sell. What does this mean?

A.   He has given you the first opportunity to purchase it before he offers it for sale to others
B.   He expects you to refuse to buy it
C.   He expects you to pay more for it than anyone else
D.   None of the above

174. You are selling the house you live in, but the house you're moving to is not completed. You need to stay on in the house a while after closing. You work out a deal with the new purchaser called a

A.   no-rent lease agreement
B.   delayed possession for the new purchaser
C.   sale-leaseback
D.   lease for one year past closing

175. In a tenancy in common

A.   ownership passes to the survivors in the event of death

B.   ownership does not pass to the survivors in the event of death

C.   there are no provisions made for the death of the owners

D.   when one person dies, the others have to move

176. The duties of a "servicer" include

A.   collecting principal and interest payments from borrowers

B.   managing borrowers' escrow accounts

C.   usually a servicer services mortgages purchased by an investor in the secondary mortgage market

D.   all of the above

177. In "third-party origination"

A.   an independent political party originates a loan

B.   a lender uses another party to completely or partially originate, process, underwrite, close, fund, or package the mortgages it plans to deliver to the secondary mortgage market.

C.   three parties are involved in the loan process

D.   all of the above

178. A title search of a property would show the following to be true:

A. the seller is the legal owner of the property
B. there are no liens or other claims against the property
C. the previous owners came over on the Mayflower
D. both A and B

179. A trustee

A. is known to be trustworthy
B. is someone who has a great deal of trust in others
C. is a fiduciary who holds or controls property for the benefit of another
D. is usually a job for relatives

180. When a person is "vested" he can

A. use a portion of a fund such as an individual retirement fund
B. use a portion of a fund without paying taxes on it
C. have access to a bulletproof vest when in dangerous situations
D. both A and C

181. Which of the following is not true of the term "appraised value"?

A. It usually comes out lower than the purchase price when using comparable sales

B.   It is an opinion of a property's fair market value

C.   It is based on comparable sales

D.   None of the above

182. If a buyer qualifies and is able to take over the seller's mortgage when buying his home, this type of mortgage is called

A.   "pass on down" mortgage

B.   assumable mortgage

C.   owner financing

D.   both B and C

183. A call option is most similar to

A.   a lifetime cap

B.   a buy-down

C.   an acceleration clause

D.   all of the above

184. A "chain of title" would show

A.   the transfers of title to a piece of property over the years

B.   members of the "chain gang" who had previously owned the property

C.   neither A nor B

D.   both A and B

185. Which of the following is true of a cloud on title?

A.   It usually cannot be removed except by deed, release, or court action

B.   It is the result of conditions revealed by a title search that adversely affect the title to real estate

C.   both A and B

D.   neither A nor B

186. Which of the following applies to "closing costs"?

A.   They are divided into two categories—"non-recurring closing costs" and "pre-paid items"

B.   Lenders try to estimate the amounts of non-recurring and pre-paids on a Good Faith Estimate shortly after receiving the loan application

C.   Pre-paids are items which recur over time, such as property taxes and homeowners insurance

D.   All of the above

187. What is "community property"?

A.   Property that is owned by an entire condominium development

B.   Property that is owned by an entire subdivision of single-family homes

C. Property acquired by a married couple during the marriage and considered to be jointly owned
D. Both A and B

188. If an apartment complex is converted to a condominium, this is called

A. a condominium conversion
B. an apartment conversion
C. either an apartment or condominium conversion
D. fewer options for people to rent

189. This is an adjustable rate mortgage that allows the borrower to change the ARM to a fixed rate mortgage within a specific time.

A. due-to-change ARM
B. convertible ARM
C. fixed rate ARM
D. two-fold mortgage

190. If someone gives you "credit," you are

A. agreeing to receive something of value in exchange for a promise to repay the lender at a later date
B. getting something you deserve for something you did
C. very lucky, because this doesn't happen often

D.   both B and C

191. In an effort to avoid foreclosure (which may or may not happen), you might give the lender

A.   the payments he is due, all at one time
B.   your car and any other valuable personal property you have
C.   a "deed in lieu" (of foreclosure)
D.   a "deed in lieu" (of foreclosure), which then will not affect your credit badly

192. When a lender performs this calculation annually to make sure the correct amount of money for anticipated expenditures is being collected, the lender is performing

A.   checks and balances
B.   an escrow analysis
C.   a detailed loan analysis
D.   lenders don't do this

193. The report on the title of a property from the public records or an abstract of the title is called

A.   a title report
B.   an examination of title

C.   an examination of deed, survey and title
D.   title insurance

194. A consumer protection law that regulates the disclosure of consumer credit reports by consumer/credit reporting agencies and establishes procedures for correcting mistakes on one's credit record is called the

A.   Credit Reporting Act
B.   Fair Credit Reporting Act
C.   Consumer Protection Act
D.   Truth-in-Lending Act

195. If you inherit from someone, the best type of estate to inherit is called

A.   a fee simple estate
B.   general, all-encompassing estate
C.   life estate
D.   none of the above

196. A homeowner's association does which the following?

A.   It manages the common areas of a condominium project or planned unit development
B.   It owns title to the common elements in a condominium development

C.   It doesn't own title to the common elements in a planned unit development

D.   All of the above

197. In simple terms a judgment is

A.   a personal opinion about real estate

B.   an individual's way of making decisions about legal matters

C.   a decision made by a court of law

D.   an opinion of an attorney

198. This is a way of holding title to a property wherein the mortgagor does not actually own the property but rather has a recorded long-term lease on it.

A.   contract for deed

B.   rent-to-own contract

C.   long-term lease

D.   leasehold estate

199. Which of the following are duties of a loan officer?

A.   The solicitation of loans

B.   Representation of the lending institution

C.   Representation of the borrower to the lending institution

D.   All of the above

200. The amount paid by a mortgagor for mortgage insurance, either government or private is called

A.   mortgage insurance premium
B.   private mortgage insurance premium
C.   FHA insurance premium
D.   VA insurance premium

201. Which of the following statements is not true of mortgage life and disability insurance?

A.   It begins immediately after someone becomes disabled
B.   It pays off the entire debt if someone dies during the life of the mortgage
C.   It is a type of term life insurance often bought by borrowers
D.   In this type insurance, the amount of coverage decreases as the principal declines

202. Which is the best definition of "multi-dwelling units"?

A.   They are properties that provide separate housing units for more than one family with several different mortgages
B.   They are properties that provide separate housing units for more than one family, but with a single mortgage

C.   They are properties that provide separate housing units for more than one family, but are leased rather than owned

D.   They are properties that provide separate housing units for more than one family on a lease-option basis

203. Which of the following is true of "negative amortization"?

A.   It is also called "deferred interest"

B.   Because some ARM's allow the interest rate to fluctuate, the borrower's minimum payment may not cover all the interest

C.   The unpaid interest is added to the balance of the loan and the loan balance grows larger instead of smaller

D.   All of the above

204. For someone to be determined to be "pre-qualified" for a loan, what has taken place?

A.   The person has given a written statement saying he can afford the loan

B.   A loan officer has given a written opinion of the borrower's ability to qualify based on debt, income, or savings

C.   The loan officer has reviewed a credit report on the borrower

D.   The information given to the loan officer is in the form of written documentation

205. The four components of a monthly mortgage payment on impounded loans are

A.   principal, interest, taxes, maintenance
B.   principal, interest, insurance, bank fees
C.   principal, interest, taxes, miscellaneous charge
D.   principal, interest, taxes, insurance

206. The term "periodic rate cap" refers to

A.   an adjustable rate mortgage
B.   a limit on the amount the interest rate can increase or decrease during any one adjustment period
C.   conventional fixed-rate loans
D.   both A and B

207. The acquisition of property through the payment of money or its equivalent is called

A.   a purchase money transaction
B.   having a down payment and mortgage
C.   simply, buying property
D.   a sales transaction

208. What is a recording?

A.   A sound file of music to study real estate by

B.   Details of a properly executed legal document noted in the registrar's office

C.   A document, such as a deed or mortgage note which becomes public record

D.   Both B and C

209. If a landlord wants to protect himself against loss or rent or rental value due to fire or other casualty that would render the premises unusable for a time he would purchase

A.   hazard insurance
B.   fire insurance
C.   rent-loss insurance
D.   there is no such insurance

210. The right to enter or leave designated premises is called

A.   the right of ingress or egress
B.   the right to enter or leave
C.   the right of non-trespass
D.   an easement

211. "Secondary market" means

A.   a market which is not as important as the primary market
B.   the buying and selling of existing mortgages, usually as part of a "pool" of mortgages

C.   a market of lower real estate values

D.   none of the above

212. The property that will be pledged as collateral for a loan is called

A.   the back-up plan
B.   the credit
C.   security
D.   the borrower's former home

213. If you were purchasing a piece of property, either you or your bank would want to know if you were paying a fair price and would order

A.   a market analysis by a realtor
B.   an appraisal
C.   survey
D.   termite inspection

214. Which of the following is an example of "transfer of ownership"?

A.   The purchase of property "subject to" the mortgage
B.   Joint tenancy
C.   The assumption of the mortgage debt by the property

purchaser

D.   Both A and C

215. Which of the following does not apply the Treasury index?

A.   An index used to determine interest rate changes for certain fixed-rate loans

B.   It is based on the results of auctions that the U. S. Treasury holds for its Treasury bills and securities

C.   derived from the U. S. Treasury's daily yield curve

D.   None of the above

216. What are assets?

A.   Items of value owned by an individual

B.   Items that can be quickly converted into cash are called "liquid assets"

C.   Real estate, personal property, and debts owed to someone by others

D.   All of the above.

217. One who establishes the value of a property for taxation purposes is called

A.   a government tax appraiser

B.   an assessor

C. an appraiser
D. all of the above

218. A certificate of deposit index is

A. one of the indexes used for determining interest rate changes on some adjustable rate mortgages
B. is an average of what banks are paying on certificates of deposit
C. both A and B
D. neither A nor B

219. Which of the following is true of "common areas"?

A. They include swimming pools, tennis courts, and other recreational facilities
B. They are portions of a building, land, and amenities owned or managed by a planned unit development or condominium project's homeowners' association
C. They have shared expenses by the project owners for the operation and maintenance
D. all of the above

220. In a condominium hotel you would find the following:

A. Rental or registrations desks

B.   Daily cleaning services
C.   No individual ownership
D.   Both A and B

221. A type of multiple ownership where the residents of a multi-unit housing complex own shares in the cooperative corporation that owns the property and gives each resident the right to occupy a specific apartment or unit is called

A.   an investment condominium
B.   an investment planned unit development
C.   a cooperative
D.   a government-run housing project

222. Which is true of the cost of funds index (COFI)?

A.   It represents the weighted-average cost of savings, borrowings, and advances of the financial institutions such as banks and savings & loans in the 11th District of the Federal Home Loan Bank
B.   It is one of the indexes used to determine interest rate changes for certain government fixed rate mortgages
C.   It is an index used to determine interest rate changes for certain adjustable-rate mortgages
D.   Both A and C

223. Once you buy a house, the amount you pay each month includes an extra amount above principal and interest. This extra money is held in a special account to pay your taxes and homeowners insurance when it comes due. This account is called

A. an escrow account
B. a savings account
C. a regular checking account
D. both B and C

224. Which of the following does the Federal Housing Administration do?

A. Lends money and plans and constructs housing
B. Insures residential mortgage loans made by government lenders
C. Sets standards for construction and underwriting
D. None of the above

225. If you purchase a type of insurance called homeowner's warranty, you would do so because

A. It will cover repairs to certain items, such as heating or air conditioning if they break down within the coverage period
B. The seller will sometimes pay for it
C. Both A and B

D.   Neither A nor B

226. A type of foreclosure proceeding used in some states that is handled as a civil lawsuit and conducted entirely under the auspices of a court is called

A.   a legal foreclosure
B.   a court-appointed foreclosure
C.   a judicial foreclosure
D.   a civil foreclosure

227. Which of the following is not part of loan servicing?

A.   Processing payments, sending statements
B.   Managing the escrow account
C.   Handling pay-offs and assumptions
D.   Sending a monthly statement to the owner

228. A period payment cap applies to

A.   any mortgage taken out in the U.S.
B.   adjustable rate mortgages
C.   fixed-rate loans
D.   government loans

229. The commitment issued by a lender to borrower or other mortgage originator guaranteeing a specified interest

rate for a specified period of time at a specific cost is called

A.   a rate lock
B.   under lock and key
C.   a promissory note
D.   a deed of trust

230. A fund set aside for replacement of common property in a condominium, PUD, or cooperative project, particularly that which has a short life expectancy, such as carpet or furniture is called

A.   a capital improvements fund
B.   a replacement reserve fund
C.   a savings fund
D.   a contingency fund

231   The term "servicing" describes

A.   the collection of mortgage payments from borrowers
B.   what the mechanic does to your car
C.   duties of a loan servicer
D.   both A and C

232. A two- to-four family property

A.   consists of a structure that provides living space for two to four families and ownership is evidenced by two to four deeds

B.   consists of a structure that provides living space for two to four families and ownership is evidenced by a single deed

C.   is not a deeded property

D.   is an illegal form of ownership

1. Many states determine the order of water rights according to which users of the water hold a recorded beneficial use permit. This allocation of water rights is determined by:

A. accretion.
B. riparian theory.
C. littoral theory.
D. the doctrine of prior appropriation.

2. The right to control one's property includes all of the following EXCEPT:

A. the right to invite people on the property for a political fund-raiser.
B. the right to exclude the utilities meter reader.
C. the right to erect "no trespassing" signs.
D. the right to enjoy pride of ownership.

3. Which of the following types of ownership CANNOT be created by operation of law, but must be created by the parties' expressed intent?

A. community property
B. tenancy in common
C. condominium ownership
D. tenancy by the entireties

4. Which of the following is/are considered to be personal property?

A. wood-burning fireplace
B. furnace
C. bathtubs
D. patio furniture

5. The word "improvement" would refer to all of the following EXCEPT:

A. streets.
B. a sanitary sewer system.
C. trade fixtures.
D. the foundation.

6. All of the following are physical characteristics of land EXCEPT:

A. indestructibility.
B. uniqueness.
C. immobility.
D. scarcity.

7. Certain items on the premises that are installed by the tenant and are related to the tenant's business are called:

A. fixtures.
B. emblements.
C. trade fixtures.
D. easements.

8. Personal property includes all of the following EXCEPT:

A. chattels.
B. fructus industriales.
C. emblements.
D. fixtures.

9. A person who has complete control over a parcel of real estate is said to own a:

A. leasehold estate.
B. fee simple estate.
C. life estate.
D. defeasible fee estate.

10. A portion of Wendell's building was inadvertently built on Ginny's land. This is called an:

A. accretion.
B. avulsion.
C. encroachment.
D. easement.

11. The purchase of a ticket for a professional sporting event gives the bearer what?

A. an easement right to park his car
B. a license to enter and claim a seat for the duration of the game

C. an easement in gross interest in the professional sporting team

D. a license to sell food and beverages at the sporting event

12. If the owner of the dominant tenement becomes the owner of the servient tenement and merges the two properties, what happens?

A. The easement becomes dormant.
B. The easement is unaffected.
C. The easement is terminated.
D. The properties retain their former status.

13. Homeowner Ginny acquired the ownership of land that was deposited by a river running through her property by:

A. reliction.
B. succession.
C. avulsion.
D. accretion.

14. The rights of the owner of property located along the banks of a river are called:

A. littoral rights.
B. prior appropriation rights.
C. riparian rights.
D. hereditament.

15. The local utility company dug up Frank's garden to install a natural gas line. The company claimed it had a valid easement and proved it through the county records. Frank claimed the easement was not valid because he did not know about it. The easement:

A. Was valid even though the owner did not know about it.
B. Was an appurtenant easement owned by the utility company.
C. Was not valid because it had not been used during the entire time that Frank owned the property.
D. Was not valid because Frank was not informed of its existence when he purchased the property.

16. Jim and Sandy are next-door neighbors. Sandy tells Jim that he can store his camper in her yard for a few weeks

until she needs the space. Sandy did not charge Jim rent for the use of her yard. Sandy has given Jim a(n) what?

A. easement appurtenant
B. easement by necessity
C. estate in land
D. license

17. Your neighbors use your driveway to reach their garage on their property. Your attorney explains that the ownership of the neighbors' real estate includes an easement appurtenant giving them the driveway right. Your property is the:

A. leasehold interest.
B. dominant tenement.
C. servient tenement.
D. license property.

18. Quintin owned two acres of land. He sold one acre to Frank and reserved for himself an appurtenant easement over Frank's land for ingress and egress. Frank's land:

A. Is the dominant tenement.
B. Is the servient tenement.

C. Can be cleared of the easement when Quintin sells the withheld acre to a third party.

D. Is subject to an easement in gross.

19. Ginny owns 50 acres of land with 500 feet of frontage on a desirable recreational lake. She wishes to subdivide the parcel into salable lots, but she wants to retain control over the lake frontage while allowing lot owners to have access to the lake. Which of the following types of access rights would provide the greatest protection for a prospective purchaser?

A. an easement in gross

B. an appurtenant easement

C. an easement by necessity

D. a license

20. Sam and Nancy bought a store building and took title as joint tenants. Nancy died testate. Sam now owns the store:

A. as a joint tenant with rights of survivorship.

B. in severalty.

C. as a tenant in common with Nancy's heirs.

D. in trust.

21. When real estate under an estate for years is sold, what happens to the lease?

A. It expires with the conveyance.
B. It binds the new owner.
C. It is subject to termination with proper notice.
D. It is valid but unenforceable.

22. Evan lives in an apartment building. The land and structures are owned by a corporation, with one mortgage loan covering the entire property. Like the other residents, Evan owns stock in the corporation and has a lease on his apartment. This type of ownership is called a(n):

A. condominium.
B. planned unit development.
C. time-share.
D. cooperative.

23. Tom leases store space to Kim for a restaurant, and Kim installs her ovens, booths, counters, and other equipment. When do these items become real property?

A. when they are installed
B. when Kim defaults on her rental payments
C. when the lease takes effect
D. when the lease expires, if the items are not taken by the tenant

24. Jim, Manny and Harry are joint tenants owning a parcel of land. Harry conveys his interest to his long-time friend Wendell. After the conveyance, Jim and Manny:

A. become tenants in common.
B. continue to be joint tenants with Harry.
C. become joint tenants with Wendell.
D. remain joint tenants owning a two-thirds interest.

25. In a gift of a parcel of real estate, one of the two owners was given an undivided 60 percent interest and the other received an undivided 40 percent interest. The two owners hold their interests as what?

A. cooperative owners
B. joint tenants
C. community property owners

D. tenants in common

26. To create a joint tenancy relationship in the ownership of real estate, there must be unities of:

A. grantees, ownership, claim of right, and possession.
B. title, interest, encumbrance, and survivorship.
C. possession, time, interest, and title.
D. ownership, possession, heirs, and title.

27. What is a Schedule of Exceptions on a title policy?

A. encumbrances
B. tax liens
C. list of things not insured in the policy
D. defects

28. When a company furnishes materials for the construction of a house and is subsequently not paid, it may file a(n):

A. deficiency judgment.

B. lis pendens.

C. estoppel certificate.

D. mechanic's lien.

29. Which of the following liens does not need to be recorded to be valid?

A. materialman's lien

B. real estate tax lien

C. judgment lien

D. mechanic's lien

30. The system of ownership of real property in the United States is what?

A. incorporeal

B. allodial

C. inchoate

D. feudal

31. mechanic's lien would be properly classified as a(n):

A. equitable lien.
B. voluntary lien.
C. general lien.
D. statutory lien.

32. Under which of the following types of liens can both the real property and the personal property of the debtor be sold to pay the debt?

A. real estate tax lien
B. mechanic's lien
C. judgment lien
D. assessment lien

33. A homeowner owned a house on a lot. The front ten feet of the lot were taken by eminent domain for a sidewalk. Would the homeowner be entitled to compensation?

A. Yes. The land was taken for public use by eminent domain.
B. Yes. He must be paid for the use of the sidewalk.
C. No. He still had use of the house and lot.
D. No. Compensation is not given on land taken for public use.

34. The covenant in a deed which states that the grantor is the owner and has the right to convey the title is called:

A. covenant of further assurance.
B. Yes. He must be paid for the use of the sidewalk.
C. covenant of seisin.
D. covenant against encumbrances.

35. The recording of a deed:

A. Is all that is required to transfer the title to real estate.
B. Gives constructive notice of the ownership of real property.
C. Insures the interest in a parcel of real estate.
D. Warrants the title to real property.

36. Which of the following provides a buyer with the best assurance of clear, marketable title?

A. certificate of title
B. title insurance
C. abstract of title
D. general warranty deed

37. What do liens and easements have in common?

A. Both are encumbrances.
B. Both must be on public record to be valid.
C. Neither can be done without the consent of the owner.
D. Both are money claims against the property.

38. The title to real estate passes when a valid deed is:

A. signed and recorded.
B. delivered and accepted.
C. filed and microfilmed.
D. executed and mailed.

39. The primary purpose of a deed is to:

A. Prove ownership.
B. Transfer title rights.
C. Give constructive notice.
D. Prevent adverse possession.

40. A special warranty deed differs from a general warranty deed in that the grantor's covenant in the special warranty deed:

A. Applies only to a definite limited time.
B. Covers the time back to the original title.
C. Is implied and is not written in full.
D. Protects all subsequent owners of the property.

41. Which of the following deeds contains no expressed or implied warranties?

A. a bargain and sale deed
B. a quitclaim deed
C. a warranty deed
D. a grant deed

42. When the grantor does not wish to convey certain property rights, he or she:

A. must note the exceptions in a separate document.
B. may not do so, since the deed conveys the entire premises.
C. may note the exceptions in the deed of conveyance.

D. must convey the entire premises and have the grantee reconvey the rights to be retained by the grantor.

43. A partition suit is used for which of the following?

A. determination of party fences
B. to allow construction of party walls
C. to force a division of property without all the owners' consents
D. to change a tenancy by entireties to some other form of ownership

44. The condemnation of private property for public use is exercised under which government right?

A. taxation
B. escheat
C. manifest destiny
D. eminent domain

45. When a claim is settled by a title insurance company, the company acquires all rights and claims of the insured

against any other person who is responsible for the loss. This
is known as what?

A. caveat emptor
B. surety bonding
C. subordination
D. subrogation

**46. Which of the following would be used to clear a defect
from the title records?**

A. a lis pendens
B. an estoppel certificate
C. a suit to quiet title
D. a writ of attachment

47. A bill of sale is used to transfer the ownership of what?

A. real property
B. fixtures
C. personal property
D. appurtenances

48. A written summary of the history of all conveyances and legal proceedings affecting a specific parcel of real estate is called a(n):

A. affidavit of title.
B. certificate of title.
C. abstract of title.
D. title insurance policy.

49. When the preliminary title report reveals the existence of an easement on the property, it indicates that the easement is a(n):

A. lien.
B. encumbrance.
C. encroachment.
D. tenement.

50. The list of previous owners of conveyance from whom the present real estate owner derives his or her title is known as the:

A. chain of title.

B. certificate of title.

C. title insurance policy.

D. abstract of title.

51. A person agrees to sell a property for $500,000. The buyer gives the seller $150 as valuable consideration for a six-month option. Which of the following statements is true?

A. The $150 is valuable consideration if the seller accepted it.

B. The buyer must have at least 5% down as valuable consideration.

C. The buyer must have at least 20% down.

D. The seller cannot accept money for the option.

52 . Which of the following activities is a violation of the Federal Fair Housing Act?

A. a nonprofit church that denies access to its retirement home to any person because of race

B. a nonprofit private club that gives preference in renting units to its members at lower rates

C. the owner of a single-family residence selling his/her own home who gives preference to a buyer based on his/her sex

D. discrimination in the sale of a warehouse based on the prospective purchaser's gender

53. A Savings & Loan institution would be violating the Federal Fair Housing Act by denying a loan to Mr. and Mrs. Happy Borrower for which of the following reasons?

A. low earnings
B. too old
C. too many loans
D. minority background

54. The Civil Rights Act of 1866 prohibits discrimination in housing based on which of the following reasons?

A. race
B. religion
C. sex
D. marital status

55. An agent working as a subagent of the seller would suggest that the buyer hire an inspector from an outside service in all of the following cases EXCEPT:

A. when they smell gas in the basement.
B. when there is a slow drain in the toilet.
C. when a hinge is off the door.
D. when there is sawdust in the kitchen cabinets.

56. The federal anti-discriminatory laws apply to which of the following?

A. a broker selling a single-family home
B. a private club not open to the general public
C. office building sales
D. the rental of industrial property

57. A tenant complained to HUD about his landlord's discriminatory practices in his/her building. A week later the landlord gave the tenant an eviction notice. Under which of the following situations would the Federal Fair Housing Act be violated?

A. when the tenant is two months behind in his/her rent

B. when the landlord evicts the tenant for reporting him to HUD

C. when the tenant has damaged the premises

D. when the tenant is conducting an illegal use on the premises

58. The Federal Fair Housing Act states that a prima facie (at first view) case against a broker for discrimination be established after a complaint has been received because the broker has failed to do which of the following?

A. The broker has failed to display a HUD Equal Opportunity poster.

B. The broker has failed to join an affirmative marketing program.

C. The broker has failed to join the HUD anti-discriminatory task force.

D. The broker has failed to attend mandatory classes on fair housing.

59. A broker is discussing a new listing with a prospective Mexican American buyer. The buyer wants to inspect the property immediately, but the owner of said property has instructed the broker, in writing, not to show the house during the owner's three-week absence. The buyer insists on viewing the property. The broker should:

A. Show the property to avoid a violation of the Federal Fair Housing Act.
B. Request the Real Estate Commission arbitrate the problem.
C. Inform the buyer of the seller's instructions.
D. Notify the nearest HUD office.

60. A three-story apartment complex built in 1965 does not meet with the handicapped access provisions for the 1988 Fair Housing Act. The owner must:

A. Make the ground floor handicapped accessible.
B. Make the 1st and 2nd floors accessible.
C. Make the entire building accessible.
D. The owner doesn't have to comply since it's less than 4 stories.

61. What type of a listing agreement allows the owner to appoint an exclusive agent to sell his property, but retains the right to sell the property himself?

A. open
B. exclusive right to sell
C. multiple listing

D. exclusive agency

62. Under an Exclusive Right to Sell Listing agreement, if the seller produces a ready, willing and able buyer he:

A. will not have to pay a commission since he produced the buyer.
B. will only have to pay the broker half the commission since he produced the buyer.
C. owes the listing broker a full commission.
D. will not be able to turn the buyer over to the listing agent since the agent has the exclusive right to sell the property.

63. Which of the following would not terminate an agency relationship?

A. abandonment by the agent
B. revocation by the principal
C. submission by the agent of two offers at the same time
D. fulfillment of the agency purpose

64. The buyer of an apartment complex is told that the refrigerator in one of the apartments goes with the sale.

After taking title, he discovered that the refrigerator belonged to the tenant. Which is true about this situation?

A. Since the refrigerator was in the apartment, it automatically belongs to the new owner.
B. The refrigerator is the personal property of the tenant. The seller had no right to offer it to the buyer.
C. The refrigerator was plugged into the wall and that makes it real property.
D. The tenant will have to get permission from the new owner to remove the refrigerator.

65. The illegal process of a banker refusing to approve loans for a neighborhood based on the racial composition of the area is:

A. blockbusting.
B. steering.
C. redlining.
D. panic peddling.

66. The illegal practice of directing minorities to areas populated by the same race or religion is called:

A. steering.
B. blockbusting.
C. redlining.
D. panic peddling.

67. Carl Chauvinist, the owner of an apartment complex, lives in one unit of a triplex and routinely refuses to rent either of the other two units to a female. Can he do this?

A. Yes. He may do this if he does not use a broker or discriminate in advertising.
B. Yes. He may do this if he doesn't ask the tenant's age.
C. No. Carl can never discriminate on sex.
D. No. Carl must live in a single family home to discriminate.

68. An aggrieved party with a Fair Housing violation claim has how long to file a complaint with the Department of Housing and Urban Development?

A. 1 month
B. 1 week
C. 1 year
D. 7 years

69. Jim Jones, the landlord, rents a property to Tom Smith, a handicapped person. Mr. Smith, with Mr. Jones' permission, modifies the house to suit his needs. When the lease expires, which of the following requirements would not have to be met by Mr. Smith?

A. Mr. Smith must remove the "grab rails" in the bathroom that were installed for his use.
B. Mr. Smith must raise the kitchen cabinets that were lowered for his use.
C. Mr. Smith must repair the walls where the "grab rails" in the bathroom were removed.
D. Mr. Smith must restore the wide doorways, that were installed for him, to the original size.

70. All of the following are duties of the property manager EXCEPT:

A. reporting to the owner all notices of building violations.
B. providing upkeep and maintenance on the property.
C. maintaining financial records and accounts.
D. securing tenants of a particular ethnic origin in accordance with the owner's wishes.

71. A mobility impaired person was renting a unit in an apartment complex. Half the units had been assigned parking spaces near the door; the other half had not. The owner:

A. may charge extra money to the handicapped person for providing the parking space near the door.

B. must take a vote of all tenants to see if they want to allow the handicapped person a parking space.

C. must give a parking space near the door to the handicapped person, if one is available and a need is demonstrated.

D. must allow the handicapped person to live there for a month and if a space becomes available during that time, give the parking space to the handicapped person.

72. A salesperson is involved in a transaction where an individual wishes a six-month lease with an option to buy. What is true about this situation?

A. The individual must go to an attorney since it is too complicated a transaction for a salesperson.

B. This transaction is too complicated for a salesperson. Only a person with a broker's license should handle this transaction.

C. A salesperson could use two standard forms, fill in the blanks and request that his or her broker review the forms before signing.
D. The salesperson should write the purchase offer. A lease for 6 months does not need to be in writing.

73. A void contract is one that is:

A. not in writing.
B. not legally enforceable.
C. rescindable by agreement.
D. voidable by only one of the parties.

74. The essential elements of a contract include all of the following EXCEPT:

A. offer and acceptance.
B. notarized signatures.
C. competent parties.
D. consideration.

75. If, upon the receipt of an offer to purchase his property under certain conditions, the seller makes a counteroffer, the prospective buyer is:

A. bound by his original offer.
B. bound to accept the counteroffer.
C. bound by whichever offer is lower.
D. relieved of his original offer.

76. The amount of earnest money deposit is determined by:

A. the real estate licensing statutes.
B. an agreement between the parties.
C. the broker's office policy on such matters.
D. the acceptable minimum of 5 percent of the purchase price.

77. If the buyer defaulted some time ago on a written contract to purchase a seller's real estate, the seller can still sue for damages, if he is not prohibited from doing so by the:

A. statute of frauds.
B. law of agency.
C. statute of limitations.
D. broker-attorney accord.

78. A competent and disinterested person who is authorized by another person to act in his or her place and sign a contract of sale is called:

A. an attorney in fact.
B. a substitute grantor.
C. a vendor.
D. an agent.

79. An option:

A. requires the optionor to complete the transaction.
B. gives the optionee an easement on the property.
C. does not keep the offer open for a specified time.
D. makes the seller liable for a commission.

80. When a prospective buyer makes a written purchase offer that the seller accepts, then the:

A. Buyer may take possession of the real estate.
B. Seller grants the buyer ownership rights.

C. Buyer receives legal title to the property.
D. Buyer receives equitable title to the property.

81. H agrees to purchase V's real estate for $230,000 and deposits $6,900 earnest money with Broker L. However, V is unable to clear the title to the property, and H demands the return of his earnest money as provided in the purchase contract. Broker L should:

A. Deduct his commission and return the balance to H.
B. Deduct his commission and give the balance to V.
C. Return the entire amount to H.
D. Give the entire amount to V to dispose of as he decides.

82. A buyer makes an earnest money deposit of $1,500 on a $15,000 property and then withdraws her offer before the seller can accept it. The broker is responsible for disposing of the earnest money by:

A. turning it over to the seller.
B. deducting the commission and giving the balance to the seller.
C. returning it to the buyer.
D. depositing it in his or her trust account.

83. Broker K arrives to present a purchase offer to Mrs. D, an 80 year old invalid who is not always of sound mind, and finds her son and her daughter-in-law present. In the presence of Broker K, both individuals persistently urge D to accept the offer, even though it is much lower than the price she has been asking for her home. If D accepts the offer, she may later claim that:

A. Broker K should not have brought her such a low offer for her property.
B. She was under undue duress from her son and daughter-in-law, and, therefore, the contract is voidable.
C. Broker K defrauded her by allowing her son and daughter-in-law to see the purchase offer he brought to her.
D. Her consumer protection rights have been usurped by her son and daughter-in-law.

84. The law that requires real estate contracts to be in writing to be enforceable is the:

A. law of descent and distribution.
B. statute of frauds.
C. parole evidence rule.

D. statute of limitations.

85. A(n) _____ is when an owner takes his property off the market for a definite period of time in exchange for some consideration, but he grants the right to purchase the property within that period for a stated price.

A. option
B. contract of sale
C. right of first refusal
D. installment agreement

86. A breach of contract is a refusal or a failure to comply with the terms of the contract. If the seller breaches the purchase contract, the buyer may do all of the following EXCEPT:

A. Sue the seller for specific performance.
B. Rescind the contract and recover the earnest money.
C. Sue the seller for damages.
D. Sue the broker for non-performance.

87. To assign a contract for the sale of real estate means to:

A. Record the contract with the county recorder's office.
B. Permit another broker to act as agent for the principal.
C. Transfer one's rights under the contract.
D. Allow the seller and the buyer to exchange positions.

88. The property manager suspects that the tenants in a property are engaging in illegal drug trafficking. What should the property manager do?

A. Cancel the property management agreement.
B. Observe the property for 30 days and then tell the owner.
C. Notify the owner immediately of the suspicious activity.
D. Don't worry. It's the owner's problem.

89. A zoning change has been announced that will result in the loss of value of the property to a property owner. What should a property manager do?

A. Advise the owner immediately.
B. Terminate the property management agreement.
C. Follow the owner's instructions that were previously given.
D. Keep his/her mouth shut.

90. A broker and seller terminate the listing contract. An offer is received in the mail by the broker after the termination of the listing contract. The offer is for full price and includes all of the terms and conditions of the seller. Why is this NOT a valid contract?

A. There is no consideration involved.
B. No acceptance has been given.
C. No earnest money has been enclosed.
D. There is no current listing agreement.

91. Which of the following activities does NOT require a real estate license?

A. Holding a real estate auction.
B. Selling property listed by other brokers or agencies.
C. Showing and selling one's own property.
D. Offering to buy properties on behalf of third parties.

92. In addition to selling one's own property, which of the following is also exempt from normal licensing requirements?

A. Acting as a guardian.
B. Acting as a trustee.
C. Acting as an attorney-in-fact.
D. Each of the above.

93. As long as it is specified as part of his or her duties, is it legal for an unlicensed salaried assistant to solicit listings for the broker?

A. Yes, if it is part of a written job description.
B. No, soliciting listings is the exclusive responsibility of the broker-in-charge.
C. Yes, because she is being paid a salary, not commissions.
D. No, active participation in real estate transactions requires a license.

94. Regarding the North Carolina Real Estate Commission, which of these statements is true?

A. A monthly salary plus expenses is paid to each member.

B. The North Carolina Association of Realtors® appoints the members.
C. The governor appoints members for a three-year term.
D. The Commission consists of seven members, all of whom must be active in real estate.

95. Which of these is a requirement to hold a real estate license in North Carolina? 1) Be a resident in good standing of the state. 2) Be at least 21 years old.

A. Only #1.
B. Only #2.
C. Neither #1 nor #2.
D. Both #1 and #2.

96. Licensees must notify the Real Estate Commission when which of these events occur?

A. There is a significant change in sales volume.
B. The business tradename has changed within the past ten days.
C. The business trade-name has changed within the past thirty days.
D. The licensee has received more than two traffic violations within the past eighteen months.

97. What is the first point at which a person may begin practicing real estate in North Carolina?

A. When a broker activates his or her license.
B. Upon successful completion of all course and exam work.
C. Upon completion of all education requirements.
D. Upon completion of course work requirements, successfully pass the exam and finish a recognized training program.

98. Which of these is required to be a broker-in-charge? 1) An active broker's license for the state of North Carolina. 2) Eight hours of continuing education each year.

A. Only #1.
B. Only #2.
C. Neither #1 nor #2.
D. Both #1 and #2.

99. What is "first substantial contact?"

A. An initial meeting to formalize a client-agency relationship.

B. A flexible standard for establishing client-agency relationships.

C. A new agent's first listing agreement or sales contract.

D. The point at which buyers or sellers must be given the North Carolina consumers' real estate disclosure document.

100. What is the definition of "dual agency" in North Carolina?

A. One firm represents both the buyer and the seller equally.

B. One firm represents the seller and another represents the buyer in the same transaction.

C. One firm represents both the buyer and the seller, but owes primary loyalty to seller.

D. One firm represents both the buyer and the seller, but owes primary loyalty to the buyer.

101. What is "designated agency" in North Carolina?

A. An alternative to dual agency.

B. A form of dual agency.

C. A minimum standard for client representation.

D. A form of representation that every company in NC must practice.

102. Who may practice designated agency?

A. Only one firm.
B. Only two firms involved in the same transaction.
C. Only brokers.
D. Only brokers or salespeople from separate firms.

103. Sally Lennox, a provisional broker working under the guidance of XYZ Real Estate Company, and with the owner's knowledge, deliberately fails to disclose that there is a dispute regarding title to the property. Who, if anyone, is liable in this situation?

A. No one is liable, since the dispute has not yet been resolved.
B. No one is liable since it's the buyer's responsibility to verify all representations, including title.
C. Only Sally is liable for her own actions.
D. Sally, the owner of the property, and the broker of XYZ Real Estate Company can all be held liable for Sally's lack of disclosure.

104. Which of the following is NOT a responsibility of a broker in North Carolina?

A. Disclosing property defects to the buyer.
B. Disclosing the seller's reasons for selling.
C. Accounting for all funds in the transaction.
D. Loyalty to his or her client.

105. Bill Timmons has a listing agreement to sell Paula Robinson's home. So far, Paula has turned down all offers, including those Bill thought were good. A new offer comes in the Friday before a weekend open house that's less than 70% of the asking price. Bill is certain it wont be accepted. What should he do?

A. Let Paula know he has a low offer, but deliver it to her anyway as soon as possible.
B. Tell the buyer it won't be accepted and refuse the offer.
C. Accept the offer, but don't present it.
D. Accept the offer, but hold it until after the open house to see if a better one comes along.

106. In which of these capacities may an agent represent a client?

A. As a buyer's agent.

B. As a seller's subagent.

C. As a dual agent.

D. Any of these relationships is acceptable.

107. When may a provisional broker represent both the buyer and the seller in the same transaction?

A. Never.

B. If the provisional broker's broker approves.

C. If the provisional broker informs both parties.

D. None of these situations are acceptable.

108. Before a person can receive compensation in a real estate transaction, he or she must have which of these credentials?

A. An MLS membership.

B. An agency-exclusive agreement.

C. An active license.

D. An active or inactive license and certificates of completion for all course and examination requirements.

109. Phil Patterson is the broker-in-charge of Patterson-Stark Realty, a firm that practices dual agency. One of his agents, Barb, is working with a client as a buyer's agent. Another P&S agent, Rebecca, has one of the company's listings that Barb's client is interested in. How should they proceed to complete a transaction?

A. They cannot proceed because it would create conflicts of interest and confidentiality.
B. The listing relationship takes precedence, so Phil and Rebecca can only represent the seller and Barb can only represent the buyer.
C. If all parties agree, each can function as a dual agent.
D. As the listing firm, Phil, Rebecca and Barb must represent the seller.

110. Which of these is required to practice designated agency? 1) The firm has a policy of dual agency. 2) The firm has a policy of designated agency. 3) There are at least two licensees in the firm.

A. #1 only.
B. #2 only.
C. #1 and #2.

D. #1, #2 and #3.

111. At what point should associates at Bay Head Realty discuss the possibility of dual agency?

A. When they meet a fellow associate they'd like to partner with.
B. At the point of first substantial contact with a prospective client.
C. When one associate agrees to show some properties to a prospective client he met at an open house and who, as it turns out is also working with another agent in the firm.
D. As soon as a new client signs an agreement.

112. What is the rule describing brokers and trust accounts?

A. Brokers may have trust accounts if and as needed.
B. Firms, not brokers, hold trust accounts.
C. A broker must have a trust account for every client.
D. Brokers must always have a trust account.

113. If a dispute over monies in a trust account arises between a buyer and seller, what action must a broker take?

A. Hold the monies in the trust account until the parties reach agreement.
B. Turn the monies over to an attorney.
C. Return all monies to the buyer.
D. Split the monies between the buyer and seller.

114. Which of the following is NOT considered trust money?

A. Earnest money.
B. Broker funds for service charges.
C. Down payments.
D. Funds for final settlement.

115. Are interest-bearing trust accounts permissible?

A. No, any interest that accrues in a trust account goes to the state to fund real estate programs and studies.
B. Yes, and the interest is split between the buyer and seller as well as the broker to cover administrative expenses.
C. Yes, and the interest is split between the seller and broker.
D. Yes, in certain conditions.

116. What is the maximum amount of personal funds a provisional broker may keep in a trust account

A. 100
B. 300
C. Enough to cover service charges.
D. None of the above.

117. What is the deadline for depositing monies into a trust account?

A. The same day they are received.
B. Within three banking days of receipt.
C. As stipulated in the contract.
D. It varies with the type of deposit (earnest money, downpayment, etc.).

118. When may a licensee pay a referral fee?

A. If it is $50 or less.
B. If there is a written agreement between the parties.
C. If it is to a licensee.
D. Never.

119. When it comes to financing theory, what kind of state is North Carolina?

A. A title theory state.
B. A lien theory state.
C. Both 1 and 2.
D. Neither 1 nor 2.

120. Rita Spenser is a provisional broker completing a transaction with her seller when she discovers an error on the closing statement. Who is responsible for ensuring the accuracy of closing statements?

A. Rita, as the provisional broker, is responsible.
B. Rita's broker is responsible.
C. The title company.
D. The attorney.

121. Bob is a recent college graduate planning on a career in real estate. Although not yet licensed, he proceeds to show a

property for the experience, even though it's a violation of real estate law. Who is subject to disciplinary action?

A. Bob.
B. The principal of the firm.
C. Bob's broker.
D. No one, since Bob is not yet licensed and thus exempt from the rules.

122. There is strong evidence a licensee embezzled from his firm. What action may the Real Estate Commission take?

A. None, unless the embezzlement was from a trust account and directly related to real estate transactions.
B. If found guilty, he can be fined by the Commission.
C. He can be prosecuted by the Commission and, if found guilty, is subject to criminal penalties including possible jail time.
D. He can be prosecuted by the Commission and, if found guilty, is subject to noncriminal licensure penalties.

123. An unhappy seller took a licensee to court which found in the seller's favor. Which of the following would NOT occur as a result?

A. The licensee could be fined.
B. The court could recommend disciplinary action against the licensee to the chairman of the Real Estate Commission.
C. The court could revoke his or her license.
D. The seller could file an additional complaint with the Real Estate Commission.

124. Vicky is a real estate licensee whose friend Thomas is a home inspector with an excellent reputation. When Vicky has a buyer interested in a property, she sends them to Thomas, who pays her brokerage a $50 referral fee. Is this a legal practice?

A. Under no circumstances.
B. Yes, with the permission of Vicky's broker, and if the buyer knows of and agrees to the arrangement.
C. Yes, if the money is paid to Vicky through the broker-in-charge.
D. Yes, because small amounts of $50 or less are viewed as "honorariums," not fees or commissions.

125. Violations of license law tend to be which of the following?

A. Misdemeanors.

B. Felonies.

C. Civil violations that result in loss of license.

D. Civil violations that result in license suspension.

126. Can Lance, a successful provisional broker ambitious to move to the "next level," place a series of ads in the newspaper?

A. Yes, if his broker approves and the ads carry the name of the firm or broker in addition to Lance's.

B. Yes, if the ads only feature Lance's name and don't attempt to "borrow equity" by including the firm's name.

C. No, only firms can place ads.

D. No, other than classifieds, newspapers only accept ads from recognized advertising agencies.

127. Provisional broker Jackie Revson-Smith receives an earnest money deposit on a major property. What must she do with the check?

A. Deposit it into a trust account within three banking days.

B. Give it to her broker as soon as possible.

C. Present it to the seller within twenty-four hours.
D. Give it to the closing attorney to hold.

128. Brokers-in-charge are responsible for all of the following, EXCEPT:

A. Other brokers associated with his or her office.
B. Part-time provisional brokers.
C. Unlicensed support staff.
D. Trust accounts.

129. What actions are required of agents regarding "material facts?"

A. They are deemed confidential between the agent and client and should be protected.
B. They should generally be disclosed to the public although in some instances they may be considered minor or confidential and need not be disclosed.
C. Must always be disclosed.
D. Should be disclosed to serious buyers.

130. Sheila Rittenhouse knows that a property she hopes to sell is in foreclosure but fails to disclose the fact to potential buyers. Since she also knows this is a material fact, what violation is she guilty of?

A. Negligent omission.
B. Willful omission.
C. Negligent misrepresentation.
D. Willful misrepresentation.

131. The widening of a highway adjacent to a large subdivision has been proposed. There is a 20-foot buffer of mature trees sheltering the subdivision from the highway that is unlikely to be affected. Is this a material fact that needs to be disclosed.

A. No, since the subdivision is unlikely to be affected.
B. Yes, but only if the proposal passes.
C. No, it is not material since it does not pertain to the actual property or the ability of parties to perform as promised.
D. Yes, it must be disclosed.

132. Peggy buys her new home through Fred Priori an agent for Eastern Shore Realty. Fred assures Peggy her utility bills

will be low since the house is newly built, although he has no actual knowledge of the property's utility costs. Peggy's bills turn out to be much higher than average because of poor construction and materials. Is Fred guilty of any violation?

A. Yes, willful omission.
B. Yes, willful misrepresentation.
C. No, Fred made a reasonable assumption that simply turned out to be incorrect.
D. No, because Fred was not representing the builder.

133. John Martin assures real estate provisional broker, Alison Jacoby, that the home he's selling has hardwood floors throughout. This appears to be true, since it is exposed in all rooms but two of the bedrooms which have wall-to-wall carpeting. Alison passes these assurances on to buyers who later discover that one of the bedrooms does not have hardwood. What, if anything, is Allison guilty of.

A. She's not guilty of anything since she made a good faith effort to discover the truth and relied on the owner's assurance.
B. She's guilty of willful omission.
C. She's guilty of negligent misrepresentation.
D. She's guilty of willful misrepresentation.

134. A buyer enthusiastically tells a provisional broker that his reason for purchasing a particular property is its peace and quiet. The provisional broker knows construction will soon start on a major shopping center immediately behind the property but says nothing because the buyer didn't ask about future development or surrounding properties. What, if anything, is the provisional broker guilty of?

A. Nothing, the buyer didn't ask.
B. He is guilty of negligent misrepresentation.
C. He's guilty of willful omission.
D. He's guilty of willful misrepresentation.

135. When a real estate firm practices dual agency, which of these statements is true? 1) It must make full disclosure to all parties when an offer is written. 2) Dual agency must be explained to all parties at the first substantial contact.

A. Only #1 is true.
B. Only #2 is true.
C. Both #1 and #2 are true.
D. Neither #1 or #2 is true.

136. Which of these can define "first substantial contact?" 1) A person calls a real estate company to ask about a listed property. 2) A person attends an open house and speaks with an agent.

A. Only #1.
B. Only #2
C. Both #1 and #2.
D. Neither #1 or #2.

137. Which of these are relevant disclosures that must be addressed at time of first substantial contact? 1) The concept of agency is discussed and disclosed to members of the general public. 2) The agent's duties and responsibilities to clients are discussed and disclosed to members of the general public. 2) The agents duties and responibilities to clients are discussed and disclosed to members of the public.

A. Only #1.
B. Only #2.
C. Both #1 and #2.
D. Neither #1 or #2.

138. What is the violation when a broker should know that a statement about a material fact is false, but unintentionally misinforms a party in a real estate transaction?

A. Negligent misrepresentation.
B. Negligent omission.
C. Willful misrepresentation.
D. Willful omission.

139. What is the violation when a broker has information about a property that could impact the decision of a party in a real estate transaction but fails to disclose it?

A. Negligent misrepresentation.
B. Negligent omission.
C. Willful misrepresentation.
D. Willful omission.

140. Which of these statements about the Residential Property Disclosure Statement is true? 1) All sellers must provide the form to potential buyers. 2) Non-licensed owners selling their own property are exempt from this law.

A. Only #1.

B. Only #2.
C. Both #1 and #2.
D. Neither #1 or #2.

141. If the Residential Property Disclosure Statement is not delivered to a buyer before or at the time of offer, the buyer may cancel the offer under which of these circumstances?

A. If the seller does not give the buyer a copy of the form by the time he/she makes an offer to purchase the property.
B. If the buyer personally delivers his/her decision to cancel to the owner or the owner's agent within three calendar days following receipt of the Statement.
C. If the buyer personally delivers his/her decision to cancel to the owner or the owner's agent within three calendar days following receipt of the Statement, or the date of the contract, whichever occurs first.
D. All apply.

142. If the Disclosure Statement is properly delivered, when may potential buyers still cancel a contract? 1) If properly informed by the Disclosure Statement, buyers may not cancel any resulting contracts. 2) Under certain circumstances a buyer may still cancel a contract.

A. Only #1.
B. Only #2.
C. Both #1 and #2.
D. Neither #1 or #2.

143. Jerome Billings tells a buyer he represents that a property is served by city water. He believes this is true because several nearby homes he sold did have city water service, although this property does not. Is he guilty of any violation?

A. No, he had reasonable grounds for believing the statement was true and did not intend to misrepresent the facts.
B. Yes, although unintentional, he is still guilty of fraudulent misrepresentation.
C. Yes, he is guilty of willful misrepresentation because water service is a matter of record he had a fiduciary responsibility to verify.
D. Yes, he is guilt of negligent misrepresentation.

144. Which of these provisions must be included in North Carolina listing agreements? 1) A defined period of time for which they are active. 2) An automatic right of renewal.

A. #1 only.

B. #2 only.

C. Both #1 and #2.

D. Neither #1 or #2.

145. What is another name for a "quitclaim deed?"

A. A "limited warranty" deed.

B. A non-warranty deed.

C. A special warranty deed.

D. A "sweetheart sale" deed.

146. A North Carolina sales contract is viewed to be which of the following? 1) Bilateral. 2) Unilateral.

A. Only #1.

B. Only #2.

C. Both #1 and #2.

D. Neither #1 or #2.

147. What is the name of the clause in a listing agreement granting brokers a protection period beyond the expiration date? 1) An override clause. 2) An extender clause.

A. Only #1.
B. Only #2.
C. Both #1 and #2.
D. Neither #1 or #2.

148. What does "parol evidence" mean? 1) Oral agreements can be part of a contract. 2) Hand-written notes and addendums to a contract take precedence over printed portions.

A. Only #1.
B. Only #2.
C. Both #1 and #2.
D. Neither #1 or #2.

149. According to the North Carolina Statute of Fraud, which of these real estate agreements must be in writing? 1) Installment land contracts. 2) Sales contracts. 3) Property management agreements. 4) Lease or rental agreements of more than one year.

A. Only #1.
B. Both #1 and #2.
C. All of the above.
D. None of the above.

150. Which, if any, of these forms of buyer agency are allowable in North Carolina?

A. Non-exclusive buyer agency.
B. Exclusive buyer agency.
C. 24-hour buyer agency.
D. All of the above.

1. Which of the following activities does NOT require a real estate license?

A. Holding a real estate auction.
B. Selling property listed by other brokers or agencies.
C. Showing and selling one's own property.
D. Offering to buy properties on behalf of third parties.

2. In addition to selling one's own property, which of the following is also exempt from normal licensing requirements?

A. Acting as a guardian.
B. Acting as a trustee.
C. Acting as an attorney-in-fact.
D. Each of the above.

3. As long as it is specified as part of his or her duties, is it legal for an unlicensed salaried assistant to solicit listings for the broker?

A. Yes, if it is part of a written job description.

B. No, soliciting listings is the exclusive responsibility of the broker-in-charge.

C. Yes, because she is being paid a salary, not commissions.

D. No, active participation in real estate transactions requires a license.

4. Regarding the North Carolina Real Estate Commission, which of these statements is true?

A. A monthly salary plus expenses is paid to each member.

B. The North Carolina Association of Realtors® appoints the members.

C. The governor appoints members for a three-year term.

D. The Commission consists of seven members, all of whom must be active in real estate.

5. Which of these is a requirement to hold a real estate license in North Carolina? 1) Be a resident in good standing of the state. 2) Be at least 21 years old.

A. Only #1.

B. Only #2.

C. Neither #1 nor #2.

D. Both #1 and #2.

6. Licensees must notify the Real Estate Commission when which of these events occur?

A. There is a significant change in sales volume.
B. The business tradename has changed within the past ten days.
C. The business trade-name has changed within the past thirty days.
D. The licensee has received more than two traffic violations within the past eighteen months.

7. What is the first point at which a person may begin practicing real estate in North Carolina?

A. When a broker activates his or her license.
B. Upon successful completion of all course and exam work.
C. Upon completion of all education requirements.
D. Upon completion of course work requirements, successfully pass the exam and finish a recognized training program.

8. Which of these is required to be a broker-in-charge? 1) An active broker's license for the state of North Carolina. 2) Eight hours of continuing education each year.

A. Only #1.
B. Only #2.
C. Neither #1 nor #2.
D. Both #1 and #2.

9. What is "first substantial contact?"

A. An initial meeting to formalize a client-agency relationship.
B. A flexible standard for establishing client-agency relationships.
C. A new agent's first listing agreement or sales contract.
D. The point at which buyers or sellers must be given the North Carolina consumers' real estate disclosure document.

10. What is the definition of "dual agency" in North Carolina?

A. One firm represents both the buyer and the seller equally.
B. One firm represents the seller and another represents the buyer in the same transaction.

C. One firm represents both the buyer and the seller, but owes primary loyalty to seller.

D. One firm represents both the buyer and the seller, but owes primary loyalty to the buyer.

11. What is "designated agency" in North Carolina?

A. An alternative to dual agency.

B. A form of dual agency.

C. A minimum standard for client representation.

D. A form of representation that every company in NC must practice.

12. Who may practice designated agency?

A. Only one firm representing the buyer and seller in the same transaction.

B. Only two firms involved in the same transaction.

C. Only brokers.

D. Designated agency can be practiced by firms who do not practice dual agency in North Carolina.

13. Sally Lennox, a provisional broker working under the guidance of XYZ Real Estate Company, and with the owner's knowledge, deliberately fails to disclose that there is a dispute regarding title to the property. Who, if anyone, is liable in this situation?

A. No one is liable, since the dispute has not yet been resolved.
B. No one is liable since it's the buyer's responsibility to verify all representations, including title.
C. Only Sally is liable for her own actions.
D. Sally, the owner of the property, and the broker of XYZ Real Estate Company can all be held liable for Sally's lack of disclosure.

14. Which of the following is NOT a responsibility of a broker in North Carolina?

A. Disclosing property defects to the buyer.
B. Disclosing the seller's reasons for selling.
C. Accounting for all funds in the transaction.
D. Accounting for all funds belonging to both parties to a transaction.

15. Bill Timmons has a listing agreement to sell Paula Robinson's home. So far, Paula has turned down all offers, including those Bill thought were good. A new offer comes in the Friday before a weekend open house that's less than 70% of the asking price. Bill is certain it won't be accepted. What should he do?

A. Let Paula know he has a low offer, but deliver it to her anyway as soon as possible.
B. Tell the buyer it won't be accepted and refuse the offer.
C. Accept the offer, but don't present it.
D. Bill is a knowledgeable licensee, and is fully aware of what Paula will or will not accept. Bill should sit down with the buyer and negotiate for a higher price even at the risk of losing the sale for Paula.

16. In which of these capacities may an agent represent a client?

A. As a buyer's agent.
B. As a seller's subagent.
C. As a dual agent.
D. Any of these relationships is acceptable.

17. When may a provisional broker represent both the buyer and the seller in the same transaction?

A. Never.
B. If the provisional broker's broker approves.
C. If the provisional broker informs both parties.
D. None of these situations are acceptable.

18. Before a person can receive compensation in a real estate transaction, he or she must have which of these credentials?

A. An MLS membership.
B. An agency-exclusive agreement.
C. An active license.
D. An active or inactive license and certificates of completion for all course and examination requirements.

19. Phil Patterson is the broker-in-charge of Patterson-Stark Realty, a firm that practices dual agency. One of his agents, Barb, is working with a client as a buyer's agent. Another P&S agent, Rebecca, has one of the company's listings that Barb's client is interested in. How should they proceed to complete a transaction?

A. They cannot proceed because it would create conflicts of interest and confidentiality.

B. The listing relationship takes precedence, so Phil and Rebecca can only represent the seller and Barb can only represent the buyer.

C. If all parties agree, each can function as a dual agent.

D. As the listing firm, Phil, Rebecca and Barb must represent the seller.

20. Which of these is required to practice designated agency? 1) The firm has a policy of dual agency. 2) The firm has a policy of designated agency. 3) There are at least two licensees in the firm.

A. #1 only.

B. #2 only.

C. #1 and #2.

D. #1, #2 and #3.

21. At what point should associates at Bay Head Realty discuss the possibility of dual agency?

A. When they meet a fellow associate they'd like to partner with.

B. At the point of first substantial contact with a prospective client.

C. When one associate agrees to show some properties to a prospective client he met at an open house and who, as it turns out is also working with another agent in the firm.

D. As soon as a new client signs an agreement.

22. What is the rule describing brokers and trust accounts?

A. Brokers may have trust accounts if and as needed.

B. Firms, not brokers, hold trust accounts.

C. A broker must have a trust account for every client.

D. Brokers must always have a trust account.

23. If a dispute over monies in a trust account arises between a buyer and seller, what action must a broker take?

A. Hold the monies in the trust account until the parties reach agreement.

B. Turn the monies over to an attorney.

C. Return all monies to the buyer.

D. Split the monies between the buyer and seller.

24. Which of the following is NOT considered trust money?

A. Earnest money.
B. Broker funds for service charges.
C. Down payments.
D. Funds for final settlement.

25. Are interest-bearing trust accounts permissible?

A. No, any interest that accrues in a trust account goes to the state to fund real estate programs and studies.
B. Yes, and the interest is split between the buyer and seller as well as the broker to cover administrative expenses.
C. Yes, and the interest is split between the seller and broker.
D. Yes, in certain conditions.

26. What is the maximum amount of personal funds a provisional broker may keep in a trust account?

A. $100.00
B. $300.00
C. Enough to cover service charges.
D. None of the above.

27. What is the deadline for depositing monies into a trust account?

A. The same day they are received.
B. Within three banking days of receipt.
C. As stipulated in the contract.
D. It varies with the type of deposit (earnest money, downpayment, etc.).

28. When may a licensee pay a referral fee?

A. If it is $50 or less.
B. If there is a written agreement between the parties.
C. If it is to a licensee.
D. Never.

29. When it comes to financing theory, what kind of state is North Carolina?

A. A title theory state.
B. A lien theory state.

C. Both 1 and 2.
D. Neither 1 nor 2.

30. Rita Spenser is a provisional broker completing a transaction with her seller when she discovers an error on the closing statement. Who is responsible for ensuring the accuracy of closing statements?

A. Rita, as the provisional broker, is responsible.
B. Rita's broker is responsible.
C. The title company.
D. The attorney.

31. Bob is a recent college graduate planning on a career in real estate. Bob is working as an unlicensed assistant in a real estate office while he is studying for his real estate exam. Although not yet licensed, he proceeds to show a property for the experience even though it's a violation of real estate law. Who is subject to disciplinary action?

A. Bob.
B. The principal of the firm.
C. Bob's broker.

D. No one, since Bob is not yet licensed and thus exempt from the rules.

32. There is strong evidence a licensee embezzled from his firm. What action may the Real Estate Commission take?

A. None, unless the embezzlement was from a trust account and directly related to real estate transactions.
B. If found guilty, he can be fined by the Commission.
C. He can be prosecuted by the Commission and, if found guilty, is subject to criminal penalties including possible jail time.
D. He can be prosecuted by the Commission and, if found guilty, is subject to noncriminal
licensure penalties.

33. An unhappy seller took a licensee to court which found in the seller's favor. Which of the following would NOT occur as a result?

A. The licensee could be fined.
B. The court could recommend disciplinary action against the licensee to the chairman of the Real Estate Commission.
C. The court could revoke his or her license.

D. The seller could file an additional complaint with the Real Estate Commission.

34. Vicky is a real estate licensee whose friend Thomas is a home inspector with an excellent reputation. When Vicky has a buyer interested in a property, she sends them to Thomas, who pays her brokerage a $50 referral fee. Is this a legal practice?

A. Under no circumstances.
B. Yes, with the permission of Vicky's broker, and if the buyer knows of and agrees to the arrangement.
C. Yes, if the money is paid to Vicky through the broker-in-charge.
D. Yes, because small amounts of $50 or less are viewed as "honorariums," not fees or commissions.

35. Violations of license law tend to be which of the following?

A. Misdemeanors.
B. Felonies.
C. Civil violations that result in loss of license.
D. Civil violations that result in license suspension.

36. Can Lance, a successful provisional broker ambitious to move to the "next level," place a series of ads in the newspaper?

A. Yes, if his broker approves and the ads carry the name of the firm or broker in addition to Lance's.
B. Yes, if the ads only feature Lance's name and don't attempt to "borrow equity" by including the firm's name.
C. No, only firms can place ads.
D. No, other than classifieds, newspapers only accept ads from recognized advertising agencies.

37. Provisional broker Jackie Revson-Smith receives an earnest money deposit on a major property. What must she do with the check?

A. Deposit it into a trust account within three banking days.
B. Give it to her broker as soon as possible.
C. Present it to the seller within twenty-four hours.
D. Give it to the closing attorney to hold.

38. Brokers-in-charge are responsible for all of the following, EXCEPT:

A. Other brokers associated with his or her office.
B. Part-time provisional brokers.
C. Unlicensed support staff.
D. Trust accounts.

39. What actions are required of agents regarding "material facts?"

A. They are deemed confidential between the agent and client and should be protected.
B. They should generally be disclosed to the public although in some instances they may be considered minor or confidential and need not be disclosed.
C. Must always be disclosed.
D. Should be disclosed to serious buyers.

40. Sheila Rittenhouse knows that a property she hopes to sell is in foreclosure but fails to disclose the fact to potential buyers. Since she also knows this is a material fact, what violation is she guilty of?

A. Negligent omission.
B. Willful omission.
C. Negligent misrepresentation.
D. Willful misrepresentation.

41. The widening of a highway adjacent to a large subdivision has been proposed. There is a 20-foot buffer of mature trees sheltering the subdivision from the highway that is unlikely to be affected. Is this a material fact that needs to be disclosed.

A. No, since the subdivision is unlikely to be affected.
B. Yes, but only if the proposal passes.
C. No, it is not material since it does not pertain to the actual property or the ability of parties to perform as promised.
D. Yes, it must be disclosed.

42. Peggy buys her new home through Fred Priori an agent for Eastern Shore Realty. Fred assures Peggy her utility bills will be low since the house is newly built, although he has no actual knowledge of the property's utility costs. Peggy's bills turn out to be much higher than average because of poor construction and materials. Is Fred guilty of any violation?

A. Yes, willful omission.
B. Yes, willful misrepresentation.
C. No, Fred made a reasonable assumption that simply turned out to be incorrect.
D. No, because Fred was not representing the builder.

43. John Martin assures real estate provisional broker, Alison Jacoby, that the home he's selling has hardwood floors throughout. This appears to be true, since it is exposed in all rooms but two of the bedrooms which have wall-to-wall. Alison passes these assurances on to the buyers who later discover that one of the bedrooms does not have hardwood. What, if anything is Alison guilty of?

A. She's not guilty of anything since she made a good faith effort to discover the truth and relied on the owner's assurance.
B. She's guilty of willful omission.
C. She's guilty of negligent misrepresentation.
D. She's guilty of willful misrepresentation.

44. A buyer enthusiastically tells a provisional broker that his reason for purchasing a particular property is its peace and quiet. The provisional broker knows construction will soon start on a major shopping center immediately behind

the property but says nothing because the buyer didn't ask about future development or surrounding properties. What, if anything, is the provisional broker guilty of?

A. Nothing, the buyer didn't ask.
B. He is guilty of negligent misrepresentation.
C. He's guilty of willful omission.
D. He's guilty of willful misrepresentation.

45. When a real estate firm practices dual agency, which of these statements is true? 1) It must make full disclosure to all parties when an offer is written. 2) Dual agency must be explained to all parties at the first substantial contact.

A. Only #1 is true.
B. Only #2 is true.
C. Both #1 and #2 are true.
D. Neither #1 or #2 is true.

46. Which of these can define "first substantial contact?" 1) A person calls a real estate company to ask about a listed property. 2) A person attends an open house and speaks with an agent.

A. Only #1.
B. Only #2
C. Both #1 and #2.
D. Neither #1 or #2.

47. Which of these are relevant disclosures that must be addressed at time of first substantial contact? 1) The concept of agency is discussed and disclosed to members of the general public. 2) The agent's duties and responsibilities to clients are discussed and disclosed to members of the public.

A. Only #1.
B. Only #2.
C. Both #1 and #2.
D. Neither #1 or #2.

48. What is the violation when a broker should know that a statement about a material fact is false, but unintentionally misinforms a party in a real estate transaction?

A. Negligent misrepresentation.
B. Negligent omission.
C. Willful misrepresentation.
D. Willful omission.

49. What is the violation when a broker has information about a property that could impact the decision of a party in a real estate transaction but fails to disclose it?

A. Negligent misrepresentation.
B. Negligent omission.
C. Willful misrepresentation.
D. Willful omission.

50. Which of these statements about the Residential Property Disclosure Statement is true? 1) All sellers must provide the form to potential buyers. 2) Non-licensed owners selling their own property are exempt from this law.

A. Only #1.
B. Only #2.
C. Both #1 and #2.
D. Neither #1 or #2.

51. If the Residential Property Disclosure Statement is not delivered to a buyer before or at the time of offer, the buyer may cancel the offer under which of these circumstances?

A. If the seller does not give the buyer a copy of the form by the time he/she makes an offer to purchase the property.
B. If the buyer personally delivers his/her decision to cancel to the owner or the owner's agent within three calendar days following receipt of the Statement.
C. If the buyer personally delivers his/her decision to cancel to the owner or the owner's agent within three calendar days following receipt of the Statement, or the date of the contract, whichever occurs first.
D. All apply.

52. If the Disclosure Statement is properly delivered, when may potential buyers still cancel a contract? 1) If properly informed by the Disclosure Statement, buyers may not cancel any resulting contracts. 2) Under certain circumstances a buyer may still cancel a contract.

A. Only #1.
B. Only #2.
C. Both #1 and #2.
D. Neither #1 or #2.

53. Jerome Billings tells a buyer he represents that a property is served by city water. He believes this is true because several nearby homes he sold did have city water service, although this property does not. Is he guilty of any violation?

A. No, he had reasonable grounds for believing the statement was true and did not intend to misrepresent the facts.
B. Yes, although unintentional, he is still guilty of fraudulent misrepresentation.
C. Yes, he is guilty of willful misrepresentation because water service is a matter of record he had a fiduciary responsibility to verify.
D. Yes, he is guilt of negligent misrepresentation.

54. Which of these provisions must be included in North Carolina listing agreements? 1) A defined period of time for which they are active. 2) An automatic right of renewal.

A. #1 only.
B. #2 only.
C. Both #1 and #2.
D. Neither #1 or #2.

55. What is another name for a "quitclaim deed?"

A. A "limited warranty" deed.
B. A non-warranty deed.
C. A special warranty deed.
D. A "sweetheart sale" deed.

56. A North Carolina sales contract is viewed to be which of the following? 1) Bilateral. 2) Unilateral.

A. Only #1.
B. Only #2.
C. Both #1 and #2.
D. Neither #1 or #2.

57. What is the name of the clause in a listing agreement granting brokers a protection period beyond the expiration date? 1) An override clause. 2) An extender clause.

A. Only #1.
B. Only #2.
C. Both #1 and #2.

D. Neither #1 or #2.

58. What does "parol evidence" mean? 1) Oral agreements can be part of a contract. 2) Hand-written notes and addendums to a contract take precedence over printed portions.

A. Only #1.
B. Only #2.
C. Both #1 and #2.
D. Neither #1 or #2.

59. According to the North Carolina Statute of Fraud, which of these real estate agreements must be in writing? 1) Installment land contracts. 2) Sales contracts. 3) Property management agreements. 4) Lease or rental agreements of more than one year.

A. Only #1.
B. Both #1 and #2.
C. All of the above.
D. None of the above.

60. Which, if any, of these forms of buyer agency are allowable in North Carolina?

A. Non-exclusive buyer agency.
B. Exclusive buyer agency.
C. 24-hour buyer agency.
D. All of the above.

61. Melissa is listing a house for sale and needs to know its square footage. Which of these methods is acceptable?

A. Consulting tax records.
B. Consulting previous sales or listing agreements.
C. Measuring the house herself.
D. All of the above.

62. Melissa's new listing is a standard two-story home. In calculating square footage, she can measure the outside of the house and deduct which of the following?

A. Closets.
B. Stairs.
C. Any space with standing headroom of less than five feet.
D. All of the above.

63. Which of these characteristics must be present to include a space in square footage calculations.

A. It must be heated and cooled by a conventional HVAC system.
B. It must be intended to be used as a living area.
C. It must be finished.
D. All of the above.

64. Melissa's partner, Terri, has another listing that includes a 600 square-foot guest house at the rear of the property. According to the Real Estate Commission's guidelines, how should it be reported?

A. It may be listed as additional space, but not included as part of the primary home's square footage.
B. It can be included in the main home's square footage as long if qualified by expressions such as, "3,700 square feet of total living area."
C. It should not be combined with the main house in any way.
D. Any of these options is allowable.

65. Mark and Phyllis want to list their home. It has a huge bonus room over the garage they want to include as part of the square footage. Under what conditions may they do so?

A. A minimum percentage of its total space must have a ceiling height of at least seven feet.
B. Walls, floors and ceilings must all be finished and the room must be directly accessible from inside the home.
C. It must have a conventional heating system.
D. All of the above.

66. Which, if either, of these elements MUST be in every buyer agency agreement? 1) A written termination date. 2) A clause stating the agent will not discriminate.

A. Only #1.
B. Only #2.
C. Both #1 and #2.
D. Neither #1 or #2.

67. Rob wants to cancel his contract to buy Peter's property. Assuming all other conditions are met, to whom must Rob give written notice? 1) The owner's agent. 2) The owner.

A. Only #1.
B. Only #2.
C. Either #1 or #2.
D. Neither #1 or #2.

68. Which type of listing agreement provides the most protection for brokers?

A. An open listing.
B. An exclusive right-to-sell listing.
C. An exclusive agency listing.
D. A net listing.

69. When are licensees allowed to draft simple paragraphs and addendums to contracts for their clients?

A. Never.
B. When asked to do so and all parties initial the change or addendum.
C. At the request of their broker-in-charge.
D. With the approval of their broker-in-charge.

70. Nate is using an attorney-approved preprinted offer/sales contract for his client. Which of the following should NOT be included in the agreement's language?

A. Agency disclosures to the other side of the transaction.
B. How the buyer intends to use the property.
C. How the agent is to be compensated.
D. Who is responsible for paying closing costs.

71. Deborah sees a property she likes and makes an offer with a $2,500 earnest money binder. The owner makes a counter offer, but Deborah then sees another property she likes better. Which of these situations apply?

A. Deborah is entitled to have her money returned immediately.
B. The seller is entitled to the binder, since Deborah backed out of the agreement.
C. The seller can decide to accept Deborah's first offer and thus create a binding contract.
D. The broker is entitled to hold Deborah's money for thirty days as a "contingency contract."

72. A property is going to closing with delinquent property taxes. What is the correct entry on the closing documents?

A. Debit seller and credit buyer the entire amount.
B. Debit seller the entire amount.
C. Prorate the entire amount between seller and buyer.
D. Deduct taxes owed from purchase price.

73. How would an attorney's closing fee of $450 typically be entered on the closing statement?

A. Buyer is debited $450.
B. Seller is debited $450.
C. Debit seller and buyer $225 each.
D. Debit buyer $450 and seller $450.

74. Jake and Nancy Lopresso have annual association dues of $600 and they paid the entire year in advance on January 2. They've sold their home and will close on April 30. How will this fee be reflected on the closing statement?

A. The seller will be credited $400 and the buyer debited $400.
B. The seller will be debited $200 and the buyer credited $400.
C. The seller will be credited $600 and the buyer debited $600.

D. The seller will be debited $600 and the buyer credited $600.

75. A homeowner is allowing the buyers to assume his existing mortgage of $65,000 at 8%. Payments are due on the first of the month, but closing is on August 10th. What portion of the August interest will be owed by the buyer and what portion by the seller at closing to the nearest dollar?

A. The seller will be credited $144 and the buyer debited $144.
B. The seller will be credited $289 and the buyer debited $289.
C. The seller will be debited $144 and the buyer credited $144.
D. The seller will be debited $289 and the buyer credited $289.

76. Bill and Joan Wellbridge are selling their home for $125,000 and the buyers are assuming their existing $67,215 mortgage. How will the loan assumption amount be entered in the closing statement?

A. The seller will be credited $57,785 and the buyer will be debited $57,785.
B. The seller will be debited $67,215 and the buyer credited $67,215.
C. The seller will be debited $57,785 and the buyer credited $57,785.

D. The seller will be credited $67,215 and the buyer debited $67,215.

77. Rick is selling one of the rental properties he owns. It brings $570 a month in rent, which is paid on the first of every month and closing is on the 10th of the month. How would the entries read?

A. Debit the seller $380 and credit the buyer $380.
B. Credit the seller $190 and debit the buyer $190.
C. Debit the seller $190 and credit the buyer $190.
D. Credit the seller $380 and debit the buyer $380.

78. Rick has also agreed to sell another income property that rents for $1,200 a month. Rent is due on the 1st of the month and Rick is closing on the 7th, but has not yet collected that month's rent. How will the closing entries read in this situation?

A. The seller will be debited $280 and the buyer credited $280.
B. The buyer will be credited $920 and the seller debited 280.
C. The buyer will be debited $920 and the seller credited $920.
D. The seller will be credited $280 and the buyer debited $280.

79. A buyer made an EMD (earnest money deposit) of $2,500 on a house he's now closing on. How will the EMD entry read on the closing document?

A. The buyer will be debited $2,500.
B. The Seller will be debited $2,500.
C. The seller will be credited $2,500.
D. The buyer will be credited $2,500.

80. The buyers of an existing home have secured an 80% loan on the $95,000 property. How will the entries for the loan read in the closing documents?

A. Credit buyer $76,000 and debit the seller $19,000.
B. Credit the buyer $76,000
C. Credit the buyer $76,000 and debit the seller $76,0000.
D. Debit the buyer $76,000.

81. A couple is selling their house for $137,500 on which they have a mortgage balance of $79,315. How will this portion of the transaction be entered on the closing documents?

A. Debit the seller $79,315 and credit the buyer $79,315.

B. Credit the seller $58,185.
C. Debit the seller $79,315.
D. Credit the seller $79,315.

82. To help a young couple purchase their home, sellers are giving the buyers a $25,000 purchase money mortgage (PMM). What are the entries?

A. Debit the sellers $25,000 and credit that amount to the buyers.
B. Debit the sellers $25,000.
C. Credit the buyers $25,000.
D. None of the above.

83. The obligations of an apartment lessor and lesee are governed by which state law?

A. The North Carolina Landlord and Tenant Act.
B. The North Carolina Fair Housing Statute.
C. The North Carolina Apartment and Renters Act.
D. The North Carolina Residential Agreements Act.

84. Which of these is a provision of the North Carolina Residential Rental Agreements Act?

A. A fair and equitable security deposit must be charged before a lease is considered valid.

B. Tenants have the right to withhold rent if heat or other basic services are unavailable for more than three days.

C. Landlords must provide and maintain premises that are fit and habitable.

D. Leases in shopping centers may be cancelled by tenants if business is poor.

85. Which act requires tenants to properly maintain his or her dwelling unit?

A. The North Carolina Tenants Responsibilities Act.

B. The North Carolina Residential Rental Agreements Act.

C. The Fair Housing Opportunity Act.

D. The Joint Tenants and Landlords Responsibilities Statutes.

86. How does the sale of a property with long-term lease agreements affect existing tenants?

A. The tenants must negotiate new leases with the new owner(s).
B. The new owners may terminate existing leases with three months notice.
C. It has no effect on the current tenants.
D. The tenants may terminate their leases with three months notice to the new owners.

87. Which of the following statements is NOT TRUE of the Tenant Security Deposit Act?

A. Landlords must make requested repairs within thirty days.
B. Security deposits cannot exceed two months' rent.
C. Security deposits belong to the renter but are under control of the landlord.
D. Landlords must return deposits within a specified period of time after a tenant vacates a unit or specify reasons why all or any portion of the deposit is being withheld.

88. Which of the following is NOT TRUE about the ways in which a security deposit may be handled?

A. A real estate agent may place the deposit in a trust account.
B. A landlord may place the deposit in a trust account.

C. A landlord may use the deposit to obtain a bond as a guarantee.
D. A real estate agent may use the deposit to obtain a bond as a guarantee.

89. Which of the following are considered "ordinary wear and tear" when a tenant moves out at the end of his lease and gives proper notice? 1) Windows need cleaning. 2) Walls have crayon marks. 3) Plumbing fixtures leak. 4) Drapes or blinds are worn.

A. All are normal wear and tear.
B. Only #1, #3 and #4.
C. Only #3 and #4.
D. None.

90. Jim moves out of his apartment before the lease expires, but leaves it in excellent condition. The landlord is able to find a new tenant in only three days. How much of Jim's security deposit may he keep?

A. Only that amount equal to lost rent and the cost of securing a new tenant.
B. Only that portion equal to lost rent.

C. All of it.

D. None of it.

91. Rachel Prentiss owns a beach-front property she rents out. What are her responsibilities under the North Carolina Vacation Rental Act?

A. Provide a fit and habitable premises.

B. Place all deposits and other monies received in advance in a trust or escrow account.

C. Have written rental agreements.

D. All of the above.

92. Which of the following is NOT an example of ordinary wear and tear?

A. Paint that's peeling.

B. Plumbing fixtures leak.

C. Broken plumbing fixtures.

D. Carpet that needs cleaning.

93. What is the definition of a time-share?

A. Five or more time periods of use.
B. Five or more separate periods of use over five or more years.
C. Beachfront property rented out to different tenants over five or more years.
D. Vacation property intended for rental for five years or less.

94. Which of the following is required to develop a time-share in North Carolina?

A. A certificate of registration and a project broker.
B. A certificate of registration from the state.
C. A project broker.
D. A real estate license.

95. Which is true regarding time-share developers and registration certificates?

A. It is the project broker's responsibility to obtain registrations.
B. Registrations must be obtained before 10% of the units are committed.
C. Registrations must be obtained by developers before any units are offered for sale or they are guilty of a felony.
D. #1 and #2 are both true.

96. Who is responsible for recording the instruments conveying ownership in timeshare units?

A. The developer.
B. The registrar.
C. The project broker.
D. Either the developer or the project broker.

97. Every purchaser of a time-share unit is entitled to which of the following?

A. A guarantee that they will be able to trade weeks with other owners.
B. A free weekend to evaluate the property.
C. A three-day right of rescission to make certain they want to complete the transaction.
D. None of the above.

98. How long must a purchaser's monies be kept in a time-share escrow account?

A. At least five days.
B. At least seven days.
C. At least ten days.
D. At least thirty days.

99. Time-share project brokers who violate provisions of G.S. 93A are subject to disciplinary action by which of the following?

A. The SEC.
B. The Justice Department.
C. The attorney general.
D. The Real Estate Commission.

100. Which of the following is NOT an obligation of developers under the North Carolina Condominium Act of 1986?

A. Give prospective buyers the right of rescission.
B. Arrange financing for prospective buyers.
C. Give buyers a set of bylaws.
D. File a plan of the property or plat map.

101. Which of the following IS an obligation of the seller of a condominium who is not the developer and owns a unit built after 1986?

A. Provide dues and assessments information to the buyer.
B. Provide the buyer with the original or updated plat map or plan of the property.
C. Give the buyer a seven day right of rescission.
D. All of the above.

102. Who prepares the bylaws that govern the operation of a condominium community?

A. The developer.
B. The condominium's board of managers.
C. The condominium board's executive committee.
D. The registrar in the county where the condominium is located.

103. In terms of house construction, what does the home's foundation rest on?

A. Studs.

B. Sills.
C. Footings.
D. Joists.

104. What is the term for columns that add extra support to the flooring between foundation walls.

A. Interior footings.
B. Piers.
C. Support walls.
D. Support joists.

105. Which of these statements about a home's insulation materials is true? 1) A higher "R-value" means the material is more resistant to the transfer of heat. 2) The higher the R-value, the less the material resists heat transfer. 3) The most efficient R-value should be in the roof?

A. #1 only.
B. #2 only.
C. Both #1 and #2.
D. Both #1 and #3.

106. What determines the pitch of a roof?

A. The ridge beam.
B. Ceiling joists.
C. Rafters.
D. Piers.

107. What is the name for the wooden or composite material that covers the exterior wall and roof framing of a home?

A. Siding.
B. Sheathing.
C. Vapor barrier.
D. Façade.

108. Which of these home styles is the most economical to build?

A. A two-story home.
B. A one-and-a-half story home.
C. A ranch home.
D. A ranch home with basement.

109. What document does a local building inspector issue stating that a home is complete?

A. A certificate of completion.
B. A Certificate of approval.
C. A certificate habitability.
D. A certificate of occupancy.

110. What is the term for the ordinance that specifies minimum standards of construction and materials?

A. A building code.
B. A construction code.
C. Variances.
D. Covenants.

111. What is the name for a heavy material placed on top of the sheathing to insulate and waterproof the roof?

A. Roofing boards.
B. Roofing felt.
C. Shingles.

D. Insulation.

112. What is "slab?"

A. Dirt graded in preparation for foundation work.
B. Bricks delivered on palates prior to installation.
C. Concrete material.
D. Wooden decking material.

113. What is the name for an insurance policy that covers more risks than the basic form, including such hazards such as weight of ice, snow or sleet, falling objects, damage from accidental discharges of water or artificially-generated electricity? 1) Broad form insurance. 2) Extended all-risk insurance.

A. Either #1 or #2.
B. Neither #1 or #2.
C. #1 only.
D. #2 only.

114. What is the most commonly-used, all-risk policy used today?

A. HO-5
B. HO-4
C. HO-3
D. HO-2

115. What kind of policy provides protection against damage to a homeowner's property and improvements? 1) Property insurance. 2) Casualty insurance.

A. Neither #1 or #2.
B. Either #1 or #2.
C. #1 only.
D. #2 only.

116. What is the name of the clause in most insurance policies that requires a homeowner to maintain fire insurance equal to or greater than 80% of his property's replacement cost? 1) Coinsurance clause. 2) Subrogation clause.

A. #1 only.
B. #2 only.

C. Both #1 and #2.
D. Neither #1 or #2.

117. What is the term for provisions excluding certain hazards from coverage under a particular insurance policy?

A. Exclusions.
B. Riders.
C. Endorsements.
D. Both #2 and #3.

118. Which of these is covered by most standard homeowner policies? 1) Liability. 2) Fire. 3) Theft.

A. Only #1.
B. Only #1 and #2.
C. All of the above.
D. Only #2 and #3

119. A $100,000 property sustains $60,000 in fire damage, but is only covered for $40,000. Under the terms of the

insurance policy's 80% coinsurance requirement how much will the insured receive?

A. $60,000
B. $48,000
C. $40,000
D. $30,000.00

120. Ross and Amanda Troutman own a $199,999 home that's insured with a $120,000 policy that includes an 80% coinsurance requirement. What amount will they receive from the insurance company if they sustain a loss of $175,000?

A. $165,000
B. $120,000
C. $175,000
D. $131,250.66

121. Rachel Prentiss owns a beach-front property she rents out. What are her responsibilities under the North Carolina Vacation Rental Act?

A. Provide a fit and habitable premises.

B. Place all deposits and other monies received in advance in a trust or escrow account.

C. Have written rental agreements.

D. All of the above.

122. Which of the following is NOT an example of ordinary wear and tear?

A. Paint that's peeling.

B. Plumbing fixtures leak.

C. Broken plumbing fixtures.

D. Carpet that needs cleaning.

123. What is the definition of a time-share?

A. Five or more time periods of use.

B. Five or more separate periods of use over five or more years.

C. Beachfront property rented out to different tenants over five or more years.

D. Vacation property intended for rental for five years or less.

124. Which of the following is required to develop a time-share in North Carolina?

A. A certificate of registration and a project broker.
B. A certificate of registration from the state.
C. A project broker.
D. A real estate license.

125. Which is true regarding time-share developers and registration certificates?

A. It is the project broker's responsibility to obtain registrations.
B. Registrations must be obtained before 10% of the units are committed.
C. Registrations must be obtained by developers before any units are offered for sale or they are guilty of a felony.
D. #1 and #2 are both true.

126. Who is responsible for recording the instruments conveying ownership in timeshare units?

A. The developer.
B. The registrar.
C. The project broker.

D. Either the developer or the project broker.

127. Every purchaser of a time-share unit is entitled to which of the following?

A. A guarantee that they will be able to trade weeks with other owners.
B. A free weekend to evaluate the property.
C. A three-day right of rescission to make certain they want to complete the transaction.
D. None of the above.

128. How long must a purchaser's monies be kept in a time-share escrow account?

A. At least five days.
B. At least seven days.
C. At least ten days.
D. At least thirty days.

129. Time-share project brokers who violate provisions of G.S. 93A are subject to disciplinary action by which of the following?

A. The SEC.
B. The Justice Department.
C. The attorney general.
D. The Real Estate Commission.

130. Which of the following is NOT an obligation of developers under the North Carolina Condominium Act of 1986?

A. Give prospective buyers the right of rescission.
B. Arrange financing for prospective buyers.
C. Give buyers a set of bylaws.
D. File a plan of the property or plat map.

131. Which of the following IS an obligation of the seller of a condominium who is not the developer and owns a unit built after 1986?

A. Provide dues and assessments information to the buyer.

B. Provide the buyer with the original or updated plat map or plan of the property.
C. Give the buyer a seven day right of rescission.
D. All of the above.

132. Who prepares the bylaws that govern the operation of a condominium community?

A. The developer.
B. The condominium's board of managers.
C. The condominium board's executive committee.
D. The registrar in the county where the condominium is located.

133. In terms of house construction, what does the home's foundation rest on?

A. Studs.
B. Sills.
C. Footings.
D. Joists.

134. What is the term for columns that add extra support to the flooring between foundation walls.

A. Interior footings.
B. Piers.
C. Support walls.
D. Support joists.

135. Which of these statements about a home's insulation materials is true? 1) A higher "R-value" means the material is more resistant to the transfer of heat. 2) The higher the R-value, the less the material resists heat transfer. 3) The most efficient R-value should be in the roof.

A. #1 only.
B. #2 only.
C. Both #1 and #2.
D. Both #1 and #3.

136. What determines the pitch of a roof?

A. The ridge beam.
B. Ceiling joists.
C. Rafters.

D. Piers.

137. What is the name for the wooden or composite material that covers the exterior wall and roof framing of a home?

A. Siding.
B. Sheathing.
C. Vapor barrier.
D. Façade.

138. Which of these home styles is the most economical to build?

A. A two-story home.
B. A one-and-a-half story home.
C. A ranch home.
D. A ranch home with basement.

139. What document does a local building inspector issue stating that a home is complete?

A. A certificate of completion.

B. A Certificate of approval.
C. A certificate habitability.
D. A certificate of occupancy.

140. What is the term for the ordinance that specifies minimum standards of construction and materials?

A. A building code.
B. A construction code.
C. Variances.
D. Covenants.

141. What is the name for a heavy material placed on top of the sheathing to insulate and waterproof the roof?

A. Roofing boards.
B. Roofing felt.
C. Shingles.
D. Insulation.

142. What is "slab?"

A. Dirt graded in preparation for foundation work.
B. Bricks delivered on palates prior to installation.
C. Concrete material.
D. Wooden decking material.

143. What is the name for an insurance policy that covers more risks than the basic form, including such hazards such as weight of ice, snow or sleet, falling objects, damage from accidental discharges of water or artificially-generated electricity? 1) Broad form insurance. 2) Extended all-risk insurance.

A. Either #1 or #2.
B. Neither #1 or #2.
C. #1 only.
D. #2 only.

144. What is the most commonly-used, all-risk policy used today?

A. HO-5
B. HO-4
C. HO-3
D. HO-2

145. What kind of policy provides protection against damage to a homeowner's property and improvements? 1) Property insurance. 2) Casualty insurance.

A. Neither #1 or #2.
B. Either #1 or #2.
C. #1 only.
D. #2 only.

146. What is the name of the clause in most insurance policies that requires a homeowner to maintain fire insurance equal to or greater than 80% of his property's replacement cost? 1) Coinsurance clause. 2) Subrogation clause.

A. #1 only.
B. #2 only.
C. Both #1 and #2.
D. Neither #1 or #2.

147. What is the term for provisions excluding certain hazards from coverage under a particular insurance policy?

A. Exclusions.
B. Riders.
C. Endorsements.
D. Both #2 and #3.

148. Which of these is covered by most standard homeowner policies? 1) Liability. 2) Fire. 3) Theft.

A. Only #1.
B. Only #1 and #2.
C. All of the above.
D. Only #2 and #3

149. A $100,000 property sustains $60,000 in fire damage, but is only covered for $40,000. Under the terms of the insurance policy's 80% coinsurance requirement how much will the insured receive?

A. $60,000
B. $48,000
C. $40,000

D. $30,000.00

150. Ross and Amanda Troutman own a $199,999 home that's insured with a $120,000 policy that includes an 80% coinsurance requirement. What amount will they receive from the insurance company if they sustain a loss of $175,000?

A. $165,000
B. $120,000
C. $175,000
D. $131,250.66

1. The fastest way to calculate one month's interest on a real estate loan with an interest rate of 7.2% interest per annum is to multiply the principal balance by:

A.   0.006
B.   0.6
C.   7.2% and divide by 12
D.   12 and divide by 7.2%

2. A duplex with a fair market value of $20,000 and an outstanding loan balance of $12,000 was exchanged for a four-plex with a market value of $35,000 and an outstanding $18,000 loan balance. The owner of the duplex would pay in cash or secondary financing

A. $6,100
B. $8,100
C. $9,100
D. $15,100

3. Mr. Brown, licensed broker, took an offer from Mr. Green on land for $6,000 with the following terms: $2,000 down and purchase money trust deed and note for the

balance, payable $70 per month including interest at 7.2%.
If the offer was accepted by the seller, what is the balance of
the loan after the first 3 months payment?

A. $3,186
B. $3,467
C. $3,861
D. $3,790

4. After subtracting $140.00 escrow fees and 6% commission
on gross sales price, a seller receives $13,584.00. What is the
selling price?

A. $12,770
B. $14,440
C. $14,540
D. $14,600

5. Keith Johnson purchased a property at 20% less than the
listed price and later sold the property for the original listed
price. What was the percentage of profit?

A.   10%
B.   20%
C.   25%

D.   40%

6. Lots "A", "B" and "C" sold for a total price of $39,000. If lot "B" was priced at $6,400 more than lot "A", and lot "C" was priced at $7,100 more than lot "B", the price of lot "A" was:

A. $13,000.00
B. $6,366.67
C. $5,433.33
D. $4,633.00

7. Assume a real estate salesman sold a residence for $31,000. If the broker's commission was 6% and the salesman was to receive 45% of the total commission for selling the property, the salesman would receive:

A. $837.70
B. $959.95
C. $1,860.00
D.   None of the above

8. Smith and Allen wish to exchange real property. Smith owns a property valued at $150,000 against which there is a $35,000 trust deed. Allen owns property worth $105,000 on which there is an existing first trust deed of $25,000 and a

second trust deed of $20,000. Allen has $15,000 in cash which he is willing to pay towards the exchange. If Smith is willing to accept a second trust deed and note from Allen in order to effect the exchange, the amount of the note would be:

A. $20,000
B. $40,000
C. $50,000
D. $70,000

9. An apartment house property costs $240,000 and this price has been verified to be an accurate estimate of the property value. In comparable circumstances it is also verified that the owner may use a 10% capitalization rate to the purchase price in determining his net income. Should there be a 10% increase in rental income with no increase in the owner's expense and should the capitalization rate of the property be increased to 12%, what would be the estimated value of the property be?

A. $220,000
B. $240,000
C. $264,000
D. None of the above

10. Able purchased a $15,000 home. His down payment amounted to 6 2/3% of the purchase price; the balance was carried as a first trust deed bearing interest at 8.4% per annum. The principal is to be repaid at $50.00 per month. A three-year insurance policy costs $72.00; the property taxes are $360.00 per year. Able is required to make a proportionate monthly payment to a loan trust fund for these items. The total amount of the first monthly payment most nearly would be:

A. $267
B. $182
C. $186
D. $188

11. A husband and wife own a vacation home in the mountains. The annual taxes on the property are $400.00. Since the total taxes cannot exceed 1% of the full cash value of the property, the "full cash value" of the property would be:

A. $10,000
B. $20,000
C. $40,000
D. $80,000

12. A house sold for $16,350, which amount was 9% more than the cost of the house. The cost of the house was:

A. $14,878.50
B. $15,000.00
C. $16,000.00
D. $17,821.50

13. The Southern Pacific Railroad Company sold ABS Developers three sections of land that had been divided into 20 acre parcels. 16 sold at $4,000 each and the remainder sold at $5,000 each. Which of the following was most nearly the total amount realized by the seller?

A. $350,000
B. $358,000
C. $475,000
D. $500,000

14. An acre is to be divided into four equal lots. If the lots are parallel to each other, rectangular, and 200 feet deep, the width of each lot would most nearly be:

A.   15 feet
B.   55 feet

C. 200 feet

D. 218 feet

15. A prospect is considering the purchase of an income property which has an operating statement showing $94,500.00 deducted from gross income to arrive at the net income. The deductions amount to 60% of the gross income. If the prospect wants a 12% return on the purchase price of any investments he makes, what should he pay for the property?

A. $81,000

B. $196,000

C. $504,000

D. $720,000

16. Richard Rock sold his residence which was unencumbered. Total deductions in escrow amounted to $215.30 in addition to a broker's commission of 6% of the selling price. The selling price was the only credit item. Richard Rock received a check for escrow amounting to $15,290. The selling price was most nearly:

A. $16,200

B. $16,266

C. $16,430

D. $16,495

17. Mr. and Mrs. Smith acquired a home in 1977 for $48,000. In 1987 they sold it for $60,500 and moved into an apartment unit. During the ten year period of ownership, permanent improvements totaling $12,750 were made to their house. If Mr. Smith's income consists entirely of wages, how would the sale affect his 1987 federal income return?

A.   No affect
B. $125.00 loss
C. $250.00 loss
D. $12,500 gain

18. Eddie Ronquillo sold his house and took back a note for $4,200 secure a second deed of trust. He promptly sold the note for $2,730. This represents a discount of:

A.   28%
B.   35%
C.   55%
D.   65%

19. An owner depreciated the improvements based on a cost basis of $160,000 using the straight line method. Improvements are depreciated 37.5% to date and the remaining economic life is estimated to be 15 years. Which of the following is correct? The:

A.   Rate of depreciation exceeds 4% per annum
B.   Time of depreciation to date is over ten years
C.   Value of the building is $120,000
D.   Rate of depreciation cannot be determined from the data
given

20. What is the monthly return on an income property with a 6 1/2% return on its value of $46,500?

A. $251.88
B. $302.50
C. $151.25
D. $3,630.00

21. Andrew Blacker was the owner of a straight note with an annual interest rate of 8.4%. In 5 years, he had received $5,460 in interest. What was the principal amount of the note?

A. $1,092
B. $13,000
C. $6,500
D. $3,250

22. The Phillips sold their home for $36,850, which represents a 17% profit over the original price. What was the original price?

A. $31,495
B. $35,000
C. $53,540
D. $19,850

23. If a building's costs increased 20 percent, the value of the investor's dollar has decreased by:

A. 16 and 2/3%
B. 20%
C. 25%
D. 33 and 1/3%

24. One month's interest on a 5 year straight note amounted to $225.00. At a 7 1/2% per year interest rate, what was the face amount of the note?

A. $2,700
B. $1,688
C. $36,000
D. $44,000

25. Escrow closed May 1 with interest on a $4,415 second trust deed paid to June 1. The interest rate is 7 2/10%. What is the debt to the buyer, if the buyer assumes the loan?

A. $22.09
B. $26.49
C. $4,415.00
D.   None of the above

26. A man owns an apartment building with 20,000 square feet of living space and wants to carpet 60% of the area. If the carpet costs $6.00 a square yard, what is the total cost of the carpeting?

A. $3,996
B. $4,000
C. $7,998
D. $24,000

27. One month's interest on a straight note amounted to $45. At 4 1/2% per year, what was the face amount of the note?

A. $2,025
B. $1,200
C. $12,000
D. $24,000

28. If the interest is paid at a rate of $60 per month and the rate of interest is 8% per year, what is the principal amount of the loan?

A. $5,760
B. $8,560
C. $9,000
D. $90,000

29. Mr. Morton paid $945 interest on a straight note loan of $7,000, at a rate of 9%. What was the term of the loan?

A.   18 months
B.   36 months
C.   48 months
D.   60 months

30. A man paid $140 in interest for a 90 day period on a $7,000 loan. What was the interest rate on the loan?

A.   6%
B.   8%
C.   10%
D.   11%

31. A rectangular parcel containing 540 square yards which has a frontage of 45' would be how many feet deep?

A. 54' deep
B. 108' deep
C. 270' deep
D. 540' deep

32. How many acres are contained in a parcel of land 1,320' by 2,640'?

A. 40 acres
B. 60 acres
C. 80 acres
D. 120 acres

33. If $150 interest is paid in 8 months on a straight note loan of $2,500, what is the annual rate of interest?

A. 9%
B. 10%
C. 11.50%
D. 12%

34. A parcel of land 1/4 mile by 1/4 mile is how many acres?

A. Ten acres

B.   Twenty acres
C.   Forty acres
D.   Eighty acres

35. A man bought a home for $31,680 and now wishes to sell. He is informed that the cost of selling will amount to 12% of the selling price. He wishes to sell at a price so as not to have a loss. How much would the home have had to appreciate in order to offset the selling costs?

A. $1,080
B. $2,160
C. $4,320
D. $5,400

36. A building that has interior dimensions of 26' x 30' and has 6" walls would cover how much square footage of land?

A.   58
B.   428
C.   837
D.   3,680

37. A rectangular parcel of land measures 1,780' x 1,780' and contains how many acres?

A. 73
B. 316
C. 632
D. 1,780

38. A borrower paid $120 interest on a 90-day straight note. The principal was $6,000. What was the interest rate?

A. 6%
B. 7%
C. 8%
D. 9%

39. A man borrowed $750 on a straight note at an interest rate of 7.2%. If his total interest payment was $67.50, the length of the loan was?

A. Twelve months
B. Fifteen months
C. Twenty four months
D. Thirty months

40. A house sold for $16,350 which was 9% more than its original cost. What was the original cost?

A. $15,000

B. $20,000
C. $25,000
D. $30,000

41. A homeowner sold his house for $23,000. This selling price represented a 15% profit over what he had originally paid for the house. What was the original price of the home?

A. $15,000
B. $20,000
C. $25,000
D. $30,000

42. Assume that a second trust deed of $1,000 was to be paid in annual installments of $300 plus 6% interest, with a balloon payment of the balance at the end of the third year. The remaining balance of the principal after the second annual installment was paid would be:

A. $400.00
B. $424.00
C. $505.60
D. $520.00

43. Mr. John listed his home with Broker Bob for $35,000. The broker was to receive a commission rate of 6%. The broker brought an offer at 10% less than the listed price.

The owner agreed to accept the offer if the broker reduced his commission by 20%. If they all agree to these terms, what amount of commission would the broker receive?

A. $812
B. $1,012
C. $1,312
D. $1,512

44. A man had an income property which suffered a $300 monthly loss of net income when a freeway was built nearby. At a capitalization rate of 12%, how much did his property lose in value?

A. $20,000
B. $30,000
C. $40,000
D. $50,000

45. Kent was the owner of a straight note with an annual interest rate of 8.4%. In five years he had received $5,460 in interest. The principal amount of the note was most nearly?

A. $12,000
B. $13,000
C. $14,000
D. $15,000

46. An investor owns a 20-unit apartment house. When compared to comparable apartment properties he loses $200 net income a month because his property is located next to a busy freeway. Appraisers are using a 12% capitalization rate for this neighborhood of income properties. The subject property has suffered a loss in value in the amount of:

A. $20,000
B. $25,000
C. $30,000
D. $35,000

47. In order to earn $208 per month from an investment that yields a 6% return you would have to invest approximately:

A.   12480
B. $20,800
C. $24,960
D. $41,600

48. A man bought two 60 foot lots for $18,000 each and divided them into three lots which he sold for $15,000 each. What was his percentage of profit?

A.   15.00%

B.   25.00%
C.   28.00%
D.   30.00%

49. If a man paid $50,000 for a business which gave him a 6% return on his money, how much did he make during the first year that he owned it?

A. $1,500
B. $3,000
C. $4,500
D. $6,000

50. An investor was going to have a building constructed which was to cost $150,000 and could, when completed, be leased for $2,500 per month. The annual operating expenses for the property would be $6,000. The amount he could invest in the land to realize a 12% return would be:

A. $50,000
B. $75,000
C. $100,000
D. $150,000

51. An investor purchased property for a total price of $72,000, paying $20,000 down and financing the balance of

$52,000 using a straight note. If the investor eventually sold the property after it had doubled in value and had made no principal payments on the loan, each dollar invested would show a return of:

A. $2.00
B. $4.60
C. $5.60
D. $8.70

52. Which of the following contains the largest area?

A.   4 square miles
B.   5,280' X 10,560'
C.   2 sections
D.   1/10 of a township

53. Harris obtained a loan in the amount of $20,000 and paid the mortgage lender four discount points and an origination fee of 2%. If the payments on the loan were $163.00 per month, including 8% interest and the average balance over a five year period was $18,500, the gross amount earned by the lender is the 5 years was most nearly:

A. $5,100
B. $6,000

C. $7,400
D. $8,600

54. An individual who receives $225 per month on a money market savings account that pays 7 1/2% per year, has invested which of the following amounts?

A. $12,500
B. $27,000
C. $36,000
D. $48,000

55. A seller took back a second trust deed and note in the amount of $11,400 payable $240 per month, including interest at 7% per annum. If interest on the note begins July 15 and the first payment is made on August 15, the amount of the first payment that is applied to the principal is:

A. $66.50
B. $79.80
C. $173.50
D. $240.00

56. Humphreys sold his residence which was unencumbered. Total deductions in escrow amounted to $215.30 in addition

to a broker's commission of 6% of the selling price. The selling price was the only credit item. Humphreys received a check from escrow amounting to $15,290. The selling price was most nearly:

A. $16,200
B. $16,266
C. $16,430
D. $16,495

57. Ms. Rodgers sold her house and took back a note for $4200 secured by a second deed of trust. She promptly sold the note for $2730. This represents a discount of:

A. 28%
B. 35%
C. 51%
D. 73%

58. After subtracting $140 escrow fees and 6% commission on gross sales price, a seller receives $13,584. What is the selling price?

A. $12,770
B. $14,440
C. $14,540
D. $14,600

59. A man purchased a property at 20% less than the listed price and later sold the property for the original listed price. What was the percentage of profit?

A.   10%
B.   20%
C.   25%
D.   40%

60. Escrow closed May 1st with interest on a $4415 second trust deed paid to June 1st. If the interest rate is 7.2%, the debit to the buyer, if the buyer assumed the loan, would be:

A. $22.09
B. $26.49
C. $4,415.00
D.   None of the above

61. A board foot of lumber could be obtained from a piece of lumber that is:

A.   6" X 6" X 1"
B.   6" X 12" X 1"
C.   12" X 1" X 1"
D.   6" X 12" X 12"

62. Assume that a second trust deed of $1000 was to be paid in annual installments of $300 plus 6% interest, with a balloon payment of the balance at the end of the third year. The remaining balance of the principal after the annual installment had been paid was:

A. $400
B. $424
C. $506
D. $520

63. Assume a real estate salesman sold a residence for $31,000. If the broker's commission was 6% and the salesman was to receive 45% of the total commission for selling the property, the salesman would receive:

A. $837.70
B. $959.95
C. $1,860.00
D.   None of the above

64. If Broker Christianson brought in an offer of 10% less than the listing price of $15,300 and the seller would agree to the price if the broker would accept a 20% reduction of his commission, the broker's commission would amount to:

A. $660.96
B. $689.85
C. $735.84
D. $827.82

65. A man enters into a lease agreement on a grocery store with the following terms: $350 minimum monthly rent or 5% grocery sales, 7% of meat sales, 6% of deli sales, and 8% of produce sales, whichever is greater. The grocery sales were $27,000 annually, meat sales $500 per month, deli sales $300 per month and produce sales $3,000 annually. What was the annual rent on the store?

A. $3,180
B. $4,200
C. $4,386
D. $5,120

66. A building was insured for $19,500 at a rate of .18 per hundred. If the three year policy was 2 1/2 times the one year rate, what amount per month should be added to the monthly payments to properly cover the insurance cost?

A. $7.31
B. $2.92
C. $2.44

D. $1.46

67. What is the annual interest rate on a $16,000 loan when the interest payments are $160.00 per quarter on the full amount? At least:

A.   3%, but less than 4%
B.   4%, but less than 5%
C.   5%, but less than 6%
D.   6%, but less than 7%

68. A homeowner sold his house for $23,000. If the selling price represented a 15% profit over what he had originally paid for the house, the original price of the home was:

A. $19,550
B. $20,000
C. $27,000
D.   None of the above

69. An owner of a section of land dedicates an easement for a road along the south side of his section. The easement contained 3 acres. The width of the road was approximately:

A.   Twenty feet
B.   Thirty feet

C. Forty feet
D. Fifty feet

70. There are five units in a condo. Smith paid $12,600, Jones paid $13,500, Kahn paid $13,750, Poe paid $14,400 and Clark paid $15,250. If there was an $1800 annual maintenance fee and each owner was to pay his proportionate share based upon the ratio of his unit purchase price to the total purchase price of all units, the monthly share of Smith's unit would be:

A. $8.00
B. $27.00
C. $32.40
D. $36.00

71. A property in probate was offered for sale and an offer of $12,000 was received. If anyone else wishes to bid on the property at the time of the confirmation, the initial minimum overbid must be:

A. $12,000
B. $13,000
C. $13,100
D. $13,500

72. The total number of lineal feet on one side of a Section is:

A.   1,000
B.   2,640
C.   5,280
D.   43,560

73. Arnold held a straight note which carried an annual interest rate of 8.4%. If in five years he had received $5,460 in interest, the principal amount of the note was:

A. $10,000
B. $11,500
C. $13,000
D. $15,000

74. Escrow companies normally base their prorations on an escrow year of:

A.   350 days
B.   355 days
C.   360 days
D.   365 days

75. Eddie Ronquillo sold his home for $17,200. If this represents 9% more than what he paid for it, the cost of the home was most nearly:

A. $15,424
B. $15,500
C. $15,800
D. $16,000

76. An individual borrowed $750 on a straight note at an interest rate of 7.2%. If the total interest payment on the loan was $81.00, the term of the loan was:

A.   15 months
B.   18 months
C.   21 months
D.   24 months

77. The Richard Rock sold his home and had to carry back a second trust deed and note of $5310. If he sold the note for $3823.20 before any payments had been made on the note, the rate of discount amounted to:

A.   25%
B.   28%
C.   54%

D.   72%

78. A real estate syndicate paid $193,600 for a lot on which they planned to build a high rise apartment. If the lot was 200 feet deep and they paid $4.40 per square foot, the cost per front foot was:

A. $220
B. $440
C. $880
D. $960

79. A rectangular parcel of land that measures 220' X 330' contains most nearly:

A.   1 1/4 acres
B.   1 3/5 acres
C.   1 2/3 acres
D.   2 acres

80. A borrower signed a straight note for a term of eight months in the amount of $2500. If she paid $150 in interest on the loan, the interest rate was:

A.   8%
B.   9%

C.   9%
D.   10%

81. An income property was appraised for $100,000 based on a 6% capitalization rate. If an investor used an 8% cap rate, the value of the property would be:

A. $60,000
B. $75,000
C. $80,000
D. $90,000

82. If a note in the amount of $22,250 specifies monthly payments over a period of 30 years at 6.6% interest per annum, what is the first month's interest payment?

A. $111.25
B. $122.38
C. $130.71
D. $140.50

83. If Haeli McDonald paid a commission of 6% of the selling price of a property valued at $54,375, the selling broker would receive:

A. $4,275.00
B. $3,375.00
C. $3,262.50
D. $3,191.50

84. A bank agreed to lend the owner of a piece of property a sum equal to 66 2/3% of its appraised valuation. The interest rate charged on the amount borrowed is 5% per annum. The first year's interest amounted to $200.00. What was the valuation placed upon the property by the bank?

A. $3,000.00
B. $4,000.00
C. $5,333.33
D. $6,000.00

85. A married couple purchased a property for a total price of $18,000, paying $5000 down and having the seller take back a first trust deed in the amount of $13,000. The terms of the $13,000 trust deed called for no payments in the first year. If at the end of the first year, they were to sell the property at twice its original cost, their original dollar is now worth:

A. $2.00
B. $4.60

C. $7.20
D. $8.00

86. If a borrower pays $1650 interest per quarter on a straight note of $60,000, the interest rate would be:

A.   8.50%
B.   9.00%
C.   10.50%
D.   11.00%

87. Maria Watson sold a residence that was free and clear of all liens and received a check for $30,580. If closing costs of $430.60 had been deducted as well as the broker's 6& commission, the actual selling price would have been most nearly:

A. $31,590
B. $31,825
C. $32,885
D. $32,990

88. The number of townships in a tract of land that is 28 miles square is most nearly:

A.   Eleven

B.   Seventeen
C.   Twenty two
D.   Fifteen

89. Clever executed a promissory note in the amount of $7000. If the note called for the payment of interest only and Clever paid off the entire sum in 90 days together with interest of $210, the interest rate on the note was most nearly:

A.   9%
B.   10%
C.   11%
D.   12%

90. Broker Thomas is listing a property owned by Gibson. Gibson has advised Thomas that he wished to realize $37,000 cash from the sale after paying Thomas a 4% commission and paying $600 in closing costs. To accomplish this and assuming that the property is free and clear, the selling price must be at least:

A. $37,856
B. $38,480
C. $39,110
D. $39,167

91. The interest rate on a straight note in the amount of $27,000 that calls for interest payments of $573.75 each quarter would most nearly be:

A.   6.6%
B.   7.2%
C.   8.6%
D.   9.2%

92. A commercial office building yields an annual net income of $174,000. If an appraiser applied a capitalization rate of 8% to the property, the market value of the property would most nearly be:

A. $1,392,000
B. $1,666,000
C. $1,932,000
D. $2,175,000

93. An individual who receives $225.00 per month on a money market savings account that pays 7.5% per year, has invested which of the following amounts?

A. $125,000
B. $27,000
C. $36,000

D. $48,000

94. A holder of a second trust deed and straight note with a face amount of $3740 sold it for $2431. This amounted to a discount of:

A.   26%
B.   35%
C.   45%
D.   55%

95. A seller took back a second trust deed and note in the amount of $11,400, payable $240 per month, including interest at 7% per annum. If interest on the note begins July 15 and the first payment is made on August 15, the amount of the first payment that is applied to the principal is:

A. $66.50
B. $79.80
C. $173.50
D. $240.00

96. A homeowner made a regular monthly payment of $550 on her home loan. Out of the total payment, the lender deducted the interest that was due for the month and applied the remaining balance of $43.85 to the principal. If the outstanding balance of the loan was $56,500, the interest

rate on the load was most nearly:

A. 8.50%
B. 9.25%
C. 10.75%
D. 12.50%

97. A square parcel of land that is 1780' X 1780' contains most nearly:

A. 27 acres
B. 54 acres
C. 65 acres
D. 73 acres

98. An investor purchased two lots and paid $18,000 for each one. Since each lot had a 60' frontage he was able to subdivide the combined parcels in 3 lots with equal front footage. If the 3 lots sold for $15,000 each, his rate of profit on his investment was:

A. 20%
B. 25%
C. 33%
D. 40%

99. A one acre parcel of land that is square is divided into four lots of equal size. If the lots are rectangular, parallel to each other and are 240' deep, the width of each lot is most nearly:

A.   45.4'
B.   90.8'
C.   181'
D.   240'

100. Natalie Johnson owns a $100,000 property based on a 6% capitalization rate. If due to changes in economic conditions investors now require a higher capitalization rate or 8%, what would the value of the property be using the same dollar income?

A. $90,000
B. $75,000
C. $80,000
D. $60,000

SECRETS TO PASSING THE REAL ESTATE EXAM

Studying by itself is not always enough. Learning good examination habits and techniques is also important. Good "examinationship" will mean extra points for you.

Knowing how to take an examination can make the difference between passing and failing. Many people fail the real estate exam before they enter the examination room. Be prepared and be confident.

Don't study late the night before your examination. If you have done your preparation, the few extra hours of rest will mean more in being fresh for the examination.

Avoid the use of amphetamines. They frequently give a false sense of understanding.

They cause students to jump at an answer without carefully weighing alternative possibilities.

Allow yourself plenty of time to get to the examination location. Plan for traffic problems, parking, etc. Murphy's Law states: "Whatever can go wrong, will go wrong!" and O'Brian's Law states: "Murphy was an optimist!"

People are nervous at test time. Avoid pre-examination socializing. Talking with a group of nervous people will only tend to heighten your anxiety. Fear is contagious. Don't listen to the "expert" who knows the ropes simply because he has taken the exam several times.

He is obviously doing something wrong. Remain calm and confident. This is key!

Take a seat as far forward in the examination room as possible. You are less likely to be distracted by students moving in front of you.

The Department of Real Estate allows the use of non-programmable electronic calculators. Make sure you have one and you fully understand its operation. Go through sample problems with it in advance. Some calculators will give wrong answers when the batteries are low. Remember "Murphy": Have new batteries in your calculator.

Bring several sharp pencils to use for the examination. However, if the state supplies you with a pencil, USE IT, not your own. The test is electronically scored and your own pencil mark may not register. Different pencil manufacturers use different types of graphite in their pencils.

Pay attention to all instructions given by the examination tutor as well as those written on the examination.

If you are right-handed, place the examination answer sheet to the right of the examination booklet. If you are left-handed, place the answer sheet to the left. This way your arm does not crowd over the examination booklet while answering a question. Not only will it save time in finding your place, but it will also reduce the possibility of answering a question in the wrong section of the answer sheet. You DO NOT want to suddenly find yourself out of sequence by marking the answer to question 100 in the section for question 99 and find out you have been marking the wrong section for the past 15 questions.

Frequently among the first few questions it seems that there are some of the most difficulty. Physiologically it will throw you off pace and the Department of Real Estate has coldly done this on purpose. What you will want to do is skip the first 5 questions and start with question number 6. Once you have finished all the questions, then go back and do questions 1 through 5. Also, you will want to skip all the math questions in your first run through. You will want to wait to answer any math questions until the very end. This reason for this is that the brain takes about 10 to minutes to completed go from a comprehensive thinking to analytical mathematical thinking. Your exam will be timed and you will only have about a minute and a half for each question. So your time will be valuable.

Here is a run down of how you should approach the exam process:

You will be allowed one sheet of scratch paper. On this sheet make 3 columns labeled A, MATH and GUESS. Write the numbers 1, 2, 3, 4, 5 in column A and draw a line under number 5. These are the first 5 questions you are going to skip and come back to. Remember we mentioned this earlier in the beginning of this book. On this first run through you are NOT going to guess at any questions. Start with question number 6. Let's say you know the answer and you answer it correctly. Then go to the next question, number 7. You do not know the answer right away and it might cause you to think about it for awhile. Remember time is valuable. Write the number 7 on your sheet of scratch paper in column A with the other numbers. You will come back to this later. You go on to question number 8. This one you know, and answer it correctly. You continue on answering correctly until you come to question number 15. It is a math question. Place this in the MATH column and any other math questions you come across on this first run through.

From now on in this first run through you will place all questions you do not know right away in the column A, any math questions in column labeled MATH. The column labeled GUESS will be for the second run through. Your scratch paper should now look like the image on the next page.

A	Math	Guess	
1 2 3 4 5 — 7	15		

Continue with your first run through of the exam, placing math questions in the MATH column and unknown questing in column A until you get to the end. You will find that there will be very few math question on the exam. They do not weigh very heavily on the exam.

Now you are ready for the second run through. Look at your scratch paper. Go to column A and start with the first question below the line under the number 5. This question has now had some time to incubate in your mind, or there was another question like it in the exam that you answered correctly. You now know the answer and answer it correctly.

Cross out the number 7 and go to the next one in the column. Continue until you come across one in this column that you still do not know or absolutely have not clue. Let's say it was question number 37. Cross out number 37 and place it in the GUESS column.

Continue on this second run though. Answering the ones you now know and crossing them out, and placing the ones that you still do not know in the GUESS column until you reach the end again. Your scratch paper should look something like the image on the next page.

A	Math	Guess	
1	15	37	
2	21		
3	35		
4	45		
5	67		
~~X~~			
~~18~~			
~~26~~			
~~37~~			
42			
63			

Now for the third run through. Go back to column A and answer the first 5 questions. Do the same as before. The ones you do not know place them in column labeled GUESS.

Once you have gone through the first 5 you are now ready to go on to the MATH column.

Do the same with this column. If you absolutely do not know one of the math questions, place it in the GUESS column. Your scratch paper should now look like the one on the next page.

A	Math	Guess	
~~1~~	~~15~~	37	
2	~~21~~	4	
~~3~~	35	21	
~~4~~	~~45~~		
5	~~67~~		
~~7~~			
~~18~~			
~~26~~			
~~37~~			
42			
63			

Now you are ready to attack the GUESS column. First go to the math question. If the math question has answers that look like the ones below, you will see that nothing in residential real estate costs $36.00 and hardly anything in residential real estate costs $360,000,000.00. So, you can eliminate A and D. This leaves B and C and a 50/50 chance at getting it correct. Take a look at the question once more. Look at the numbers that are being used in the question and the type of question it is. Is the math question about commission or annual interest? If so, the answer may be C. Or, is the math question about fees, penalties, monthly payments, monthly savings, or monthly interest? If so, then the answer to this question is probably B.

A. $36.00

B. $360.00

C. $3600.00

D. $360,000,000.00

Finally, finish the GUESS column with the comprehensive questions you had no clue about. Can you play the elimination game with those and give yourself a 50/50 chance on those too? If so, great! But still do not answer it. Locate the question on your answer sheet. Look at the answers you bubbled in for the 3 before it and the 3 after it. Does there seem to be a pattern? In the Department of Real Estate's exam there are patterns and they usually happen in 4's. If you see that there is a pattern of 4 with the answers like the ones below, continue that pattern.

35. B

36. B

37. (this one you did not know and is in your GUESS column)

38. B

39. C

So, for number 37 you will mark it B. If you do not see a pattern, and you cannot eliminate to make a 50/50 chance, do as the old college saying goes, "if you don't know it, mark it C". You will be amazed at how many question on ANY exam has the letter C as the answer.

So, now you have the tools to take your exam with even more confidence knowing that you have a better chance at passing your exam than anyone else there in the exam room.

Many people consider the examination which they took to become a real estate license tougher than any examination they ever had in college. You can see that there are hundreds of unfamiliar terms and phrases too be learned which cover a wide spectrum of areas.

Do not be intimidated by the size of the task before you. You do not need to have an exceptional intellect or memory to pass your examination. What you must have is dedication to continue with your studies and plan to get the most of your study time. As said before, confidence is the key.

Many students are discouraged because of confusion. During your first few lessons, confusion is the normal situation not the exception. Many students have stated that they are confused and unsure until they start their reviews. Then things start to clarify and make sense.

Teenagers and octogenarians have passed real estate examinations, and you can too. A positive attitude and learning how to study and take an examination can mean your success.

Closing

The Department of Real Estate or Real Estate Commission regularly changes the real estate exam. However, they do not write new questions for each new exam. The state keeps a test bank of real estate questions. Each real estate exam is composed from this bank of questions. Questions are dropped from the bank that are either seldom answered correctly or nearly always answered correctly. Consequently, the majority of the questions are repeated again and again. Often questions will be changed slightly to call for a "negative" rather than a "positive" answer. Other times the question will remain the same, but the answer will be worded differently. The questions offered in this Real Estate Exam Prep book are questions from this "test bank". Studying these questions and answers (with explanations) is a great way to familiarize yourself with the examination you will receive by the Department of Real Estate or Real Estate Commission, and will substantially increase your odds of passing the exam on the first try.

As mentioned before, confidence is the key. What better why to give yourself confidence than to have this book along with the questions and answers BEFORE you take the exam. Knowing exactly what to expect on the day of your exam will boost your confidence level.

Thank you again! We hope this book will give you the confidence needed to pass your real estate exam and become a successful real estate agent.

LIMITS OF LIABILITY

MAY 2020

CPSIA information can be obtained
at www.ICGtesting.com
Printed in the USA
LVHW061509230120
644586LV00010B/460